The Sound of Innovation

Inside Technology

edited by Wiebe E. Bijker, W. Bernard Carlson, and Trevor Pinch

A complete list of the series appears at the back of the book.

The Sound of Innovation

Stanford and the Computer Music Revolution

Andrew J. Nelson

The MIT Press
Cambridge, Massachusetts
London, England

This book was set in Stone by the MIT Press.

Library of Congress Cataloging-in-Publication Data

Nelson, Andrew J.
The sound of innovation : Stanford and the computer music revolution / Andrew J. Nelson.
pages cm.—(Inside technology series)
Includes bibliographical references and index.
ISBN 978-0-262-02876-9 (hardcover : alk. paper)
ISBN 978-0-262-54894-6 (paperback)
1. Stanford University. Center for Computer Research in Music and Acoustics. 2. Computer music—History and criticism. 3. Music—Computer programs—History. 4. Music and technology—History. I. Title.
ML33.S73C464 2015
786.7'60979473—dc23
2014031506

Contents

Acknowledgments

In 1986, at the age of eleven, I started a newspaper route. My motivation was singular: To save the roughly $2,000 required to purchase a Yamaha DX7 synthesizer—the most intriguing and beautiful musical instrument I had ever encountered. After several months of progress, my parents lent me the rest of the money needed for the purchase, on the condition that I pay it back—with interest. I did.

Seven years later, I arrived at Stanford University as a freshman. One of my first stops was the Center for Computer Research in Music and Acoustics (CCRMA), where I encountered a dizzying array of advanced sound technologies. I immediately began coursework for a major in Music, Science and Technology. Though I didn't know at the time, CCRMA had developed many of the innovations underlying the computer music revolution, including the technology at the heart of the DX7. In fact, a decades-long relationship with Yamaha was essential to the center's existence.

In light of this history, it might be accurate to say that the origins of this book stretch back nearly thirty years. More recently, however, the immediate impetus for this book lies in a statement that Woody Powell made in a 2001 Stanford PhD seminar, during my first year in the Management Science and Engineering (MS&E) doctoral program: "Few people recognize that one of Stanford's most lucrative technology licenses stems from the music department." I recognized immediately that he was referencing the CCRMA–Yamaha relationship. With Woody's guidance, I produced a term paper on this history. The term paper became my doctoral qualifying paper, which in turn became my first peer-reviewed journal article. In many ways, this book is the product of Woody's continued guidance and encouragement over many years. I'm indebted to him.

In the fourteen years that I've been researching various facets of CCRMA, countless other individuals also have enabled and encouraged my work. The members of my dissertation committee—Steve Barley, Woody Powell, Kathy Eisenhardt, and Mark Granovetter—encouraged me to appreciate and explore the complexities of the relationships between the "technical" and the "social." The Powell "lab group"—including Jeannette Colyvas, James Evans, Stine Grodal, Jason Owen-Smith, Kelley Packalen, Kaisa Snellman, and Kjersten Bunker Whittington—offered a simultaneously challenging and supportive environment in which to try out many of this book's core themes.

This book never would have materialized without the support of a wide range of other groups. First and foremost, CCRMA students, staff, faculty, and alumni have been overly generous in sharing their time, insights, and even personal collections of historical documents. I'm indebted to each of the interviewees listed in the appendix—and especially to John Chowning, Chris Chafe, and Julius Smith, each of whom spent days guiding me through the intricacies of CCRMA's history and read drafts of the manuscript. (John also taught a sound synthesis course that I took at CCRMA in 1994, and Chris served as my undergraduate advisor at Stanford.) A large number of other CCRMA participants also contributed to this book through informal conversations and extended email exchanges, including Marina Bosi, Al Cohen, Les Earnest, John Granzow, Hiro Kato, David Kerr, Don Knuth, Sasha Leitman, Chryssie Nanou, Nick Porcaro, Jean-Claude Risset, Loren Rush, Craig Sapp, Gary Scavone, Tricia Schroeter, Carr Wilkerson, Linnea Williams, Patte Wood, Bill Verplank, and Nette Worthy. Patte Wood, in particular, deserves tremendous thanks for her foresight in saving several boxes of documents from her many years as CCRMA's administrator and for depositing these historical treasures with the Stanford University Special Collections and University Archives. A reality of any book is that it cannot capture and reflect each perspective in the richness that it deserves; undoubtedly, each of these participants would tell CCRMA's story differently, highlighting other aspects of the center and interpreting the same events in different ways. In fact, as I argue throughout this text, there is great power in things like books, histories, computers, and compositions precisely because they afford such multiple interpretations. I hope, therefore, that my own interpretations will be received with openness.

At the Stanford Archives, Maggie Kimball, Polly Armstrong, Jerry McBride, and Paul Mustain offered frequent assistance. At Stanford's Office of Technology Licensing, Kathy Ku was gracious in sharing documents and data. At Stanford's Office of Development, Julia Hartung and Belinda Kuo helped me understand both the composition of CCRMA alumni and the role of individual and corporate giving. Arthur Patterson of Stanford's News Service, John Strawn, and Patte Wood worked to identify key photographs. At the National Association of Music Merchants, Dan Del Fiorentino and Tony Arambarri enabled access to recorded interviews and other historical materials. Finally, at the Paris-based IRCAM, Hugues Vinet was a gracious host as I toured facilities and spoke with participants in an effort to understand how CCRMA compared to another leading computer music center.

Conducting this research over great distances and many years required substantial financial resources. I am particularly grateful to the Kauffman Foundation, which provided generous financial support and early encouragement through the award of a Kauffman Junior Faculty Fellowship.

At MIT Press, editor Margy Avery and series editors Wiebe Bijker, W. Bernard Carlson, and Trevor Pinch shared my vision in this project and encouraged its further development into the present version. Paul Leonardi, Jonathan Sterne, and Steve Kahl each read the full manuscript and provided valuable guidance in this process.

Closer to home, my University of Oregon colleagues supported a curiosity-driven research environment, while Jon Bellona and Stephan Nance offered valuable research assistance.

And closest to home, Ann, thank you for your ceaseless encouragement to write this book, despite the many evenings, weekends, and "vacations" sacrificed. To Elizabeth, who was born in the midst of this project, thank you for introducing me to the wonders of encountering new sounds and new music for the very first time. And to Mom and Dad—thanks for the loan and the encouragement. I'll bet you never thought my fascination with the DX7 would lead to this.

1 Introduction

Eight musicians filed into the chamber music hall, dressed in all black and wearing focused expressions. Silently, they fanned into a semicircle across the front of the room, just feet away from the closest audience members. The sound of creaking chairs accompanied fumbling efforts by the last few attendees to turn off their mobile phones. What happened next, however, resulted from the musicians' failure to turn off their *own* phones. It was not an accident.

The musicians' focus turned to their iPhones, each held snugly in one hand. Small, amplified speakers hung off each of their wrists, held in place by fingerless gloves. As the musicians waved their arms—slowly, deliberately—an otherworldly sound filled the air. The sound—like the drone of a wet finger rubbing the rim of a glass bowl—grew louder. It grew denser. It grew higher in pitch. And the audience grew mesmerized.

As the piece continued, the phone-produced sounds slowly morphed. New textures developed and swirled about one another, mimicking the musicians' own movements. A warbled hum imitated one musician's agitated wrists. A whistling melody rose and fell as another musician's right arm reached for the ceiling and dropped toward the floor. A sustained metallic buzz emerged almost unnoticed, but grew thicker, more harmonic, and more insistent until it nearly overtook the rest of collage. With the final crescendo, the musicians—eyes locked on the ensemble's director—dropped their arms in unison. The audience burst into voracious applause.

The Stanford Mobile Phone Orchestra, or MoPhO, is a special ensemble: A musical group that raises questions as to whether a phone—or any object, for that matter—is a musical instrument; a musical group that leverages cutting-edge audio technologies, available via open source yet also commercialized through a Silicon Valley startup, Smule; and a musical group whose "instruments" have been provided by the corporate technology partners of its academic home, Stanford's Center for Computer Research in Music and Acoustics, or CCRMA (pronounced "karma").[1]

Ge Wang is the thirty-something music professor who directs the MoPhO. Though each CCRMA student, faculty, and staff member comes to the center via a different route, Wang's background is representative: He is trained as both a computer scientist and a musician; he works at the intersection of technology and music; he holds a tenure-track academic appointment in Stanford's music department while simultaneously serving, for a period, as cofounder and Chief Technology Officer at Smule; and he blurs the lines between science, art, engineering, and commerce, passing almost seamlessly between these different worlds.

Wang's academic home on the Stanford campus, CCRMA, possesses these same attributes. In fact, CCRMA emerged and thrives at such diverse intersections. In turn, it has played a vital role not only in developing the new discipline of computer music, but also in ensuring that digital audio enjoys a nearly ubiquitous presence in the world today. As someone plays music on a computer, plunks keys on a keyboard, or streams songs over the Internet, chances are good that a CCRMA alum or partner is involved in some way.

CCRMA originated in the 1960s, when composer John Chowning and other pioneers latched on to both the equipment and the people at Stanford's budding Artificial Intelligence Laboratory. There, working mostly at night and on weekends ("so as not to abuse our hosts," as Chowning would explain), the team of musicians, engineers, psychologists, and computer scientists labored to apply the computer in an entirely novel way: to produce and manipulate sound and, more importantly to them, the sonic basis of new musical compositions. In the process, they helped to develop a new academic field, to invent the technologies that would underlie this field, and to transpose these inventions into broad commercial application, reaching consumers in every corner of the planet.

One of CCRMA's first inventions was Chowning's frequency modulation (FM) synthesis technique, which helped to usher in the era of digital music. In 1975, Yamaha Corporation of Japan licensed FM and used it to power one of the best-selling musical instruments in history—their DX7 synthesizer—along with countless computer soundcards for multimedia PCs and semiconductor chips that enable mobile phone ring tones. The FM license, in fact, still remains one of Stanford's most profitable technology licenses—an impressive achievement in a university that produced Google, DSL, and recombinant DNA, among other high-profile inventions. CCRMA, in turn, would plow the financial proceeds into an endowment fund that continues to sustain the center.

In the 1990s, CCRMA and Yamaha would attempt to repeat the feat, working to develop a novel type of "physical modeling" synthesis that promised to nearly eliminate computer memory requirements for sound generation. Today, CCRMA serves as a hub of free and open-source music and audio software, and CCRMA researchers apply these tools in settings ranging from the sonic exploration of archaeological ruins in Peru to the development of smartphone applications that turn mobile phones into virtual pianos and rap-music beatboxes. The center is widely recognized as a world leader in computer music and digital audio research.

Underpinning this technological history is a musical one. Indeed, CCRMA's technological contributions must be understood, first and foremost, as facilitators of compositional aims. From its inception, the center attracted some of avant-garde classical, jazz, and rock music's biggest names, including Pierre Boulez, Gyorgi Ligeti, Stan Getz, and Phil Lesh. The center's own students and faculty have composed hundreds of works, featured on stages around the world and garnering countless awards. Closer to home, as Stanford prepared in 2012 to open a new $112-million concert hall that would host Yo-Yo Ma and the San Francisco Symphony in its inaugural season, the first group to "perform" in the under-construction hall was CCRMA's "Laptop Orchestra"—a chamber ensemble in which all of the instruments are laptop computers.

The everyday practices at CCRMA are a lauded, albeit still unusual, combination: an energized interdisciplinarity that stimulates creativity and contributions at the intersections of fields; a fierce commitment to open sharing and to "users"—primarily, musicians and composers—that defines both priorities and vision; and deep commercial engagement that has resulted in numerous widely used products and in far-flung relationships with diverse organizations.

CCRMA is instructive, however, not only as an example of these activities, but also as a collective at their forefront. Thus, members of the center embraced interdisciplinarity not when boards of trustees and government agencies said that such mixing was "good," but rather when administrators and funders alike questioned whether it was appropriate; CCRMA focused relentlessly on users and on the broad diffusion of technology not only in an era of Silicon Valley marketing, but also in a period of Cold War self-sufficiency that celebrated walled-off engineers and "upstream creators" over populist tinkerers; and CCRMA developed intellectual property and engaged with industry not after 1980 US legislation encouraged such moves and new "technology transfer offices" mushroomed to support it, but rather when university patents were unusual and efforts to commercialize university research were sparse and peripheral. CCRMA, therefore, serves as both an exception and an example: an early outlier that became a model—indeed, an archetype—for later organizations.

This book focuses on two intertwined questions: First, why and how did CCRMA emerge, not only crafting success as an organization but also seeding an entirely new field, computer music, that today permeates academia, industry, and everyday life? As the account in the chapters that follow makes clear, this success was neither easy nor preordained.

Second, beyond CCRMA's early success, how has the center continued to engage in these diverse and creative activities nearly fifty years later? As countless treatises on organizational renewal and corporate entrepreneurship highlight, the continued regeneration of innovation and of an innovative culture is both precious and unusual.[2]

My analysis of CCRMA draws upon and develops three broad themes: (1) interdisciplinarity, including the rise of interdisciplinary programs and the challenges and opportunities associated with them; (2) open innovation, including user innovation, free and open source software, and technology standards; and (3) university technology transfer and research commercialization. In turn, I argue that the center's emergence, sustenance, and renewal stems from the ability of CCRMA participants to intertwine and mutually leverage these activities in unique and powerful ways.

Recent years have witnessed a surge in interest by university administrators, funders, and researchers themselves around *interdisciplinarity*—a concept whose definition varies from author to author and from setting to setting, but which typically conjures images of "unity and synthesis" among different fields, perspectives, methods.[3] In turn, scholars have investigated how interdisciplinary work offers new opportunities, owing to the insights that emerge across boundaries, but also presents new challenges, particularly in terms of perceived legitimacy among existing academic disciplines.[4]

CCRMA reflects a particular approach to interdisciplinarity that Cyrus Mody and I label *radical interdisciplinarity*—a partnership in which seemingly diverse disciplines come together on equal footing and in which the participants from these disciplines are forever changed as a result of the interaction.[5] Thus, CCRMA is not simply an example of infusing a bit of software engineering into music (or vice versa); instead, it represents a fundamental transformation of disciplines through the combinations that it engenders. To employ a cooking analogy, radical interdisciplinarity is like a purée in which each ingredient is critical and in which neither chef nor diner can pull apart the constituent ingredients again, even though they may identify the individual influences.

Of course, such interdisciplinarity can fail, too. It can be difficult to communicate across disciplinary boundaries; it can be difficult to establish credibility as an individual researcher when one's work lies between disciplines; and it can be difficult to attract resources, which often are tied to particular departments and disciplines.[6] CCRMA, too, experienced these challenges. The center's history, therefore, sheds light on the circumstances under which interdisciplinarity may open up new possibilities or result in failure.

A second theme that runs through CCRMA's history is *open innovation*. Henry Chesbrough's book, *Open Innovation*, describes open innovation as a model by which organizations look beyond their internal R&D labs and capabilities in order to identify and develop innovations.[7] Thus, "open" refers to organizational boundaries and barriers—of both physical and cognitive sorts.

Although much of the work on open innovation focuses on partnerships between organizations, end-users themselves often make important contributions, too. Thus, whereas a traditional innovation model may posit that users are mere consumers of offerings from firms, in many cases users act to modify and co-create products and services. For instance, Trevor Pinch and colleagues have documented numerous cases in which users suggest new applications and adaptations that were initially unimagined by firms.[8] Eric von Hippel and colleagues have bolstered this "user innovation" argument by emphasizing how users often create entirely new products in order to serve their own idiosyncratic needs. In turn, firms only later pick up these products, facilitating their diffusion into a broader market.[9] Similarly, CCRMA composers do not merely apply or use existing technologies from commercial firms. Instead, their own musical and compositional aims suggest new technologies that firms may later develop and diffuse.

Of course, open innovation is facilitated by sharing across boundaries, a point emphasized by the phenomenon of open source software communities.[10] In these communities, participants share the "products" themselves—typically computer code or, as with Wikipedia and YouTube, other knowledge assets—openly and freely with one another. In the CCRMA case, for example, a Bell Labs researcher, Max Mathews, shared with Chowning his program for generating music with a computer. In turn, CCRMA shared its enhancements to Mathews's program with IRCAM, a Paris-based computer music center widely viewed—alongside CCRMA—as one of the best in the world. CCRMA's sharing not only saved IRCAM years of development time, but also enabled personnel and further software developments to move easily between the groups.

As this example highlights, technical standards thus serve an important role in facilitating open innovation. Indeed, standards have a number of benefits: By enabling economies of scale and by encouraging competition on the basis of price, technical standards can drive down prices and enable broader access. Moreover, standards yield *network externalities*. These externalities may be direct, as with email: As more people adopted email, the value of email increased since each user could reach more people. Or, the externalities may be indirect. As more users purchase smartphones, for example, there is greater incentive to produce "apps" and to improve the quality and availability of service in order to address this increasing user base. Through these different effects, technical standards thus enable interoperability among technologies and collaboration among users.[11]

Standardization, however, also imposes costs. Standards can restrict customization efforts that are fine tuned to any particular user's needs, imposing a tyranny of the majority that is insensitive to important but idiosyncratic needs among a minority. For example, Jonathan Sterne describes how the MP3 audio standard addresses the desires of the majority of listeners by reducing file sizes and, therefore, enabling denser storage and faster transmission. Yet this same standard exhibits artifacts and quality limitations that a minority of listeners, such as audiophiles, find objectionable.[12]

Moreover, once established, standards can be difficult to change, even if most users would be better off under such a change. For example, economist Paul David argues that most users remain "locked in" to the QWERTY keyboard standard—the particular arrangement of keys on a typewriter or computer keyboard—even though alternative arrangements would be more efficient.[13] As a group both dependent upon standards and instrumental in developing them, CCRMA provides insight into the emergence and management of these tensions around standards and open innovation.

The commercialization of university research is a third major theme running through the CCRMA account. Stanford has given rise to some of the most prominent firms in today's economy, including Google, Yahoo, Genentech, and Hewlett-Packard. In turn, policy makers and business leaders alike have not missed the potential connections between university research and important products and organizations.[14] Concurrently, academic investigations into the commercialization of university research have mushroomed in recent years.[15] This literature has wrestled with a number of outstanding questions, including faculty involvement and perceptions; the role of university technology-transfer offices; the role of university and government policies; and the processes and mechanisms underlying commercialization.[16]

As David Mowery and others have documented, Stanford was one of the earliest universities to embrace such commercial engagement. It is an instructive example, therefore, of how market considerations came to be intertwined with university research activities.[17] Indeed, CCRMA provided some of the earliest technology disclosures to Stanford's newly formed Office of Technology Licensing in the 1960s and 1970s, and the Yamaha FM synthesis license was this office's first big hit. At the same time, however, much of the commercial engagement at CCRMA transpires through what might be termed "informal" technology transfer efforts—that is, activities beyond the formal patenting and licensing of technologies.[18] Moreover, CCRMA's experience upends the conventional wisdom that firms are primarily recipients of university technology, instead highlighting cocreation efforts and instances of firm-to-university technology transfer. Thus, commercialization at CCRMA is a multifaceted endeavor that both extends and challenges the existing literature.

These three themes—interdisciplinarity, open innovation, and commercialization—are threads that wind throughout the CCRMA account, stitching together diverse people, organizations, activities, and motivations against the backdrop of a changing and heterogeneous context. In turn, my central thesis in this book is that they must be viewed as coevolving—as mutually shaping activities whose interactions influence one another's trajectories. For example, Chowning's musically motivated invention of FM enabled Yamaha Corporation to introduce a low-cost and widely accessible digital music synthesizer. In turn, sales of this synthesizer provided licensing revenue to support academic activities at CCRMA, which also enabled a broad group of musician-engineers to generate further inventions.

As another example, Professor Ge Wang's desire to test a new music programming language with a broad user base led to his founding of a startup, Smule. In turn, Smule employs some of the same CCRMA students who compose music for the Stanford mobile-phone ensemble that Wang directs. In other words, the ties between diverse people engaged in academic research, invention, and commercialization run thick; they not only are difficult to unravel, but also doing so would remove the context in which they operate. Thus, although there is a substantial literature on each of these themes independently, as cited throughout the text, my analysis of CCRMA represents an initial attempt to pull them together into a cohesive account of how a new academic discipline can emerge at the intersection of new technologies that provide new capabilities, commercial activities that develop these technologies and that provide critical resources, and interdisciplinary engagement that draws together diverse perspectives, communities, and interests.

To explain how people, resources, activities, and ideas move across boundaries—and with what effect—I leverage the concept of *multivocality*. Multivocality, in the words of sociologist Woody Powell and his colleagues, refers to the ability to perform "multiple activities with a variety of constituents."[19] For example, Powell and colleagues leverage multivocality to describe collaborations in the biotechnology industry. In their case, universities, dedicated biotechnology firms, venture capitalists, large pharmaceutical companies, and other organizations come together through a range of different activities, including research, marketing, and funding relationships. In fact, Powell and colleagues argue that it is through these diverse constituencies engaging in multiple activities that the biotechnology industry emerged and grew; each group found ways to connect with other groups through a common activity, such that the pursuit of multiple activities formed a dense network of diverse organizations.[20]

Multivocality also suggests that these diverse participants need not interpret the same activity in the same way. Political scientists John Padgett and Christopher Ansell, for example, use multivocality to describe how the Medici family of Renaissance-era Florence maintained power through Cosimo de Medici's "sphinxlike character": Cosimo arbitrated between and leveraged diverse economic and familial networks by maintaining ambiguity as to his true desires and intentions. In turn, different participants interpreted these desires and intentions according to their own perspectives. Thus, to Padgett and Ansell, multivocality means that "single actions can be interpreted coherently from multiple perspectives simultaneously, ... single actions can be moves in many games at once, and ... public and private motivations cannot be parsed."[21]

Similarly, my investigation of CCRMA highlights the ways in which the same activities can be interpreted by different people and groups in different ways, and it shows that an emergent center like CCRMA can access resources and legitimacy by leveraging such multivocality. The CCRMA account moves beyond this point, however, by underscoring how the success of any given individual or group engaged in this system may in fact *depend* upon this diversity of perspectives, participants, and goals. Moreover, it develops an essential role for technologies and technological artifacts in facilitating such multivocality. Ultimately, therefore, the emergence and renewal of CCRMA shows how interdisciplinarity, open innovation, and commercialization not only can reinforce one another, but also can form an inseparable web of mutual fate.

My account of CCRMA reflects fourteen years of research into the center. My data include formal interviews with thirty-one people, constituting over a thousand pages of transcripts. (See the appendix.) I also held informal conversations and extended email exchanges with dozens of other current and former CCRMA students, faculty, and other affiliates. In addition, I make use of several interviews conducted by journalists and historians, stretching back to the center's early history. These various interviews, conversations, and exchanges helped to establish context, to capture specific events, and to verify and refine facts and perceptions.

I also draw upon thousands of pages of archival documents, including personal and business correspondence, minutes from various meetings, concert programs, grant proposals and reviews, interdepartmental memos, and technology licensing documentation. (These documents reside in the Stanford University Special Collections and Archives, in the Stanford Office of Technology Licensing files, and in the private collections of several

CCRMA affiliates.) I quote liberally from these sources, and from the interviews, in an attempt to provide the reader with a sense of the conversations and considerations in historic context and in the words of those people who made this history. By providing a detailed historic account of a group at the center of the computer music revolution, my intention is to infuse a grounded qualitative richness into conversations about interdisciplinarity, open innovation, and commercialization that sometimes devolve into comparative statistics and rankings.

For the interested reader, the following website contains electronic copies of hundreds of archival documents, alongside other resources, organized by their linkage to specific chapters in the text: http://www.thesoundofinnovation.com. In many cases, therefore, the reader can trace footnotes to freely accessible electronic images of the source documents. This website also includes lists of CCRMA publications and patents, along with lists of concerts and performances, compositions, recordings, and other data. As noted at various points in the text, I have leveraged these resources for various journal articles on related aspects of CCRMA, each of which also is available through the website.

The decade over which I've engaged in this research has enabled me to craft and recraft my understanding and analysis of CCRMA. It also has raised my awareness as to the many important contributions and people that are omitted, very regrettably, from this particular account. Most notably, my attention to the many compositions associated with CCRMA and to the gifted composers behind them is limited. They deserve a book of their own.

The account that I do give is crafted as follows: Chapter 2 describes how broader institutional environments shape organizational emergence. Thus, it describes the history of both Stanford University and the Stanford music department, and it focuses on the tumultuous era of the 1960s and the changes in federal funding and social priorities that facilitated CCRMA's emergence. Chapter 3 explores the history of computer music, including early activities at AT&T's Bell Labs and user-driven innovation at Stanford's artificial intelligence laboratory. Chapter 4 provides a clear sense of the early uncertainties and tensions surrounding CCRMA and interdisciplinary efforts to promote computer music, from the "low notes" of faculty dismissals and research group "divorces," to the "high notes" of faculty reinstatements and the making of major grants to the center. Chapter 5 focuses on CCRMA's four-decade-long relationship with Yamaha, exploring how university–industry collaborations can emerge and evolve to the benefit of both organizations even as they raise challenges tied to different goals and incentives. Chapter 6 describes creative projects and efforts in the 1980s and 1990s to bolster, renew and grow the center amidst shifting funding, technological and musical landscapes. Chapter 7 conveys CCRMA's attempts to commercialize another kind of sound synthesis, which raised new questions about intellectual property, open sharing, and the relationship between academic and commercial activities. Chapter 8 focuses on the new millennium, which is marked by a resurgence of free and open source sharing, and the extension of CCRMA activity into an ever-wider array of disciplines. Finally, chapter 9 reconsiders the ways in which academic disciplines, open innovation, and technology commercialization can coevolve, pointing to broader lessons for creative organizations that serve, in Chowning's words, as sites of "intellectual ventilation as well as coordination."[22]

2 Setting the Stage

To understand CCRMA's emergence, it is useful to step back to World War II. For the first years of that conflict, the Allies relied overwhelmingly on aerial bombardment as the means to engage the Germans. The casualties associated with this approach were overwhelming, with an estimated 2 to 20 percent of planes lost on any given mission. Germany's electronic air defense system—a network of radars and antiaircraft guns that enabled them to track, intercept, and destroy Allied planes—was formidable and lethal.

An intense Allied effort focused, therefore, on determining details of the German system and on further developing the Allies' own electronic warfare capabilities. At the center of these efforts was the Radio Research Laboratory (RRL) at Harvard University. Frederick Terman, a Stanford professor who would prove important to CCRMA, was the RRL's director.[1]

The RRL was one of several government-funded large-scale research efforts tied to World War II. Other examples include the Manhattan Project and the Radiation Laboratory at MIT. These programs aimed to leverage university (and industry) researchers in order to produce new technologies that many observers would credit, literally, with winning the war.[2]

As ticker tape rained down upon parades of returning US soldiers at the end of World War II, scientists and engineers thus shared in the glory. Wartime efforts, such as those undertaken at the RRL, highlighted the critical role of scientific research in addressing "practical" problems.[3] To be sure, US universities had long engaged in the pursuit of practical problems. The decentralized control of American universities—as contrasted against the centralization of many European systems—meant that funding and enrollment of American universities was dependent upon the interests of the local community. In turn, these interests tended to be practical in nature.[4] The Morrill Act of 1862 codified this arrangement, explicitly tying public universities "to the needs of local industries and to the priorities established by state legislatures."[5] Thus, the University of Oklahoma developed expertise in petroleum engineering, the University of Kentucky worked extensively on tobacco processing, and the University of Minnesota conducted research on mining, as three examples. The institutionalization of engineering and applied sciences in American universities—spurred by the rise of university-trained engineers and scientists in industry—further reinforced the role of "practical problems" in university research and teaching.[6]

In establishing their own university, which opened in 1891, Leland and Jane Stanford, too, emphasized practical interests. Their founding document decreed that the university should "qualify students for personal success and direct usefulness in life."[7] Thus, a practical orientation was baked into Stanford's origins, at least to some extent. What changed with World War II, however, was the orientation of these efforts, from regional to national, and the level of government support (which increased dramatically). Indeed, World War II dramatically boosted the prestige of American science among the public and politicians alike, leading to significant funding increases.[8]

The nexus of research activity in World War II, however, remained on the East Coast—especially around Harvard and MIT. Stanford, by comparison, played a minor role. This observation was not lost on Terman, the Stanford professor and director of the RRL. Terman returned to Stanford and became the dean of the School of Engineering in 1946.[9]

As dean of the School of Engineering, and as provost starting in 1955, Terman saw a "wonderful opportunity" in the Cold War expansion of federal research funding.[10] Indeed, the 1950 establishment of the National Science Foundation—which was proposed and first led by Terman's mentor, Vannevar Bush—provided a vehicle through which the federal government could support both basic and applied research at universities. When the Soviets launched Sputnik in 1957, the widely shared interpretation was that the United States was falling behind in science and engineering. In turn, federal support for university research again surged.[11] Building on the growth in federal funding, Terman oriented Stanford faculty hiring and university budgets around government grants and contracts.

At the same time, Terman encouraged strong ties between the university and industry. As early as the 1930s, for example, he encouraged two of his students, William Hewlett and David Packard, in their development of a new line of audio oscillators. These audio devices would become the first product for the Hewlett-Packard Company, and an early model still sits in a glass display case at Stanford's electrical engineering building. (Incidentally, multiple CCRMA participants hold joint appointments with the electrical engineering department.) Through the 1950s and 1960s, Terman amplified his efforts at industry engagement. He invited local companies onto Stanford land, in what would become the Stanford Industrial Park; he encouraged technology development collaborations between Stanford faculty and company-based researchers; he invited company-based researchers to teach Stanford courses; and he established the Honors Cooperative Program (or Honors Co-Op), whereby full-time workers at local companies could take Stanford courses and earn a Stanford degree. Terman thus established a legacy of industry engagement.[12]

Of course, Stanford focused not just on commercializing established university departments. In an effort to bridge basic and applied research, the university also established a number of nondepartmental research centers. The first such center was the Microwave Laboratory, established in 1944 as the on-campus arm of a local company, Varian Associates.[13] Next came the Applied Electronics Laboratory, the Systems Techniques Laboratory, the Solid State Electronics Laboratory, and the Center for Materials Research. Although these centers performed basic research, they also emphasized short-term defense-related applications, they drew money from defense related sources, and they maintained ties with firms in the military-industrial complex.[14]

A key feature of these centers, Terman reasoned, was interdisciplinarity. As Terman observed, "The training of engineers [up to World War II] was inadequate [and] they didn't measure up to the needs of the war. ... Most of the major advances in electronics were made by physicists ... rather than by engineers."[15] Terman thus revamped undergraduate education to emphasize fundamental math and physics, and he encouraged interdisciplinary approaches by which physics, chemistry, and math could contribute to engineering advances.[16] This approach was particularly evident in the new centers.

In short, then, Terman demonstrated a model by which external funding supported a blend of basic and applied research through a newfound interdisciplinary emphasis. Terman's approach appeared to meet with great success: fueled, in part, by dramatic increases in federal research funding,

Stanford rose in prominence from a well-respected but regionally-oriented university to a top-ranked international institution.

In the late 1960s, however, this dramatic rise in federal funding appeared to stagnate: government support declined and then remained relatively flat until the late 1970s. Moreover, university ties to the military, in particular, carried new implications as the conflict in Vietnam escalated. Across the Stanford campus, and the nation, reformers questioned the relationships between the military and university research. At the same time, they encouraged the redirection of "applications" away from military goals and toward social ones—a goal with which many faculty agreed.[17] For example, Robert Huggins, director of the Center for Materials Research (funded by the military's Advanced Research Projects Agency), spoke of his

> desire to make use of the already strong base in materials science to assist progress in some of the civilian technologies that have lain comparatively dormant in recent years, when primary attention was heavily concentrated upon those oriented primarily toward defense- and space-related matters.[18]

Holt Ashley, a professor of Aeronautics and Astronautics, wrote in an editorial:

> Throughout the School [of Engineering] and especially in a few departments, a conscious move in the direction of more *applied* subjects is needed. No doubt there exist topics of fundamental research which are more relevant to urgent social needs, in the U.S. and the world, than the current favorities [*sic*] in Stanford Engineering.[19]

These faculty and others thus encouraged a shift in focus from military applications to social needs.[20]

Campus protesters also reacted against the hierarchical and limited interdisciplinarity that seemed to accompany Terman's vision. Instead, they proposed a *radical interdisciplinarity*, as Cyrus Mody and I have labeled it, that required equal partnerships among the natural sciences, engineering, social science, and humanities.[21] Stephen Kline, who founded Stanford's Values, Technology and Society program, captured the perspective well:

> The kinds of questions that do and should concern the students are: Do you build the SST [supersonic transport], and what is being done about smog? Questions of this sort cannot be seen clearly through the viewpoint of any single discipline ... [and instead require] various combinations of scientists, engineers, philosophers, historians, anthropologists, psychologists, psychiatrists, sociologists, ethicists, and theologians—all working very closely together.[22]

Whereas Terman brought together science and engineering disciplines, the "radical" perspective encouraged incorporation of humanities, social sciences and other fields, too. As the CCRMA case would demonstrate, such mixing could not only orient diverse fields toward a common problem, like the SST or smog, but also reshape these disciplines themselves.

Through the 1960s, therefore, activists, administrators, policy makers, and faculty alike came to adopt a broader vision of interdisciplinarity and to equate this vision with applied research.[23] At the same time, the federal funding picture changed to support this view. As Stanford's President Lyman remarked in 1971, "If we succeed, as I trust we shall, in increasing the amount of multi-disciplinary, problem-oriented research that we do, this will happen in part because money is beginning to become available for such work from the Congress and from federal agencies."[24] Indeed, federal agencies placed increased emphasis on interdisciplinary and applied research, while simultaneously offering increased skepticism about the returns on basic research.[25]

One important outcome of these shifts was recognition of radical interdisciplinary work as a solution to campus unrest and a means to appeal to a wider range of funders. Accordingly, Stanford welcomed a dramatic increase in interdisciplinary centers in the late 1960s, growing from four in 1968 to ten in 1969 to fifteen in 1975, the year of CCRMA's formal establishment.[26]

Amid the turmoil, Stanford's music department seemed to play a small role. Music itself was not new to Stanford. In reporting the history of Stanford's first twenty-five years, Stanford's first registrar, Orrin Elliott, writes:

> Music perhaps came first [among extracurricular activities at the university] and was best exemplified before the public by the Encina Glee Club ... Band and Orchestra were also early organizations and have contributed much to the serious study of music in the University. There was a Roble Glee Club the first year ... the Schubert Club, organized later, represented the more serious efforts of the women students. In 1896 the student body promoted and managed successfully a Paderewski concert in San Jose, and again in 1908 one in the Assembly Hall.[27]

Similarly, in their history of Stanford, Margo Davis and Roxanne Nilan describe the role of music in the university's early years:

> Music and drama loomed large in Stanford community life even though there were no academic departments teaching the subjects, no theater or auditorium, no one in the student body or faculty with formal ... training. Just as Stanford's first varsity football players quickly learned a game that only half of them had ever played, so

did the actors and actresses, musicians, directors, and stage managers learn the crafts of dramatics and musical performance in action.[28]

All of that is to say that music was an important and visible extracurricular activity. It lacked, however, an obvious academic purpose and integration into a course of study at Stanford.

In fact, Stanford did not offer its first formal music course until the late 1920s—more than thirty years after the university's founding—and Stanford did not establish a music department until 1947, one year after Terman assumed his position as dean of the School of Engineering. We have limited historical evidence on these first years of the music department. Department members were undoubtedly influenced, however, by other examples of humanities departments that were not oriented toward externally funded research, which was Terman's clear priority. As provost, Terman stripped the Department of Classics, for example, of faculty lines, shrank its graduate program, and directed the remaining faculty to teach large, lower-level undergraduate courses.[29] It could not have helped that the relatively new music department had yet to make a national impression: Stanford remained unranked in a 1957 survey conducted by the American Council on Education on "quality of graduate faculty in music."[30]

When the central figure in CCRMA's emergence, John Chowning, arrived in 1962 as a Stanford graduate student, he thus faced a unique environment: a non-top-ranked department situated within a university that was profoundly shaped by external funding and an orientation toward Silicon Valley industry, and which was beginning to ferment a new radical interdisciplinarity. The institutional environment, as it happens, was ripe for what Chowning later accomplished.

3 The First Movement

In 1934, as the United States was deep in the Great Depression, the rural town of Salem, New Jersey welcomed its newest resident into the world: John Chowning. Chowning held an early interest in music, playing violin from the age of seven and percussion instruments from the age of twelve. His talent as a percussionist, in fact, would take him around the world—literally: after high school, he served a three-year tour as a musician in the navy.[1]

Back in the United States, Chowning attended Wittenberg University in Ohio under the GI Bill, graduating with a Bachelor of Music in 1959. He then moved to Paris to study with Nadia Boulanger—the French composer, conductor, and teacher who counted Aaron Copland among her pupils.[2]

Post–World War II Paris was the epicenter for the *musique concrète* movement. Pierre Schaeffer, an electronic engineer, played a key role in the movement. In the 1940s, he employed rudimentary recording equipment, disc cutters, to isolate and capture naturally produced sound events.[3] (Schaeffer used the term *concrete* to refer to sounds of nature or the "real world.") Schaeffer then experimented with how to manipulate and isolate portions of these sounds, removing, for example, the "attack" or initial onset of a sound and playing recordings backward. Schaeffer's *Etude de bruits* (1948), a series of five compositions, is representative of the style: the various etudes employ modified locomotive sounds, whistling toy tops, spinning saucepan lids, boats, and other sounds.[4] Public concerts of such pieces met with mixed reactions, as some critics embraced the new style and others dismissed it as valueless noise.[5]

Musique concrète compositions and concerts also presented new technical challenges. Sound engineer Jacques Poullin, for example, grew particularly interested in the problems of sound distribution in an auditorium. Taking advantage of new tape recorders that could manage five independent tracks of sound, he developed a system that consisted of two loudspeakers in the front of a space, on each side of the stage; one speaker hanging over the center of the space; and a fourth speaker on the rear wall. Poullin thus added a spatial dimension to *musique concrete* (and he offered an early demonstration of what today's home theater enthusiasts refer to as "surround sound").[6]

Meanwhile, the city of Cologne, Germany served as the epicenter of *elektronische Musik*, which arose around the same time as *musique concrète*. *Elektronische Musik* emphasized entirely synthetic means of producing sounds, drawing upon noise generators, filters, and other devices to provide the raw sounds and to manipulate these sounds. Thus, whereas composers in the *musique concrète* tradition used electronic devices to capture "real" sounds, composers in the *elektronische Musik* tradition used such devices to create the sounds themselves. As a result, *elektronische Musik* especially engaged engineers and technologists alongside composers. Author Peter Manning reports, for example, that a 1951 talk by Werner Meyer-Eppler, an early and influential player in the movement, reached an audience "of nearly a thousand technologists."[7] Meyer-Eppler himself was a scientist—director of the Department of Phonetics at Bonn University—whose interest in the field had been sparked by the demonstration of a vocoder machine (a speech analyzer and synthesizer) by a visitor from Bell Labs in New Jersey. To further the development of *elektronische Musik*, Meyer-Eppler partnered with Robert Beyer, another scientist, and Herbert Eimert, a composer.[8] *Elektronische Musik* thus sprang from collaboration between scientists and composers, a feature that would prove essential for the Stanford computer music project, too.

Despite their different roots, these two movements—*musique concrète* and *elektronische Musik*—rubbed up against one another, and they increasingly moved away from their dogmatism in the late 1950s and 1960s. Thus, as Chowning arrived in Paris in 1959, the electronic music scene was one in which composers actively sought new direction and new inspiration for musical composition, drawing upon emerging electronic tools to further their musical visions.[9] Indeed, it was in Paris that Chowning discovered electronic music, later citing Luciano Berio, Herbert Eimert, Henri Pousseur, and Karlheinz Stockhausen as influences.[10]

Chowning's time in Paris solidified his interest in pursuing a DMA in music composition. He decided to apply to schools on the West Coast of the United States. As Chowning recalled in a 1983 interview, "I had grown up in the East and gone to school in the Midwest, ... [so] Elisabeth [his then-wife] and I decided we'd go to California. So there was [the University of California at] Berkeley and Stanford."[11] Both schools offered Chowning a scholarship (as did Michigan). A friend familiar with the music program at UC Berkeley had encouraged Chowning to attend there rather than Stanford; UC Berkeley (or "Cal") had more going on in the area of new music. Yet as Chowning recalled, "There was a little more money in the Stanford grant than Cal's. So, we came here [Stanford]."[12]

At Stanford, Chowning immediately became involved in the Society for the Performance of Contemporary Music—a small group of students who put on concerts of new music. In describing the composition environment at Stanford at the time, Chowning recalled:

> There was a lot of interest in—in post–World War II, post-Webern music. [Anton Webern was an Austrian composer and a student of Arnold Schoenberg.] And we did, you know, maybe the first performance here of [Karlheinz Stockhausen's] *Kontakte.* And we did [Stockhausen's] *Refrain,* and—[Luciano] Berio's pieces, chamber music always, or solo pieces, and—I don't know, lots—[Henri] Pousser.

In other words, the major serialist and postserialist classical composers had a major influence on Stanford composers. Continuing, however, Chowning notes:

> But there was a—oh, these curiosities, too, like we had this composer, Peter Ford, who was an—really a philosopher as much as a composer, and—with a heavy interest in French existentialism. And—well, he was far out. He wrote pieces like double fugue for solo contrabassoon that [music professor] Leland [Smith] had played, and wrote an opera called *Buddha* and subtitled *Dry Dung,* and wanted it done in the church. The department wouldn't allow it. It was—oh, there were some fun times.[13]

As Chowning describes it, therefore, the music department continued to embrace a wide range of musical styles, not only performing "traditional" classical music but also experimenting with a variety of new music.

Chowning's active role in new music extended beyond Stanford, too. By virtue of his jazz percussion skills, which allowed him to play complicated styles that "straight-trained symphonic percussionists can't handle very well," Chowning had significant contact with other players in the San Francisco Bay Area new music scene.[14] In particular, he got to know musicians and performers involved with the San Francisco Tape Music Center and Mills College.[15]

Founded in 1962 by composers Morton Subotnick and Ramon Sender, the San Francisco Tape Music Center (SFTMC) served as a forum to present concerts and to learn from and collaborate with others active in tape music—similar to what Chowning had encountered in Paris. The SFTMC traced its origins to a group of composers who had assembled an improvised electronic music studio in the attic of the San Francisco Conservatory of Music. Subotnick, who was teaching at Mills College at the time, joined this group and together they formed the SFTMC. The group was highly successful in the 1960s and undertook regional and national tours that offered broad exposure for the tape music medium and the associated composers. They also influenced technological developments: one project involved a collaboration between Subotnick, Sender, and engineer Donald Buchla, who wanted to create an electronic instrument that would meet the demands of composers. The result was the first Buchla analog synthesizer. In 1966, the SFTMC moved to Mills College, where it became the Mills Tape Music Center (later renamed the Center for Contemporary Music, or CCM).[16]

At Stanford, however, Chowning was growing discouraged. The university had neither facilities for electronic music nor an interest in creating them.[17] Indeed, as far as Chowning could tell, Columbia was the only U.S. university with a studio, and electronic music certainly was not a priority in Stanford's fledgling department. As Chowning recalled in a 1987 article in *Keyboard* magazine, "An electronic music studio would have been very expensive so there was no possibility of getting the administration to support that."[18] With his composition interests increasingly oriented toward electronic music, Chowning considered stopping his studies at Stanford: "You know, get the Master's and split," as he put it in a 1983 interview.[19]

Bell Labs and the Computer

Chowning's fellow members of the Stanford Symphony Orchestra were well aware of his growing interest in electronic music. In January 1964, one of these members, Joan Mansour, passed him a copy of an article from *Science* that described how a computer could be used as a musical instrument.[20] (Mansour was a biologist and her husband, Tag, was on the faculty at Stanford Medical School.)

The author of the *Science* article, Max Mathews, based his publication on years of work that he had conducted at Bell Telephone Laboratories in

Murray Hill, New Jersey, a New York City suburb at the opposite end of the state from Chowning's hometown of Salem. There, in 1957, Mathews created some of the first computer-generated sounds.[21] As Mathews recalled in a 2005 interview, "The computer was on Madison Avenue in New York City. There were only two of them in the world at that time, one in Poughkeepsie in their research lab, and this commercial one there."[22] Mathews, who worked for Bell's Acoustic Research Department, explained the company's motivation: Bell wanted to compress speech so that they could get more voices over the same transatlantic cable. Mathews worked with converters and software to research "encoding" or compressing, which—it so happened—could also be applied to music.[23] (Indeed, this same research led to the development of the MP3 standard by Karlheinz Brandenberg at the Fraunhofer Institute and Jim Johnston at Bell Labs in the late 1980s. Brandenberg and Johnston's algorithm would facilitate the transmission and storage of digital music on an unprecedented scale, underlying services like Napster that challenged the entire record industry.[24])

Mathews, in fact, described music as one of his "great interests." In the same 2005 interview, he quipped, "I still play the violin, and enjoy it very much, although I'm not a good violin player. Probably if I were a better player, I wouldn't have bothered with computer music."[25] At Bell, Mathews worked for John Pierce, a well-known engineer who, among other accomplishments, showed that satellites could be used for communication. Pierce also shared Mathews's interest in music. As Mathews recalled:

> We were at a concert together, and we liked some of it and didn't like other parts of it. In the intermission, we turned to each other and said, "The computer could do better than this." And so he said to me, "Maxwell, I know you're supposed to be working on telephones, but take a little time on the side and write a computer program—you've already made the equipment to get computer numbers converted to sound—let's see what you can get out of it in the way of music."[26]

Mathews's article in *Science* begins with an explanation of the process by which numbers, which are the language of the computer, can be converted to sound, which is the basis of music. Fundamentally, computer music uses the numbers as "samples" of a sound pressure wave, with each sample corresponding to the state of the wave at a particular instant. The generation of sound signals, however, requires a very high sampling rate, corresponding to a large number of samples for a given period of time. The work that Mathews described in *Science*, for example, used sampling rates of 10,000 and 30,000 numbers per second, such that ten seconds of sound required specifying 100,000 to 300,000 individual numbers.[27] In turn, a "digital-to-analog" converter connected to the computer converts the sequence of numbers into a sequence of electric pulses with amplitudes that are proportional to the numbers. A filter then "smoothes" these electric pulses and a loudspeaker plays the resultant tone.

Of course, as Mathews notes in his article, "To specify individually 10,000 to 30,000 numbers for each second of music is inconceivable."[28] Thus, Mathews wrote a series of computer programs that enabled the computation of samples from a simple set of parameters, such as start time, duration, loudness, and frequency (pitch). Mathews wrote his first program, Music I, in assembly code—a low-level programming language—for an IBM 704 mainframe computer. It had a single digital oscillator, a wave generator that produced a triangle wave (a particular kind of sound wave). The following year, in 1958, Mathews wrote Music II, which had four triangle oscillators. Two years later, Mathews completed Music III, designed for the transistor-based IBM 7094 mainframe computer, a more advanced machine than the IBM 704. Music IV followed in 1962, the version that most directly informed Mathews's article in *Science*.[29]

Pierce and Mathews were interested in involving musicians in their work, and in 1961 Pierce hired the American composer James Tenney to work at Bell Labs.[30] In the time Tenney spent at Bell, from 1961 to 1964, he completed several compositions that used the computer both as a compositional tool and to make sounds directly.[31]

Chowning did not read Mathews's article right away. Instead, as he recalled in a 2008 interview:

> I stuck it in my pocket [after Joan Mansour passed it to him]. Then maybe three or four weeks later I was sending my jacket to the dry cleaner and I pulled it out and read it. And this is what I saw: [reading from the article] "There are no theoretical limitations ... The range of computer music is limited principally by the cost ... These limits are rapidly receding." So that was what caught my attention.[32]

Chowning reasoned that Mathews's insights provided a way to pursue electronic music in spite of the resource constraints he faced at Stanford. As he recalled in 1987, "Computers are general-purpose devices, and the idea of using them for music was very attractive because the computers were already there."[33] An electronic music studio required a great deal of single-purpose equipment, which Stanford would not support; a computer, however, was already in place and justified on the basis of nonmusical applications. In many ways, in fact, the roots of the Stanford computer music program would grow from repurposing nonmusical entities—equipment, programs, people, and funding agencies—in the service of musical aims. Such repurposing lies at the heart of multivocality because it takes advantage of the multiple interpretations of an activity or tool in order to facilitate novel activity and acquire resources and support for that activity.

As a first step, Chowning reasoned that he needed to learn to program. As he recalled in a 2005 interview:

> I looked in the course catalog, and there was a course for non-engineers in Algol [a computer language developed in the 1950s]. So I took the course. It was amazingly easy for me, because they taught this course not around programming engineering problems, which was the way most every programming course was taught in those days, but rather they looked for ways to engage this population of people—it was a small group of us—in terms of solving problems that we posed.

In other words, the course adopted the practical-problem orientation that emerged at Stanford more generally during this time period. Chowning, not surprisingly, identified a musical problem:

> I thought, "I'll generate a whole bunch of 12-tone rows." [Twelve-tone music uses all twelve notes of the chromatic scale equally, thus avoiding an association with any particular key.] Although I wasn't so much interested in that kind of music, it was a tractable problem. So I solved the problem, and in doing so I learned how to program, at least the basics of programming. Then when I really wanted to do something, the following summer, I was prepared.[34]

Chowning followed his spring course with a visit to Mathews in the summer of 1964. Given his own interest in music, Mathews, of course, was happy to receive another composer. Mathews provided Chowning not only with crucial direction, but also with the Music IV program on a set of punch cards.

In a 2008 interview, Mathews adopted the more recent language of "open source" to characterize his sharing:

> They [Mathews's Music programs] were all open source. That's right. We released the source code and there were no restrictions. We didn't even have a nice contract like open source programs have that says, "If you do something, you've got to give it out."[35]

In fact, Mathews later coauthored a book, *The Technology of Computer Music* (1969), intended as an instruction manual to facilitate diffusion of the subsequent Music V program.[36] As he shared in a 2008 interview:

I felt that one of the important problems in computer music was how to train musicians to use this new medium and instrument. ... [visits were] a relatively slow way of getting the media into as broad a usage as we thought was appropriate. So one of the things that I did was to write a book.[37]

Mathews's primary interest lay in encouraging the emergence of computer music and in the broad diffusion of resources that would facilitate this emergence. Thus, he engaged in free and open source sharing that enabled interested individuals—engineers and musicians, from universities and firms—to build on his own work.

SAIL and the Origins of CCRMA

The next step for Chowning was to implement this program at Stanford. In the early 1960s, computers were not common on the Stanford campus. Chowning's search for a machine quickly led him to the facilities of the Stanford Artificial Intelligence Project (Lab) or SAIL. SAIL itself was new on campus, established in 1963. Thus, SAIL appeared alongside many of the other centers from Terman's era as provost, as Terman leveraged the center model to encourage research that blended "basic" and "applied" characteristics. John McCarthy, the lab's founder, had arrived at Stanford in 1962 and immediately initiated an artificial intelligence project that built on his work at MIT in the 1950s. With support from the US military's Advanced Research Projects Agency (ARPA), SAIL rapidly grew from six people in 1963, to fifteen people in 1965, to over a hundred people in 1968.[38]

The SAIL computer system, as Chowning recalled in his characteristic dry humor, "comprised an IBM 7090 that had an enormous memory of 36k 36-bit words and a hard disk whose capacity was well over 500k words and about the size of a large refrigerator. The hard disk was shared by a DEC PDP-1 computer."[39] Chowning's graduate school advisor, Leland Smith, recalled an equipment failure a few years later at SAIL, which underscored the very early state of computer technology at the time:

The first disk drive for these IBM things, they were like wash[ing] machines. This big. [Gestures with outstretched arms around the room.] We had this thing called the Librascope. It was a giant disk. It was in a thing not quite as big as this room, but almost. [Laughter.] ...

The whole system, of course, was very flaky because of all the crazy things we were doing with the PDP-10 there at the AI lab. [The DEC PDP-10 was a successor to the IBM 7090.] ... [Once], there was a power failure. ... This disk, which was running twenty-four hours a day, had a system where if it shut down, it was supposed to open some valves to shoot in nitrogen gas to keep the heads away from the surface of the disk so they wouldn't scratch it. ...

[When the power failure happened] you could hear this disk going [Smith makes a "whoo" descending tone]. You know, slowing down [another "whoo" descending tone]. And it would go [another "whoo" descending tone]. And then we heard [Smith makes a scratching sound]. [Laughter.] ... And we were like, "My God, what's happening." [Laughter.] It turned out that some valve in the, all this billion-dollar stuff or whatever, some little valve failed. ... So they finally took this thing apart and they used this disk as a coffee table. [Laughter.][40]

To Smith, the nascent state of computer hardware was matched by the nascent state of programming knowledge. As he put it in a 2008 interview, "We were really all learning as we went along. I mean the computer science professors barely knew more about programming than the musicians did, because it was all so new."[41]

As Smith would be the first to admit, however, these computer scientists and engineers nevertheless *did* know more than Smith, Chowning, and other musicians who engaged early with computer music. Thus, although Chowning had learned some basic programming by 1964, he still lacked the skill to execute Music IV on the Stanford machine. As he recalled:

[Music IV] included of course a whole compiler, because they had a compiler called FAP [Fortran Assembly Program], but it was Bell—BE-FAP, for Bell Labs FAP, which is different from IBM FAP. So we had to load this whole compiler on the [7090], with the program, to get the object code. And he [Mathews] was not very encouraging. He said, "Well, you know, you're going to have a lot of trouble."[42]

A musician entering the world of computer science, even in the early days of computer science, did not face a straightforward transition.

Again, Chowning's participation in the orchestra proved fortuitous. As Chowning recalled, in the autumn of 1964 he made his way to SAIL. He was surprised to see David Poole there, whom he knew from the orchestra; Poole was a tuba player and Chowning a percussionist, so they sat next to one another. Neither one expected to see another orchestra member in the heart of Stanford's artificial intelligence group, leading each to exclaim: "What are you doing here? What are *you* doing here?"[43] Poole, as it happened, was an applied math major and a hacker, "sort of on the periphery of the AI lab," as Chowning recalled. Poole's skills, however, became indispensable to the growing AI lab. Moreover, the AI project's deputy director, Les Earnest, was married to a local music teacher and was sympathetic to

Chowning's attempts. With support from Earnest and "a great amount of help" from Poole, Chowning implemented Mathews's Music IV program at Stanford in September 1964, and he shifted the emphasis of his graduate studies toward computer music.[44] IBM, which had manufactured Stanford's 7090 computer, supported Chowning's early efforts through the award of an IBM student fellowship that covered his tuition and offered a small stipend for the next year.

The social, political, and economic environment surrounding these activities—a broad set of conditions that sociologists label the *institutional environment*—was critical in facilitating Chowning's pursuit.[45] Sociologists sometimes describe institutional environments as "nested" within one another, much like Russian dolls.[46] Thus, broader social, political, and economic trends, such as federal research funding and attitudes toward the Vietnam War, shaped the environment at Stanford, as discussed in the previous chapter. In turn, Stanford's relative lack of barriers between departments, schools, and programs was crucial in enabling Chowning's experimentation. As Chowning noted in a 2008 interview, not every university would have allowed a graduate student in music to access personnel and equipment from an artificial intelligence project: "That's, for me, the wonder ... that I was ever allowed to use a computer somewhere, even at night."[47] Stanford in fact may have been somewhat unique in that respect:

> Not every university [would have allowed it]. Loren Rush [who, with Chowning and others, would establish CCRMA] tried to do that [access a computer for musical purposes] at Cal [UC Berkeley] not long after I started. They wouldn't let him. He couldn't break through. Sometimes the departmental/school boundaries can't be bridged.[48]

Universities, in fact, often put up some of the most rigid departmental and disciplinary barriers.[49] Stanford, however, supported an environment that emphasizes novel research, curiosity, and exploration over departmental and disciplinary dogmatism.

The Stanford music department, too, had certain institutional features that were independent of, yet still shaped by, the broader university and national contexts. Two features of the department's institutional environment were particularly important in facilitating Chowning's pursuits. First, the department lacked a coherent identity. Stanford's music program, as described in the previous chapter, had grown organically, and it had only been an official department since 1947. The department, therefore, saw an opportunity to experiment with novel programs, since it had not yet established a reputation or devoted significant resources to any particular emphasis. In its early years, therefore, the department featured jazz studies, early dance, and performance practice—none of which were standard offerings at comparable universities.[50] At Stanford, individual faculty members had the authority to implement and oversee these experimental programs; thus, late founding and faculty autonomy combined to support experimentation and novelty in departmental offerings.

Second, the music department operated under the "chair system." Encouraged by the university, this system allowed each graduate student to pursue any topic approved by his or her immediate advisor (or "chair"), independent of department interests. In this way, the system supported identities around individual faculty rather than entire departments. In turn, it facilitated more diversity and experimentation in research topics, since students only had to convince a single faculty member to offer support (and did not need to meet a departmental common denominator). This point merits emphasis: the music department had adopted a policy that enabled creativity by tying research directions to idiosyncratic interests rather than popular, safe, or traditional topics.

Chowning's advisor was Leland Smith, an associate professor of music at the time. Smith was a bassoonist who had grown up in the Bay Area. In grammar school, he proved himself a musical prodigy but also "caused a lot of fuss," in his own words, and "got very well acquainted" with the school principal, Maud Marchant.[51] Marchant's husband, Luther, was chair of the music department at Mills College in Oakland—the same institution that would come to house the San Francisco Tape Music Center. Luther Marchant had heard not only of Smith's antics but also of his talent. At the age of fifteen, therefore, Smith was given permission to study with the French composer Darius Milhaud at Mills College.[52]

Smith maintained the Mills connection while pursuing his degrees at UC Berkeley, and he later served as an instructor at Mills in the 1950s.[53] From 1962 to 1964, Luciano Berio—the Italian composer who was one of Chowning's inspirations to pursue electronic music—also served on the music faculty at Mills, and in 1966, as noted, the San Francisco Tape Music Center moved to Mills, with Pauline Oliveros as its director. Thus, Smith's roots were tied to new music through his embedding in Mills and the Bay Area music scene. Perhaps it is not surprising, therefore, that when Chowning approached Smith with the novel suggestion of studying computer music for his doctoral degree, Smith's response, per his own recollection, was, "Well gee, that sounds interesting. That sounds great. Just so long as you teach me as you go along [laughter]."[54] Chowning was free to pursue his passion.

Buffered and supported by his advisor, Smith, Chowning began work in earnest on computer music—and Smith followed.[55] Chowning's initial work using the computer focused on the movement of sounds through four-speaker space. In this way, it continued the tradition pursued by Poullin in the *musique concrète* tradition, and by others before him, but in a much more sophisticated manner: Chowning's technique computed both Doppler shifts (the change in perception from a moving sound source, as when an ambulance siren passes a fixed point) and reverberation (the pattern of echoes that make a concert hall, for example, sound different from a gymnasium).

Smith, meanwhile, was drawn to the possibility of using the computer to print manuscripts. As Smith recalled in a 2008 interview:

> John and I sort of ended up with a tacit agreement ... that he would concentrate on the idea of how the computer made sounds and I would concentrate on how we could convey musical information into the computer to use these sounds.[56]

Smith began work, in turn, on a program to put musical notes into Mathews's Music program.

In 1966, Chowning received his DMA in composition and joined the faculty of the Stanford music department, first as a lecturer and then as an assistant professor. He and Smith continued their work in computer music through SAIL. As Chowning recalled, "We needed to use their facilities, so we became rather tenacious parasites. Leland and I had one room up there, and worked mostly at night and on weekends so as not to abuse our hosts."[57]

SAIL itself was a unique environment. Starting in 1965, it was based at the D.C. Power building, located on Stanford land but nestled in the rolling grass-covered foothills far from the heart of campus. A 1979 article in the *DCR Newsletter*, a publication for the AI community, described the environment:

> The A.I. lab is housed in the D.C. Power building (nothing to do with electricity), a semi-annular wooden barn-like structure atop a hill on Stanford land behind the campus. A bicycle ramp runs up the steps allowing one to ride right to the entrance, from whence, on a clear day, you may see San Francisco's skyline to the north and

the mountains across the bay to the east. The building is in an advanced state of decay. ... To the Australian visitor who arrived toward the end of the Californian summer, the dried grass and gum trees surrounding the lab seemed reminiscent of landscapes back home. ... Lab residents consist of A.I. hackers, music hackers (unpopular with A.I. hackers because they use lots of machine time), robots, and various animals (e.g., Marathon the SAIL cat, a Frisbee fetching dog, etc.) Facilities include the Prancing Pony (a computer controlled food vending machine), a Pepsi machine stocked with Coke and Dr. Pepper, a piano, and a sauna. A skateboard was available for intra-lab travel.[58]

Mike McNabb, who arrived at CCRMA in 1976, likened the environment at SAIL to the space station in Stanisław Lem's science fiction novel *Solaris*: "It was like Solaris. You'd think you were seeing things. All this weird music coming out of the speakers all over the room."[59]

The AI lab was intensely collaborative, and this collaboration was reinforced by the physical environment. The researchers' relative isolation in the foothills outside the main campus ensured that they interacted frequently; although their backgrounds and interests were diverse, they were the only people around, and a certain level of interaction was almost unavoidable. The architecture of the space—with floor-to-ceiling windows, semiopen spaces, and people working in close proximity to one another—also encouraged interaction. MIT professor Tom Allen argues that a building's architecture and communication patterns among its occupants are closely related. Allen claims that buildings with natural light and open spaces, and in which the occupants are physically close and have clear lines of sight, are most effective at inspiring the building's occupants and encouraging creativity.[60]

Stanford scholar Tina Seelig also argues that work environments play an important role in shaping creative behaviors. Seelig writes that environments that are "playfully disorderly," with few walls and customized work environments, spur collaboration and creativity.[61] David Kelley, head of the influential product design firm IDEO, makes a similar point:

You can tell whether a place is playful in about the first fifteen minutes as you walk down the hall. Being playful is of huge importance for being innovative. I mean if you go into a culture and there's a bunch of stiffs going around, I guarantee you they're not likely to invent anything.[62]

With the computer music project, of course, "invent anything" could refer to both technologies and compositions. The physical environment at the SAIL facility encouraged collaboration around both activities.[63]

Beyond the physical environment, however, the shared technical environment at SAIL was also critical. For instance, all SAIL participants shared the same computer—the device that facilitated their work in the first place. This sharing engendered collaboration. Bill Schottstaedt, who arrived at CCRMA in the 1970s, recalled:

> You know we had people, parties and things were going on all the time. You could come in at any time day or night and there was always the same number of people doing things, they never slowed down. ... In those days there was one [computer for music at Stanford]. If you wanted to do it [work with the computer], you had to be at that place.[64]

Similarly, Andy Moorer, who came to Stanford from MIT in 1968, explained how the physical space and shared technological tools at the AI lab facilitated diversity and openness:

> Stanford is just a very open, intellectually rich environment. The thing that attracted me about it, and [what] I continue to marvel at, was the range of the expertise of the people that work there [at the AI lab]. We had not just computer scientists, but there were doctors and musicians, obviously. And we had an ornithologist there for a while, and mechanical engineers. It was—Chowning once described it as being like the "Socratean abode." And indeed you all came together around the computer because you had to go to it, right? It didn't come to you. And everybody was together in these rooms with the consoles or with the terminals, so sharing of what you were doing was pretty common. You're walking around seeing what was on the screen of the person next to you. A very, very intense, collaborative, open atmosphere. I just really loved the intellectual openness and the range of what was going on there. It was really marvelous.[65]

As Moorer highlights, the shared use of a rare technological resource (i.e., the computer) led diverse people to congregate, while the physical environment (e.g., people in common rooms with screens that others could see) encouraged conversations and sharing among these diverse people.

Moreover, it was not just the consoles that were public, but also the sounds. Les Earnest, the AI project's deputy director, had modified the computer system so that every terminal had a loudspeaker, like a computer-controlled PA system. The setup allowed Chowning, Smith, and others to hear the sounds produced by the computer in their respective offices. That same arrangement, however, meant that *anyone* with a set of speakers in his or her office would also hear the sounds. (Incidentally, Mathews sometimes piped his computer music experiments through the intercom system at Bell Labs late at night.)[66]

The shared audio had collaborative and learning benefits. As Chowning recalled, "A lot of us learned a lot by hearing what other people were doing. [We'd hear something and ask,] 'How'd you do that?'"[67] Mike McNabb expanded on the ways in which the shared audio and shared facility led to shared knowledge:

People listened to everybody else. You never know when you might hear some interesting sound that peaks your interest and you think, "That would fit in the piece that I'm working on," and you'd go and get that instrument and code from them. ... If you hear something on the radio, you might try to do some research and figure out who produced it and what they used to get that sound. But it's hard. Usually you can't just ask around. There was a big advantage to all of us having to share a facility.[68]

The shared sounds also alerted nonmusicians as to what the musicians were doing—sometimes with humorous results. For example, Gareth Loy, a CCRMA graduate student at the time, was experimenting with the sound of breaking glass for his landmark composition, *Nekyia*. As John Strawn, another CCRMA participant in the 1970s, recalled, "It would take a while for things to compute, so you'd have silence and then, out of nowhere, this tremendous sound of breaking glass. It sent people diving for cover!" (The AI lab had floor-to-ceiling windows.)[69] The sharing of sounds with engineers, however, was critical because it translated difficult-to-observe coding activity by composers into a concrete output. In turn, this translation opened space for new collaborative relationships between engineers and composers, as the engineers better understood how and why the composers used the computer.[70]

Indeed, the technical personnel at SAIL were tremendously helpful to the musicians. As Schottstaedt recalled:

Once you got in, once John McCarthy [the lab's director] said "okay," then the people who were actually there were very open minded. ... Once you were there, you were part of a group. At least from a technical point of view, everybody was actually sharing information and helping each other out. ... The individual researchers were very helpful and very interested in what we were doing. We didn't help them very much but they helped us a lot [laughter]![71]

Of course, Schottstaedt is being modest in this passage as he, specifically, made important musical and technical contributions.

From an early date, in fact, the computer music project blurred the lines between technical and music personnel. Andy Moorer, for example, was one of the people known to be very helpful. Moorer was hired to be a systems programmer at the AI lab. Soon, however, he branched out, doing some work for the lab's video group related to robotics and building a set of converters to enable Chowning's sound spatialization work. As Moorer described it:

The one thing that was different about our converter from everybody else's is that we were four channel and everybody else's was stereo. ... It gave us the possibility of doing the spatial stuff, which otherwise just absolutely would not have been possible.[72]

Moorer's technical skill, therefore, enabled Chowning's musical experimentation. Later, to help with an experiment in timbre perception, Moorer developed a program, S (for "sound"), to illustrate and analyze sound waveforms. In turn, he invented the first digital audio workstation—an invention that would transform the worlds of music production and film scoring in the decades to come.[73]

Moorer himself came to identify closely with the computer music project. As he described these early years, "[There was a] camaraderie that we had in those early days because we [members of the computer music project] were the outlaws at that point, the misunderstood petulant little brother."[74] In fact, ironically, there was more camaraderie, in ways, among the SAIL participants than among computer music and traditional classical music. Bill Schottstaedt elaborated on the relationship between the status of early computer music and the unity of the group:

It was a really special time, I think, when a special group of people were able to come together, because computer music, or even electronic music at that time, was kind of in the periphery. If you wanted to be a straight-ahead hard-nose composer, which is what you're supposed to be doing as a graduate student, you would not waste any time on electronic music. It was very much off in left field somewhere. ... You had to be there because you were interested.[75]

The peripheral state of early computer music meant that involved individuals were deeply committed to the field—and to the other individuals crazy enough to immerse themselves in it.

In 1967, Chowning had his own technical breakthrough, which reflected the fruits of the AI lab environment: some late-night "fooling around," as Chowning described it, resulted in the discovery of frequency modulation (FM) synthesis. Chowning recalled the discovery in a 2005 interview:

I was experimenting with just a sinusoid and kept increasing the vibrato rate, so all of a sudden it didn't sound like listening to a change in pitch in time, but rather I began to hear timbral differences. So the vibrato became very, very fast, hundreds of times per second, and very, very deep, as if the violinist had a different fingerboard, and the finger was whipping up and down at very high rates and very great distances. That would be sort of a physical metaphor for this.[76]

In technical terms, FM synthesis involves varying the instantaneous frequency of a carrier wave—the pitch frequency of the violin, in Chowning's example—according to a modulating wave, or the rapid movement of the "finger" in Chowning's example. The amount the carrier varies around its average frequency—the *peak deviation*—is proportional to the amplitude of the modulating wave, akin to the great distances that the finger moves in Chowning's example.

These basics of FM were well understood as applied to radio transmission, and Chowning cites Terman's 1947 text, *Radio Engineering*, as one of the four references in his own article on the technique.[77] Engineers, however, had not yet applied the technique in meaningful ways to situations in which both the carrier and modulating frequencies fall in the range that humans can hear. (FM radio is broadcast in the range of 88 to 108 megahertz, or million Hz. Humans hear the range from 20 to 20,000 kilohertz, or thousand Hz.) Nor had engineers considered that the "un-demodulated" FM wave could itself be perceived as musically meaningful.

The "special richness" of the FM technique, as Chowning would later write in a journal article, lies in "sideband components that fall in the negative frequency domain of the spectrum." As the ratio of the peak deviation to the modulating frequency increases, energy from the carrier is redistributed among an increasing number of side frequencies, symmetrically arranged on each "side" of the carrier. For example, a 200 Hz carrier modulated at a frequency of 70 Hz would generate side bands at 270, 340, 410, 480, and 550 Hz above the carrier, and 130, 60, –10, –80, and –150 Hz below the carrier. The ear, however, perceives negative frequencies as *positive* frequencies with inverted waveforms. As these negative sidebands reflect around 0 Hz, they mix with the positive components, creating a rich inharmonic sound. Alternatively, a 200 Hz carrier modulated at a frequency of 50 Hz would generate side bands at 250, 300, 350, 400, and 450 Hz above the carrier, and 150, 50, 0, –50, and –100 Hz below the carrier. In this case, the reflected sideband components mix with positive components at the same frequencies, creating a harmonic sound.[78]

Chowning did not initially have a mathematical understanding of what he was doing, but he did understand that the ratio of frequencies determined harmonic–inharmonic spectra and that depth of modulation determined their bandwidth. He then, in his own words, "did a number of experiments and got percussive tones, brass-like tones, and woodwind-like tones. That's when I realized that there was enormous power here that was predictable."[79] As Chowning recalled, "Then I just started fooling with it crazily."[80]

Chowning made a tape of sound examples that he took to Max Mathews at Bell Labs. Chowning's tape was filled with what he described as "clangorous sounds" of limited use, but his examples proved intriguing nonetheless.

Jean-Claude Risset, a French composer, was at Bell, too. Risset later recalled being "stunned by the liveliness of the sounds and the economy and elegance of the synthesis."[81] Risset copied the data that Chowning used and he recorded the precise date of Chowning's visit as December 18, 1967. Researcher Pierre Ruiz was also present for Chowning's demonstration and he copied the algorithm. Thus, Chowning continued the tradition of open sharing that had enabled his own entry into computer music.[82]

During Chowning's visit to Bell Labs, Risset and Mathews showed him their own work on the analysis of instrument tones. Risset showed that in the trumpet tone "the bandwidth of the spectrum" and "the intensity" grow in tandem; thus, increases in one parameter are accompanied by predictable increases in the other parameter.[83] In turn, such a relationship was amenable to computer algorithms of the sort Chowning was developing.

In 1971, Chowning rethought Risset's insight into trumpet tones and realized that his FM technique could simulate the effect Risset had described.[84] One morning, after working through the night, Chowning caught his student and colleague Martin Bresnick at breakfast and enthused, "You've got to hear these brass tones I got."[85] The results were phenomenal for their realism.

The FM discovery, as Chowning would characterize it, was "an ear discovery." In a 2006 radio interview, he argued, "I think without my musical interest and musical training, I would not have stumbled upon this."[86] To Chowning, therefore, the technical breakthrough was dependent upon a musical perspective. In other words, his work was not simply the *application* of technology *to* music, but rather the *extension* or *invention* of technology *through* music. In this way, Chowning's work is emblematic of radical interdisciplinarity: by bringing together music and engineering on equal footing, Chowning developed a contribution that extended both fields simultaneously.

Despite the FM discovery, Chowning focused his ear, for the most part, on moving sound sources. In 1968, he attended his first meeting of the Audio Engineering Society (AES), held in Hollywood that year. Chowning, David Poole, and Leland Smith gave an overview of the Stanford computer music system, and they focused their comments on its application on "artificial reverberation and simulated movement of sound sources," not FM.[87] Max Mathews—who years earlier had provided Chowning with his Music IV program on punch cards—chaired the session. The presenters stemmed from a variety of institutions, but each of them focused on the intersection of music and engineering. Another panelist, for example, was Bob Moog, inventor of the Moog synthesizer.[88] That same year, 1968, Wendy Carlos had used the Moog to record *Switched-On Bach*, which became one of the bestselling classical music recordings of its era and which singlehandedly raised popular awareness of electronic music.[89]

At the 1970 AES convention in New York, Chowning again presented on moving sound sources and Doppler shift. As he recalled in a 2008 interview:

> What I didn't know was that RCA and CBS were developing quad long-play discs and they were contending for the standard. There were two different standards. One was absolutely discrete. That was RCA. CBS's was encoded. The question which was proposed, which was of great interest, was whether or not CBS's encoding would preserve the absolute localization, the azimuth information. When I walked into this room, it was packed. I had no idea. Then I played these examples and it was dead quiet. I thought something was wrong. The issue was, they were so intensely interested because these were real examples of a discrete system which would challenge or confirm one or the other technologies. ... Now, jump forward about thirty, forty years. A couple, maybe four or five years ago, I was approached by Ray Dolby [of Dolby Labs]. ... All he wanted to talk about was that meeting. At that time, he was only interested in noise reduction. That was his business, noise reduction. But he remembered that session because that finally became his thing, surround sound.[90]

Chowning's AES presentation serves as evidence not only of openness, but also of the connections between university research conducted for purposes of musical composition—as with Chowning—and emerging commercial technical standards aimed at everyday sound enthusiasts. By openly sharing his musical work in a technical forum that appealed to both university researchers and firms, Chowning enabled ties between academia and industry as well as between experimental and mainstream music.

Despite these connections, however, Chowning's own composition activities suffered in the late 1960s. Chowning's emphasis in these years was on "trying to get good sound out of the machine ... developing the computer system."[91] In addition, he maintained a full teaching load. As a result, as Chowning remembers the time period, "I didn't write any music after '66."[92]

Chowning's colleague, Loren Rush, fared better. Rush grew up in Richmond, California, near Berkeley. As a high school student, he not only wrote music and conducted at his high school, but also played with the Oakland Symphony and the Richmond Symphony. Rush completed all of his degrees in music—and all of them in the San Francisco Bay Area (his BA from San Francisco State College in 1957; his MA from UC Berkeley in 1960; and his DMA from Stanford in 1969). Rush, by chance, also was on the same ship as Chowning when Chowning returned to the United States from Europe. As Chowning recalled:

> When I told him [Rush] I was going to Stanford—he had been studying doing new music in Paris on the Prix de Rome [a scholarship for arts students awarded by the French government] from Berkeley—he put me in contact with a lot of the local people in new music. One group that was important, of course, was the [San Francisco] Tape Music Center.[93]

Thus, personal connections through people like Rush facilitated Chowning's entrance into new music in the Bay Area.

Rush also had a long-standing interest in mathematics, which may have explained his involvement in the Stanford computer music project. In fact, it was Rush who "was making strange noises" at SAIL in 1968 when Andy Moorer first arrived, attracting his attention.[94] In January 1969, Rush premiered his *Dans le Sable* at the San Francisco Museum of Art. The piece is scored for soprano soloist, a chorus of four altos, a spoken word narrator, and an instrumental ensemble.[95] It was the first major piece associated with members of the Stanford computer music project (though not a piece that used the computer) and it enjoyed performances at UC San Diego in 1969 and by the Rome Symphony Orchestra in 1970. In 1970, Rush also finished *The Cloud Messenger.* The San Francisco Symphony Orchestra would feature the piece, alongside compositions by Bernstein and Ives, on its 1973 tour of Europe.

Leland Smith, Chowning's former advisor, also completed important compositions in this time period. He premiered his landmark composition, *Machines of Loving Grace,* at Stanford in 1970. Per Smith's program notes for that piece:

> The work is really an environment of sound (and, to a certain extent, sight) for a reading of the poem, All Watched Over by Machines of Loving Grace, by Richard Brautigan. The three parts of the poem mention a "cybernetic meadow," a "cybernetic forest" and a "cybernetic ecology" in which human beings can return to their natural, mammal state under the loving protection of computers. The music is presented by a bassoon (the human-mammal) [and Smith's primary instrument] and a PDP-10 computer. The main elements ... grow out of three chords and two melodic lines which are heard in a wide variety of computer-chosen and human-chosen random deviations.[96]

Smith's composition, therefore, was a cybernetic realization of a poem about cybernetics—an interpretation possible only through computer music.

Smith's *Rhythmicana* (1971) also combined acoustic and computer-generated sounds. The piece, composed for orchestra and computer-generated stereo tape, features a computer realization of the part that composer Henry Cowell had specified for the *Rhythmicon*, a 1930 electronic rhythm machine that Cowell and Leon Theremin had coinvented. Thus, it again used cutting-edge computer music technology to reinterpret a much earlier nod to technology. In 1972, another Smith composition, *Rhapsody for Flute and Computer*, was performed in Paris, followed the next year by a New York City performance of *Machines of Loving Grace*. In short, Smith was finding success with his computer music compositions.

Finally, Chowning joined the composition fray. In 1971 he finished his landmark piece *Sabelithe*, and in 1972 he finished *Turenas*. These compositions demonstrated the power—and the beauty—of his FM technique, along with the computer's ability to transform sounds over time.[97] At one point in *Sabelithe*, for example, a drum morphs into a trumpet. The middle section of *Turenas* also focuses on strong instrumental tones and transformations using FM. At the same time, Chowning leveraged his research around spatialization, enabling the sounds in these compositions to move in space. *Turenas*, in particular, takes advantage of a Doppler shift technique that Chowning had just developed, and the first and third sections of the piece focus on sounds moving through space.[98]

For listeners accustomed to classical music—even avant-garde classical music—the computer-based compositions by Chowning, Smith, and others demonstrated musical possibilities never before heard. As the *San Francisco Chronicle* characterized Smith's *Machines of Loving Grace*, it was "like an infinitely flexible organ playing a fantasia."[99] The compositions convey a sonic atmosphere that casual listeners might describe as "spacey," mixing obviously synthetic tones with "actual" instruments and without clear and obvious melodies.[100]

To be sure, earlier work had mixed new technology-tied sonic elements with musical composition. Luigi Russolo's "noise machines" of the early twentieth century, for example, used mechanical devices to mimic industrial and natural sounds, and he employed them in his compositions *Awakening of a City* and *Meeting of Automobiles and Airplanes*. George Antheil's *Ballet Mecanique* (1927) features sirens and airplane propellers. Edgard Varèse's *Ionisation* (1929–1931) includes two sirens, originally borrowed from the New York City Fire Department, among the instrumentation.[101] Early electronic music, as in the *elektronische Musik* and *musique concrète* traditions that Chowning encountered in Europe, also introduced novel sonic components alongside compositional styles that moved away from tonality and regular rhythm. Computer music, however, afforded, at least theoretically, an unlimited sound palette with unlimited control and detail; whereas traditional instruments are objects with fixed sonic properties, the computer can create any sound you can imagine.[102] Computer music compositions, therefore, opened a never-before-heard realm of musical expression. As composer Gareth Loy, who first went to Stanford in 1974, recalled, "The music was transcendentally beautiful. ... This was not just a new technique; it was a new approach to music."[103]

User Innovation and Commercialization

The compositional activity at the computer music project underscored the project's ultimate motives. As discussed in chapter 1, recent scholarship in the management of innovation has focused on a phenomenon labeled *user innovation*: whereas traditional models of research and development place users at the end of the process—they are the consumers after engineers have already developed the product—a number of scholars document cases in which users themselves develop new products.[104] In turn, these users' motivations have been more aligned with "usefulness to self" or usefulness to their own community of practitioners rather than with the traditional model of profit seeking.

The individuals associated with the Stanford computer music project, too, were user innovators. Their primary interest lay in gaining access to new tools for composition. It just so happened that this search, in the case of Chowning and FM, led to important engineering breakthroughs that eventually made their way into widely enjoyed products. Leland Smith's development of software that would enable the computer to print music was similarly motivated by his own musical interests. As Smith recalled, referring to the 1970s:

I had gotten a pretty-much working graphics system for music. Then, to print the music, of course, we didn't have laser printers or anything like that. We [at the AI lab] had these big pen plotters that would draw scribble things out and we had a thing called a CalComp. ... It had paper like so wide [thirty inches]. So I found out from some of the people who work there [at the AI Lab] what the code would have to be to change my graphic system into pen strokes. ... Of course the pen thing would go along scribbling and to do a whole page it would take like forty-five minutes. [Smith makes "Bzzz bzzz bzzz" sound effects.] And then every now and then it would fail after about twenty minutes, and when it would go to the next stave, it would go across and not pick up the pen and you'd get a line and have to start over again. So I ended up learning how, with rubber bands or whatever, to fix this thing so it would sort of have more efficient pen motion.

In time, Smith's repurposing of the existing tools, with the help of rubber bands, and his evolving software program led to a workable system:

So in 1971 I think it was, I actually got a little set of pages, I guess six or eight pages of some piano pieces of mine called *Six Bagatelles*. I printed it out this way and then did the photo reduction down to normal size, which made it approximately four hundred dots per inch resolution, which wasn't so bad. [Given the low resolution of the plotter, Smith had to print very large sheets and then reduce them to get reasonable resolution.] ... As far as I know, that was the first printing of music by a computer where everything was done by the computer. ... I think it's in the Library of Congress now.[105]

Smith's notation program, SCORE, became a standard among professional manuscript editors. Smith's primary motivation, however, lay in developing software that would enable him and others to enter complex musical information into the computer. Thus, Smith used SCORE for his own compositions, even as he took pride in its adoption by well-known publishers.

A 1984 article on CCRMA in *Mix Magazine*, a trade magazine oriented toward audio recording professionals, emphasized this same "user innovation" orientation of the computer music project. After describing a number of CCRMA's technical research projects and technologies, the article notes:

A full accounting of [technical] accomplishments [at CCRMA] could easily fill several articles, or even a book (and hopefully will). However, as significant as these ad-

> vances are, to merely list and discuss them is to remove them from their true context and miss the real point of the work: at CCRMA, technical achievement is a means, not an end. "CCRMA exists for music," states Betsy Cohen, [a consulting] Assistant Professor of Physics at Stanford with a background equal parts music, psychoacoustics, and electrical engineering. "The research into perception, music cognition, psychoacoustics and signal processing that goes on—all that is to get the music out there." Chowning concurs, adding, "There's nothing I do in the domain of research that doesn't have some compositional value finally." In fact, most of the technical undertakings here begin as a solution to a musical or compositional need that either arises during the creation of a piece, or is seen as a limitation to that process.[106]

For Chowning and his colleagues, therefore, musical composition was both the initial motivation for projects and the ultimate outcome. In this way, CCRMA's approach is opposite that of engineers who create tools for other applications, which are then repurposed for musical applications.

At the same time, Chowning's orientation toward the musical purpose of his creations did not mean that he overlooked their commercial potential. In 1968, he filed an invention disclosure for his sound localizing technology, feeling that "there must be some application in the audio industry." The disclosure was Chowning's first to Stanford's newly created Office of Technology Licensing (OTL). Chowning does not recall how he learned of the OTL—it may have been an article in the campus newspaper—but his hope was that a collaboration with a commercial firm would enable the invention to be produced and distributed en masse.[107]

Through the 1960s, technology licensing was not commonplace at Stanford—or at any other university. In fact, Stanford had arranged for an outside firm, Research Corporation, to handle disclosed inventions starting in 1954. Through 1967, the Stanford–Research Corporation arrangement had resulted in a total financial return to Stanford of only $4,500 and in very little commercialization of the related Stanford research.[108]

Niels Reimers, an associate director at Stanford's Sponsored Projects Office or SPO (the SPO negotiated contracts with research sponsors including the US government), reasoned that there must be a better way to transfer Stanford technologies to industry. Reimers's background was in contract management in the aeronautics industry. In 1968, shortly after his arrival at Stanford, Reimers proposed a pilot program with several novel features: the program would incentivize faculty to disclose their inventions by allowing them to share in any revenue generated; it would employ designated licensing associates with relevant scientific or technical backgrounds—not lawyers—to manage cases, and it would provide them with individual authority over these cases; it would use outside law firms to handle patenting and other legal matters; and it would focus on marketing rather than legal details. Moreover, Reimers emphasized a collaborative approach with licensees from the start. As he recalled in a 2012 interview:

> Our practice at OTL was first to seek a US licensee, with the initial contact by telephone. [We'd propose] that they evaluate the commercial potential of a technology, with the objective of [establishing] a collaboration to bring the technology to commercial use. Our perceived value/significance of a technology would determine who to contact in a target company. For a small company, that generally would be the company president. And often even before a decision by us to file or not file a patent application. This drove the company patent attorneys crazy, particularly if they learned we had not filed a patent application. But throughout my career, this method of proceeding never led to a dispute as to patent rights with a company. The focus of a company patent attorney seemed to be the strength of patent claims rather than a collaboration. If we were required to go through a company patent office, I would estimate the chance of a collaboration was reduced by 75 percent.[109]

Although Reimers is careful to note the important role played by attorneys, his own experience emphasized the benefits of a collaboration focused on technology development, rather than negotiations over patent protection. With Reimers devoted to the new Stanford model half-time and with one assistant, the program produced $55,000 in its first year—more than ten times the previous total. On January 1, 1970, Stanford officially established its Office of Technology Licensing, with Reimers as the head.[110]

Chowning's 1968 disclosure for his sound-localizing technology, therefore, was one of Reimers's first invention dockets. (The pair knew each other because their children played soccer together, again underscoring the role of personal connections at CCRMA.)[111] Chowning was optimistic that the device would attract interest. As Moorer described it:

> [It was a] marvelous analog electronic contraption. ... We tried to sell it to everybody. We had those guys from ARP [an analog synthesizer company] in there, we had synthesizer [companies]. We had people in from everywhere, and it was just universally dismissed. It was really discouraging. John was so proud of having put this damn thing together and people didn't really get the idea of spatializing the sound.[112]

Indeed, Reimers initially tried to interest Disney in the technology, with the idea that surround sound could add to the movie theater experience. According to Reimers's recollection, they weren't interested.[113] (Of course, with Dolby's help, surround sound would later come to define the movie theater and home theater experiences.) Disney's lack of interest highlights a dominant theme in the scholarly literature on science and technology studies: uses for new technologies are neither obvious nor baked into the technologies themselves; instead, technologies, uses, users, and broader institutional features together shape a trajectory.[114]

Finally, GRT corporation signed a license agreement with Stanford, taking an option to commercialize the technology.[115] (The option allowed them to further investigate the technology's potential and to have first rights should they choose to pursue it further.) GRT's efforts did not prove fruitful, but the effort still netted $5,000 for Stanford for the option—more than the entirety of technology licensing earnings from the Research Corporation arrangement.[116] Underscoring his own musical motivations, Chowning put his share of the money toward a Scully tape recorder for use in his research.[117]

Not to be discouraged—and bolstered by the success of his brass tones experiments—Chowning disclosed his FM synthesis technique to Reimers's office in 1971. As Chowning recalls, upon playing the tones for John Pierce during a visit to Bell Labs, Pierce said, "Patent it!"[118] Since software could not be patented at the time, Andy Moorer designed a hardware device that embodied the technology. To aid in the task, he used a prototype CAD (computer-aided design) system, one of the first in the world, developed by the Advanced Computer Design group at the AI Lab. Thus, the association with diverse activities at the AI Lab again proved fruitful. The resultant drawings were used for the patent application. (Of course, Stanford did not have the money to actually build the device. Moorer was stunned to discover, years later, a physical prototype device based on his design: "They actually took the patent and built the device from it! … I was astonished."[119])

Reimers again set to work to find a commercialization partner, focusing on the most obvious related companies at the time: US-based organ manufacturers. Unfortunately, none of them were interested. The experience of the Hammond Organ Company was typical. Hammond was well-known for their B-3 organ used by countless jazz, rock, R&B and prog-rock artists. To create sounds, the B-3 used a tone-wheel system: toothed iron discs rotated in front of electromagnets that generated voltages, which formed the pitch for each key. Hammond sent engineers to Stanford to explore Chowning's FM technology. Sound generation through a digital computer rather than rotating discs, however, was far, far outside of Hammond's domain. As Chowning recalled, "It was just not a part of their world."[120] The manager of Hammond's Advanced Development Engineering group subsequently wrote to Stanford, "Our viewpoint is that some of the alternative approaches are more attractive in terms of design implementation, manufacturing cost, and breadth of performance."[121] Hammond declined to pursue FM any further.

While companies showed limited interest in Chowning's FM technique, musicians expressed great enthusiasm for the Stanford computer music project.[122] For example, György Ligeti, a famous Hungarian composer, served as composer-in-residence at Stanford for six months in 1972.[123] Chowning recalled how Leonard Stein, one of Schoenberg's students and a well-known concert pianist, had come to Stanford to meet with Ligeti and to see the computer music project. Chowning played *Sabelithe* for Ligeti and Stein and recalled that Ligeti was "absolutely astonished."[124] Continuing, Chowning recalled:

> He [Ligeti] was very pleased and kind of astounded that this has been going on and he didn't know it. He was just sitting down and—well, I don't think he's terribly fond of the piece as a composition, nor am I in many ways, but ... he saw a potential there that I think excited him.[125]

For composers in search of new means of expression, Chowning's use of the computer highlighted new possibilities—a bit like a painter discovering a new color palette and a new type of brush simultaneously. The fact that Chowning was a composer himself and that he could show the computer "in action" made such demonstrations all the more astonishing. Indeed, Max Mathews's early work, which he reported in his 1963 *Science* article, offered relatively simple compositions to demonstrate the potential of the computer; Chowning's demonstration through *Sabelithe* showed the marriage of the technical and the musical in rich detail.

Chowning took a sabbatical in the coming academic year, 1972–73. Ligeti arranged for him to give concerts that included his new composition, *Turenas*, in Berlin and Darmstadt in the summer of 1972. That winter, Chowning traveled around to various electronic music studios, including those in Stockholm, Utrecht, Cologne, and Milan. His visits served to strengthen the network around electronic music and enabled him to share with—and learn from—diverse approaches.

At the same time, Pierre Boulez, a renowned composer and then-director of the New York Philharmonic, was in the midst of planning an electronic music project in Paris, with significant support from the French government. Boulez had asked Jean-Claude Risset, Mathews's collaborator who had done the work on brass tones, to consider taking a position there. Ligeti, who was very well connected among modern composers, mentioned to Boulez the work at Stanford. In turn, Risset arranged for Boulez and Chowning to meet in London, a stop-off for Chowning, where they spent about an hour discussing computers and music.

Impressed, Boulez then invited Chowning to participate in the planning sessions for his Paris electronic music center, the Institut de Recherche et Coordination Acoustique/Musique (IRCAM). A planning meeting that year included a veritable "who's who" of the world of electronic music: Chowning, Risset, Ligeti, and Boulez were joined by Milton Babbitt, the famed American composer, and Luciano Berio, the Italian composer who had served on the Mills College faculty in Oakland in the early 1960s.[126] Thus, Chowning's network of personal connections—which had already proven so important—was expanding into the upper echelon of contemporary music.

Although Chowning was gaining international recognition and support through these activities, they did not immediately yield benefits back home. Instead, as he traveled Europe, Chowning received bad news from Stanford: the university had denied his case for tenure. Chowning would soon be out of a job.

4 Tension and Release

In a 2004 article in *Science,* Diane Rhoten and Andrew Parker argue that even as "interdisciplinary research has become synonymous with all things progressive about research and education," traditional disciplinary boundaries, university departmental structures, and institutional incentive systems make the practice of interdisciplinary research challenging—especially for junior scholars who may lack the resources and the protection afforded by tenure.[1] This view informs one interpretation of the difficulties that Chowning faced when his tenure case underwent review. He had published an article on the moving sound technique that appeared in the *Journal of the Audio Engineering Society* in 1971.[2] His paper on FM would appear in the same journal in 1973—reaching a wide audience of engineers, but not serving to raise Chowning's profile among musicians.[3] John Pierce of Bell Labs, one such engineer, had written a very strong letter of support for Chowning's tenure case, citing Pierce's own membership in the National Academy of Sciences, the National Academy of Engineering, the Acoustical Society of America, and a variety of other professional bodies. The text reads, in part:

> Certainly I hotly (rather than warmly) endorse John Chowning's abilities and attainments. ... In a day when many artists mouth science vainly, it is rare but extremely pleasing to find one, John Chowning, who understands and uses science. I feel that John Chowning merits a worthy and secure position, at Stanford or elsewhere, and I hope he gets one.[4]

At the same time, however, other engineers appeared uncertain of the technical quality and contributions of Chowning's work. The fact that his applications focused on musical composition may have further detracted from their consideration. At Stanford, the contribution of Chowning's *Journal of the Audio Engineering Society* papers was considered by Cal Quate. Quate is a brilliant scientist who counts invention of the scanning acoustic microscope and the atomic force microscope among his accomplishments. He also served as associate dean of Humanities and Sciences when Chowning was denied tenure. Quate, however, misunderstood Chowning's use of FM and its novelty. (As Moorer recalled, the reaction seemed to be, "We teach this to sophomore EE [electrical engineering] students. What's the big deal?"[5]) The musical applications seemed to obscure what was an important technical innovation in its own right.

Meanwhile, on the musical side, Chowning's compositions, *Sabelithe* and *Turenas*, were difficult for many musicians to interpret and understand. Chowning recalled his *Turenas* premiere at Stanford. During the performance, one of the four speaker amplifiers went out. As Chowning labored to fix it, the music department chair leaned over to another composer (Ivan Tcherepnin, who also made important contributions to electronic music) and said, "Why can't we go on? ... What does he need four [speakers] for, you know, won't three do?" As Chowning tells the story, the comment was made in good humor. Nonetheless, it underscored the lack of understanding around electronic music—and Chowning's work in particular—in the department.[6] With little history of electronic music at Stanford—and little history of computer music *anywhere*—it was difficult to assess Chowning's work, generally, and especially difficult to determine if it met the high bar required for tenure at Stanford. Chowning, in short, was caught in an interdisciplinary no-man's-land in which engineers greeted his technical contributions with skepticism because of their musical application and musicians greeted his musical contributions with skepticism because of their almost-unprecedented integration of technical advances.

In chapter 1, I reflected on the concept of *multivocality*—the ability to perform multiple activities with a variety of constituents. Existing examples in the literature highlight the benefits of multivocality, as with Powell and colleagues' study of the biotechnology industry or Padgett and Ansell's study of the Medici family: multivocality enables the focal party to draw together diverse perspectives and constituents, and to exert special influence by virtue of lying between them.[7] Chowning, too, would later benefit from this position. In the early 1970s, however, he experienced the downside of multivocality—neither group with whom he connected, at least at Stanford, fully appreciated his work in the other domain. Here, Rhoten and Parker's point in their *Science* article is particularly salient: universities are organized into departments that are bound by common disciplines and shared interests, methodologies, and epistemologies. In turn, these departments define themselves, in part, in contrast to the disciplines, interests, methodologies, and epistemologies that lie outside the department.[8] Without a strong reputation in the mainstream of either group alone, Chowning's position "between" the groups served to cast further doubt on his ability to connect with the core.

Stanford provided Chowning with two more quarters of support, to give him time to "sort things out." Chowning then planned to take a position as artist-in-residence for the City of Berlin, supported by a DAAD grant that Ligeti arranged. But his short time back at Stanford, from the fall of 1973 until the spring of 1974, proved to be critical.

With Andy Moorer, Loren Rush, and John Grey, Chowning decided to apply to the National Science Foundation (NSF) and the National Endowment for the Arts (NEA) for support for the computer music project. Chowning had applied to the NSF earlier, but without luck. As Leland Smith characterized the situation:

> I remember one time one of the people who was out here from the [National Science] Foundation said, "You know, your project is really great. We love it and all, but it's in music. If we have our limited funds and we have this guy over here with a project which is a very sort of pedestrian but useful project in mathematics or something, and we have you in music, we have to give him his project because that's science." So eventually they [Chowning and colleagues] got the idea of linking up with psychoacoustics, which is "science" [laughter].[9]

The involvement of John Grey, in particular, was crucial for the new application. Grey had double-majored in music and psychology at UCLA, where he first encountered the idea of using a computer to study how the brain processes music.[10] As a PhD student in psychology at Stanford, he focused his research on the perception of musical instrument tones.[11] The investigation of timbre was extremely difficult since, as Grey notes in a 1975 publication, perceptions depend on the spectrum of the sound, "the waveform, the sound pressure, the frequency location of the spectrum, and the temporal characteristics of the stimulus"—simultaneously.[12] Yet it was difficult to isolate these various components of timbre using traditional experimental approaches based on comparative recordings of "real" sounds. Grey's insight involved using the computer to generate instrument tones and then manipulating these various factors in order to isolate the ways in which they contributed to the perception of timbre. Thus, Grey clearly demonstrated the application of the computer to questions of both musical and scientific importance.[13]

In turn, the 1974 application to the NSF described a research project around the "computer simulation of music instrument tones in reverberant spaces," clearly building on the earlier work of Chowning, Grey, Rush, and Moorer. Pierce reviewed a draft of the application and, it appears, served as one of the official reviewers; some of the same phrases used in Pierce's letter in support of Chowning's tenure case also appear in one of the (strongly positive) grant reviews.[14]

To the NEA, the group described how "a major American contribution to present and future music exists in the application of a rapidly developing computer technology to the art and science of music."[15] Continuing, the grant application describes the computer music facility itself as a musical instrument:

> The [computer music] facility must be seen as the most flexible of musical instruments. To speak of the facility as a conventional musical instrument, however, is somewhat misleading because the system is capable of simultaneously producing a large number of independent voices having arbitrary timbral characteristics; it is much more general than a conventional musical instrument. As with any other instrument, it must be studied in order to be useful, but once learned, it is an instrument of enormous potential; it can generate any sound that can be produced by loudspeakers, modify and transform real sounds entered into the system by means of microphone, remember and modify articulated musical input, and simulate the location and movement of sounds in a variety of illusory reverberant spaces. Equally important, the facility will be capable of serving a number of composers, providing for each a direct control over his medium which was never before possible.[16]

This passage from the NEA grant is interesting for two reasons. First, it again reflects the link between multivocality and the repurposing or multipurposing of technologies. In this case, the computer can be interpreted as both a musical instrument and a scientific instrument. Second, the passage—and the grant itself—is aimed at educating the reader about the fundamentals of computer music: What constitutes an instrument? In what ways is the computer like an instrument? How does the computer instrument work? To the NEA reviewers, therefore, Chowning and colleagues worked to describe the computer in musical terms—both establishing it as a legitimate instrument and simultaneously highlighting its special characteristics.

Although the NSF application was, in Chowning's assessment, "obvious," the NEA grant was not; despite the Stanford group's education efforts, the NEA traditionally gave composer grants to individual artists, not large grants to centers. Chowning, therefore, went to Washington, DC, and met with the director of the NEA. As Chowning recalls, "I explained to him [the NEA director] what this was all about, and this was a new medium and it had a large scientific component. He believed me."[17]

As an administrative hedge, the group also proposed the formation of the Center for Computer Research in Music and Acoustics, or CCRMA. As Chowning explained:

> Because what we were doing was interdisciplinary, it didn't fit in the music department, which was dominated by musicologists. So we decided we should form some sort of center that would allow us to apply for funding. I was the one on the faculty, and so I became the director. I chose good people—the idea was to make an open, accessible system and then leave people alone.[18]

In 1974, therefore, Chowning, Grey, Moorer, Rush, and Smith prepared a formal proposal for CCRMA, which outlined the need for a proper center and described its relationship to the AI lab:

> We propose that the Department of Music continue the work with computers by organizing a center for research in acoustics and music. ... The center should be organized in such a way that it has a direct relationship to the academic program of the [music] department, but should be to some degree autonomous in determining its research projects and staff. ... There are advantages in maintaining our association with the A.I. Lab.
>
> 1. There is no requirement for additional space
> 2. We can buy a "piece" of a hardware engineer's time
> 3. Our system can be an "invisible peripheral" to the PDP-10 system
> 4. We have available to our system the PDP-10 software
> 5. We benefit from the high level of technological expertise and insights—ideas breed ideas.[19]

CCRMA was born, therefore, as a means to connect with both the AI group and the music department, while retaining a degree of autonomy in relation to each of them. In other words, the center structure provided a means to connect "loosely."[20]

At the same time, Chowning maintained his relationship with Boulez. The summer 1973 and 1974 planning meetings for IRCAM had led to a realization among the IRCAM group that a trip to Stanford would be valuable: they could receive a hands-on tutorial in the use of the computer for music. In a July 1974 letter to Al Cohen, the newly named chair of the Stanford music department, Boulez outlined his plans for the visit and

Figure 4.1
CCRMA's cofounders in 1975. Pictured standing, from left to right: Leland Smith, John Grey, John Chowning, and Loren Rush. Andy Moorer is seated. Courtesy of the Stanford University Archives.

for a general collaboration between the two groups.[21] Prior to arriving at Stanford, Cohen had taught at the University of Michigan and SUNY Buffalo, both of which featured electronic music studios. Such interest from a composer and music personality on the scale of Boulez reinforced Cohen's belief that the university might have made a mistake with Chowning's dismissal.[22] Responding to Boulez, Cohen wrote, "Please realize that I share with you recognition of the enormous promise resulting from interaction between IRCAM and the Stanford Center."[23]

As Chowning spent the summer of 1974 in Berlin, plans for the Boulez visit continued. An October 1974 letter from an IRCAM representative clarified the list of attendees: Jean-Pierre Armand, Gerald Bennett, Luciano Berio, Thomas Bever, Pierre Boulez, Yves Galmot, Vinko Globokar, Clytus Gottwald, James Lawson, Brigitte Marger, Diego Masson, Max Mathews, Jean-Claude Risset, Nicolas Ruwet, and Nicholas Snowman.[24] In other words, these were the world's leading composers and researchers in the field of computer music. As the *San Francisco Chronicle* would later describe the group, they comprised "the world's most distinguished school boys, a crème de la crème group of 13 musicians and scientists from Paris headed by Pierre Boulez, no less."[25] In turn, as Max Mathews characterized the situation, it was natural for them to visit Chowning's group: "John's group here at Stanford, CCRMA, was the only worldwide source of people who were trained in computer music techniques at that time, or at least by far the best source."[26] Increasingly, Stanford administrators felt unease with their decision to dismiss Chowning—a feeling heightened by other events that winter and spring.

No musical instrument manufacturer in the United States had been interested in Chowning's FM technique. OTL director Reimers, however, had hired an MBA student as an intern, tasked with researching potential licensors worldwide. The student identified Nippon Gakki Corporation of Japan, known as Yamaha. Though Yamaha's US market share was limited, they were a major manufacturer on a worldwide scale. Chowning and Reimers reached out to the company in 1974.

In December 1974, Yamaha's Yasunori Mochida responded to a letter from Chowning, sharing technical details of a digital synthesis system that Yamaha was developing. He included a cassette tape for Chowning to hear samples.[27] Chowning responded in January 1975, providing further technical detail on his FM system. Examining the archival records, the correspondence between Yamaha and Stanford unravels as a "dance" in which both Yamaha and Chowning reveal more and more details about their respective digital synthesis systems. Although Chowning had shared openly with colleagues at Bell Labs, as described, he was slightly more cautious with Yamaha—in large part because he lacked any personal connection with the group.

Yamaha's interest was not indicative of a "sure thing." Indeed, Cal Quate, the same engineer who had overseen Chowning's tenure case, had disclosed to the OTL a technique for converting written music to sound. The OTL, in turn, shared it with Yamaha and hoped to sign a license. Instead, Yamaha responded that they already had their own system based on work by someone at Brigham Young University and, therefore, were not interested in Quate's system.[28] Chowning's own experience with the moving sounds that GRT Corporation failed to commercialize and with an all-pass digital reverberator that Stanford decided would not be commercially competitive clearly loomed in his mind.[29] The FM sales pitch, however, was helped immensely by the three features: Yamaha was already working in this area; they had come up against a technical barrier that Chowning's system solved; and they happened to have an engineer—not a business development or marketing person—evaluate the opportunity. The engineer was Kazukiyo Ishimura.

Ishimura worked as part of Mochida's small team at Yamaha. As Mochida recalled in 1986:

> I first met Professor Chowning more than ten years ago. I then embraced a firm belief that digital processing would replace analog processing in electronic musical instruments in the future. Therefore, within Yamaha, we began conducting intensive research and study of digital processing methods, and we developed several methods of digital processing by ourselves. But every method of our own development made the hardware—in this case, electronic musical instruments—into very bulky pieces of equipment that could not be produced within our targeted cost.[30]

Chowning's FM technique reduced the computational requirements and, in turn, the bulk and cost of associated hardware. On March 19, 1975, Yamaha Corporation finalized its license for FM, with the clause that Chowning would be highly involved in its development.[31] This license would later become one of the most profitable in Stanford history. More importantly, in years that preceded recombinant DNA, DSL, the Google search engine and other important Stanford inventions, the license and development of FM would serve as a model of university technology transfer.

Just one month after Yamaha signed the license, in April 1975, the NSF wrote to Stanford's president, Richard Lyman, to notify him that they were awarding one-quarter of a million dollars to the Stanford computer music project. Alongside the NSF award, the NEA announced a grant of $160,000 to the project. Stanford, embarrassingly, had dismissed the Principal Investigator on the grants. Quickly, Stanford arranged for Chowning to return to Stanford to appeal his tenure case and they gave him the title of Research Associate to manage the computer music project. CCRMA was born.

The summer 1975 visit from Boulez and other IRCAM affiliates proved to be an important milestone for Stanford and for computer music generally. Publicly, it received considerable attention and press. When asked if the visit enhanced his standing with the university, Chowning replied, "Oh, yeah, enormously … here's this major composer-conductor [Boulez]. … He was a star, obviously. So the university had a huge reception for him and all his group."[32]

To Boulez and colleagues, however, the interest lay in new musical possibilities rather than star treatment. When making the trip arrangements, for example, the IRCAM contact noted, "We would prefer to eat in the cafeteria rather than use the more formal dining arrangements." They also arranged to stay in one of the student dormitories, Lagunita Hall, rather than a formal hotel. The IRCAM group's overwhelming desire to explore new music and to stay close to the pulse of the Stanford campus was evident in the modesty of their requests and arrangements. Indeed, as the IRCAM contact noted in arranging for the dorm rooms: "I should be especially grateful if it were possible to arrange for, perhaps, two of these [dormitory] rooms to have baths."[33] This roll-up-the-sleeves straightforwardness would prove appealing for subsequent famous and well-heeled visitors, too.

CCRMA's eventual influence on IRCAM would prove to be enormous. As Chowning would recount, rightly, in a 1979 letter to the Rockefeller Foundation:

> We have not only served to some extent as a model for Boulez's institute, but a substantial interaction and cooperation between the two centers has developed. In 1976, IRCAM acquired the same computer which we have [a PDP-10] in order to have access to all of the programs which we have developed over the years.[34]

Figure 4.2
This photograph was taken during the August 1975 visit by IRCAM personnel to CCRMA. Pierre Boulez is seated at the console and graduate student Steve Martin is seated to his left. Standing, from left to right, are Andy Moorer, John Chowning, and Max Mathews. Courtesy of the Stanford News Service. Photo by Jose Mercado.

Indeed, the CCRMA instruction manual for running Music 10 clearly notes that "in most cases this text will also apply to the program in use at the IRCAM lab in Paris."[35]

Continuing, Chowning's letter to the Rockefeller Foundation notes:

This [sharing of software] has saved IRCAM tens of man-years of development work, which in a commercial context would have resulted in a large financial return to CCRMA. In the arts such a financial transaction cannot happen nor should it, which means that the visibility of an activity such as CCRMA must find support elsewhere.[36]

Here, the suggestion of appropriate and inappropriate arenas for financial transactions is particularly interesting: Chowning wrote this passage four years *after* signing the license agreement with Yamaha (though the license had yet to yield much income since income was tied to sales of products, which were still in development). Chowning is clearly parsing, therefore, between nonprofit organizations oriented toward the arts—such as IRCAM—and for-profit organizations oriented toward technology development, such as Yamaha. As CCRMA's own experience indicates, however, the line between these activities can be difficult to draw.

The NSF and NEA grants also allowed the newly formed CCRMA to acquire a digital synthesizer. They turned to Systems Concepts, a company that specialized in making hardware peripherals for the PDP-10. Peter Samson, an MIT-trained computer scientist who had served as a contributing architect to the DEC PDP-6 computer, designed the CCRMA synthesizer. Samson proposed a synthesizer that would provide 256 "generators" (or sound wave producers with several modes and controls) and 128 modifiers (which could serve as filters, random-number generators, or other functions)—an unprecedented capability for sound synthesis. The "Samson Box," as the digital synthesizer came to be known, had 64,000 words of delay memory and functioned as a peripheral to the PDP-10, taking commands and data from the attached computer, and sending them back to the computer or to some attached analog outputs (to create sound). It resembled a green refrigerator and had a base price of $87,500 (about $380,000 in 2014 dollars).[37]

Perhaps influenced by the success of Stanford's license agreement with Yamaha, Systems Concepts proposed that they would have rights to the software developed for the machine, a request that became something of a sticking point in the agreement.[38] As Chowning explained:

That was a horrendous thing. ... Not [Pete] Samson, but the head of the company was absolutely paranoid. They thought that they could sell this thing. They were hoping to sell one to IRCAM and perhaps other places. They were trying to protect their technology ... They had a trick on doing fast multipliers and that was what made this thing so effective. It was a hardware issue or firmware. They didn't want that to become public. He [the president of Systems Concepts] worried to death about someone like David [Poole] or Tovar getting this and letting everyone else know.[39]

David Poole, of course, was the tuba player and "hacker," as Chowning would describe him, who was so instrumental in enabling Chowning to use Max Mathews's program. Tovar was the systems programmer at CCRMA in the 1970s. (His real name was John Mock. As Bill Schottstaedt, another early CCRMA participant, explained, "He chose the name Tovar because of *tovarich,* a Russian word that means 'friend and comrade.'"[40]) The concerns of Systems Concepts highlight the tremendous uncertainty surrounding computer music in the 1970s: Systems Concepts foresaw an expanding number of centers, which would require expensive custom hardware; yet, the limited number of programs in the 1970s and Chowning's own difficulties at Stanford underscored the fact that such growth was not guaranteed. Ultimately, Stanford agreed to give Systems Concepts ten years of exclusivity on the Samson Box. Systems Concepts, however, never sold another unit.

In October 1977, CCRMA took delivery of the Samson Box alongside one of the most active and influential periods of composition in the Center's history. As Max Mathews characterized the device and the creativity it engendered, "[The Samson Box gave CCRMA] a monopoly really on large-scale production of music."[41] Julius Smith, an electrical engineer who arrived at CCRMA in 1976, recalled how the Samson Box had an immediate impact:

Here you are at the AI lab, a big time-sharing facility. The music compiler runs all night just to create a few seconds of very good sound. Then this device rolls in. It looks like a big green refrigerator in the machine room next to everything else. It's just *blazingly* faster than anything you could do before. It just spurred people onwards.[42]

Smith had been an Honors Co-Op student, where he watched Stanford lectures on closed-circuit television. (Recall that Fred Terman, as provost, had started the Honors Co-Op program as a way to better integrate the university with industry.) A seminar by Andy Moorer on computer music and signal processing led Smith to conclude, "That sounds really exciting. I've got to find a way to go over there and find a way to get involved."[43] Smith, in fact, would go on to become one of CCRMA's most notable contributors. He developed a new sound synthesis technique, waveguide physical modeling, detailed in chapter 7.

Mike McNabb also arrived at CCRMA in 1976, just one year before the delivery of the Samson Box. McNabb had been at Stanford as an undergraduate. He recalled that Chowning had set up his sound spatialization system in the quadrangle at the center of Stanford's campus. Later, Chowning and Loren Rush gave a presentation in Tresidder Student Union. At the presentation, Chowning played *Sabelithe* and *Turaneus*. As McNabb recalled:

> It basically blew my mind. Since I had both this science side and music side, I had this epiphany where I thought, "Oh my God. This is it. This is the perfect thing." I just became obsessed with getting somehow into that.[44]

McNabb recalled that the Samson Box changed the paradigm of computer music composition itself:

> It was very different. As John used to put it, [it used to take] one minute to program what you wanted and then wait eight hours for it to process. Then it was reversed: You spent eight hours programming it for one minute of hearing it. [Laughter.] It was great that it was real time, but it was almost a misnomer. It took us a long time to get used to it and get used to how we needed to work. We spent a lot of time writing real software to actually control the thing. But then we were able to do some pretty amazing stuff.[45]

As McNabb highlights, new technologies—such as the Samson Box—are not mere substitutes for the artifacts they displace. Instead, as interconnected elements of a social-technical system, their introduction suggests changes in accompanying processes, such as writing software and composition.

Shortly after his arrival at CCRMA, McNabb, in fact, created one of the most iconic computer music pieces of the era: *Dreamsong* (1978). In *Dreamsong,* McNabb blends synthesized sounds and recorded natural sounds to achieve, as he describes it, "an expressive sonic continuum ranging from unaltered natural sounds to entirely new sounds—or, more poetically—from the real world to the realm of the imagination." *Dreamsong* blurs these boundaries through "constant transformations of timbre and texture, fluid shifting between familiar sounds and imaginary musical images, and illusory spatial movement." The techniques serve to draw the listener in through familiar material and then to transport him or her into "a vivid alien landscape."[46] In this way, *Dreamsong* can serve as a metaphor for CCRMA itself, leveraging the familiar while introducing novelty.

A year later, McNabb, who had a strong interest in outer space, released his *Mars Suite*, which was intended to accompany a film of NASA stereographic images of the red planet that the *Viking* lander and orbiter spacecraft had captured.[47] McNabb derived the fundamental harmonic structure for the piece from the opening bars of the last movement of Gustav Holst's *The Planets*.[48]

Chris Chafe, another key CCRMA contributor, arrived in 1977, one year after McNabb and Julius Smith. Chafe, a cellist by training, completed his undergraduate degree in music at Antioch College in Ohio, a liberal arts school known for blending practical experience with classroom education. Just prior to his arrival at CCRMA, he received a master's in composition from UC San Diego. Chafe eventually would become director of CCRMA, after Chowning.

The common thread for all of these participants—and others—was musical composition. In turn, the Samson Box and other technologies served as tools to enable the realization of new compositions. For example, Gareth Loy, who arrived as a graduate student at CCRMA in 1975, recalled that his musical background was in improvisation and that he had struggled with the slow "turnaround time" tied to the computational limits at CCRMA; the contrast between the real-time responsiveness of improvisation and the meticulous and slow process of computer music was stark. The Samson Box's speed, which made real-time synthesis possible, was thus especially appealing. In turn, Loy worked to write a Samson Box compiler (MUSBOX), which was first used for Chowning's *Turenas* and which Loy later used for creating his landmark composition, *Nekyia* (1980).[49] (A compiler is a program that turns the source code—the computer language—into an executable program.) Again, artistic aims fueled technical accomplishments.

Chowning himself created another landmark composition around the same time. His 1977 *Stria*, a commission from IRCAM, uses the FM technique to great effect. The piece, as Chowning describes it, is "a completely abstract construction. It's something that could be done by a computer but could not be done by any other electronic device."[50] As one listener describes it:

> [*Stria*'s] long, feedback-heavy tones create an ambiance and space which previously would have been impossible to create. ... It has the effect of an almost meditative-like state on the listener, gliding along your ears as if listening to a glass cabinet sing.[51]

Stria would become a classic of the genre.

CCRMA composers shared these creations widely. CCRMA held its first concert in a campus auditorium in 1976. Two years later, they put on another concert at the Stanford art museum. The event attracted 450 people. In 1980, another concert, held in the foothills surrounding the D.C. Power Lab, attracted 600 people and an NBC News team.[52]

Later, CCRMA would offer regular concerts "under the stars" at Frost Amphitheater on campus. (Starting in the late 1960s, Frost Amphitheater also hosted Jefferson Airplane, Creedence Clearwater Revival, Joan Baez, Santana, and regular concerts by the Grateful Dead.)[53] CCRMA concert materials noted that "[doors] will open at 6:30 p.m. for those who wish to picnic prior to the concert. Concertgoers are encouraged to dress warmly and to bring a blanket to sit on."[54] A 1983 concert that included saxophonist Stan Getz drew over 2,000 people. Chowning reasoned that the Silicon Valley location had something to do with these concerts' success:

> All these people who worked in the Valley then heard about these machines on which they're working also being used for a concert. And then we made it into a picnic thing at Frost. People would come early with their family and bring wine and get drunk and sit in the sun with the sunset. It became a happening, sort of. We always did really big sound systems and always quad [four-speaker surround sound]. It was a big event and lots of fun.[55]

Figure 4.3
From left to right: John Chowning, Thierry Lancino, and Chris Chafe set up an outdoor concert at the D.C. Power Lab, circa 1980. Courtesy of the Stanford News Service. Photo by Chuck Painter.

Chowning's characterization of the audience is important: Stanford is situated in the heart of Silicon Valley, which itself was experiencing dramatic growth in the 1970s and 1980s. The "Silicon" in Silicon Valley, of course, reflects the region's orientation toward semiconductors and information technology in general. Thus, many of the attendees at CCRMA concerts were engineers, largely based in industry, who came to hear a "practical application" of the kinds of technologies that they developed. Other attendees were music buffs, who longed to hear and understand this new compositional medium. Still others were counterculture participants, who found in CCRMA concerts a celebration of the nontraditional and of innovative energy focused on communal artistic outputs.[56] A critical feature of these concerts, of course, is that they brought these different groups together on picnic blankets under the stars to collectively experience the marriage of art and technology. Thus, the radical interdisciplinarity that CCRMA fermented was not limited to formal participants in the Center, but instead extended to the many people who came together to experience CCRMA compositions.

The unity of performance could span geographic boundaries, too. Given the state of computer technology at this time—very large and nonportable machines with limited real-time computation—concerts typically presented a tape recording of pieces. In turn, the performance tape could be copied by and/or shared with other groups around the world. For example, Fernando López Lezcano, who would later become the Systems Administrator at CCRMA, recalled listening to performances of CCRMA pieces at the LIPM electroacoustic music center in his native Argentina in the late 1970s and 1980s.[57] Thus, an apparent limitation of computer music—performances that relied on tape recordings and, therefore, could seem to consist of hitting the "play" button on a tape deck—could also be one of its advantages.[58]

Concerts also met the desires of funders like the NSF and NEA, who included "public outreach" among the desired outcomes of their funding. CCRMA, in turn, sought more funding from both agencies. The NSF provided two more grants in 1976 and 1977 totaling $200,000 for research into timbre, and another grant in 1977 for $175,000 to support interactive research. CCRMA received an additional $70,000 in gifts and nearly $10,000 from the Yamaha license. Thus, the center's work appeared to strike a chord with funders.

Reviews for one of the timbre perception grants highlight what funding agencies found so attractive: deep expertise in both music and science. For example, one review for the grant emphasized the scientific basis of the work, treating music as secondary:

> In past proposals the National Science Foundation has had to consider whether it was supporting music as an art or whether it was supporting a scientific study. In this proposal, there is no question about the focus of the effort. The work is entirely of a scientific nature; only the applications concern music. The personnel are appropriate for scientific work. Chowning, Grey, and Moorer are recognized leaders on purely scientific bases and Moore [*sic*] has just obtained his PhD in EE. Furthermore, the work is likely to have important implications in related scientific fields such as speech studies and multi-dimensional scaling methodology.

Another review, however, posited that music was crucial to the proposal and suggested that music tied together "the objective and subjective":

> Chowning's project is important because it addresses a very broad problem with connections from aesthetics and technology to perception, performance and listening for pleasure. Music, far more than art, is the realm where the objective and subjective can be tied together with scientific and logical rigor. Musical perception is connected to every aspect of hearing—temporal, spectral, binaural, spatial and timbre (which is so ill-defined as to be a virtually unlimited domain) and deserves investigation. … If Chowning's group can keep its impetus it may come to be a national facility for musical/psychoacoustics research.

Yet another review highlighted the "applied importance" of CCRMA's work, noting that it combined the rigor of scientific advancement with "immediate applications" (in music) that scientific studies often lacked:

> The timbre perception proposal is superb! It is a pattern for the kind of research that should be emphasized today. It is one of the too rare cases where scientific studies are making real contributions to an area of great applied importance. There are plenty of areas where good scientific methods are discovering interesting new things about the world, but often the new information does not have clear importance to applications. Likewise, there are plenty of important practical problems, but too often scientific methods can make only weak contributions to their solutions. The fundamental studies proposed here can produce information of enormous importance to music, both for immediate applications ad for the far future.[59]

The grant reviews provide evidence that Chowning and CCRMA had shifted their multivocality from a liability to an asset: now, reviewers liked, indeed *lauded*, the fact that CCRMA connected disparate areas, and they admired the applied aspects of the research. The fact that each reviewer interpreted and justified CCRMA's work on somewhat different grounds serves as evidence that CCRMA was simultaneously resonating with different interests motivated by different perspectives—a hallmark of multivocality. Internally at Stanford, CCRMA was the embodiment of Terman's vision and of the subsequent revisions to it following Vietnam War–era protests. In short, CCRMA's ability to engage across science and music, and across basic and applied research, had emerged as a new model of university research.

Part of the explanation for CCRMA's newfound success is due to the growing recognition and success of CCRMA's activities in both technology and music. Thus, CCRMA personnel found that it was not adequate simply to be engaged in diverse activities; instead, they needed to be respected in each "silo" alone in order to convince others of the benefits of working across silos. For instance, while the NSF might care only about the "scientific nature" of the work, it still mattered that the musical context was done well. In turn, when a group respected for scientific accomplishments crossed over into music, music was viewed as an added benefit that demonstrated applications. (Or, when a group respected for musical accomplishments crossed over into science, science was viewed as an added benefit that added rigor.) When the group's activity in either area was questionable, however, then engagement across boundaries only served to reinforce perceptions of peripheral contributions, as Chowning's early struggles evince.

Perhaps this shift in the respect accorded to interdisciplinary endeavors is nowhere more evident than in Chowning's own role at Stanford. Chowning, who was denied tenure in 1973 and who still listed his title as "Adjunct Professor of Music" in 1978, received an offer for a full professorship from the University of California system. This time, Stanford would not see him leave: they followed suit, promoting Chowning from an adjunct to a full professor of music—an unparalleled reversal.[60] Once again, his ally John Pierce wrote a strong letter of support:

> Chowning has contrived to show great originality and leadership. Starting from essentially nothing, he has brought diverse talents together into a field of common general interest. The work of this group in analysis of musical sounds, study of timbre by psychological techniques, digital synthesis in real time (the first effective system in the world) continues to be truly outstanding. … Chowning goes everywhere and is respected and well received everywhere. …
>
> In short, taking all things into consideration, I think that Chowning is second to none, and that you would be fortunate to retain him in a tenured position.[61]

This time, Stanford agreed with Pierce's assessment.

With his position at Stanford secure, Chowning left in late 1978 for a one-year stay at IRCAM, invited by Jean-Claude Risset to be a guest composer. Both Chowning and the IRCAM participants looked forward to such visits. As Andrew Gerszo, an IRCAM staffer since 1977 and now head of the IRCAM Education and Cultural Outreach department, recalled:

I remember very well, very vividly when John came and worked on his pieces here. Those were periods when you could really learn something—especially since he is very communicative and open about what he is doing.[62]

Inspired by a beautiful soprano tone that Mike McNabb had demonstrated at CCRMA using additive synthesis, Chowning's first activity was to pursue the synthesis of the human voice using FM. Gerald Bennett and Johann Sundberg (a talented Swedish scientist) were also at IRCAM, attempting to synthesize the voice using a different technique that Xavier Rodet was developing. At the time, IRCAM, like CCRMA, did not have an audio switch to control the distribution of sound. As with CCRMA, this setup yielded collaborative benefits. In a 2011 interview, Xavier Rodet shared:

All the main things were done on the PDP-10 [computer]. What was very interesting was the sharing of the digital to analog converter. That was a very complicated and costly and difficult piece of hardware at the time. So there was one, essentially, attached to the PDP-10. Everyone would work on the PDP-10 and send the sounds to the converter. Then, the sounds were distributed in all the rooms by analog lines, which was very interesting because it means that we were hearing the sounds done by all the others. That was fascinating because, you would hear something [and think], "Wow, this sound has something!" So, you would go to the computer and ask the guy [who made the sound], "What are you doing? What is this you have been doing?" It became an excellent exchange of knowledge. I found several of my collaborators by hearing them doing that.[63]

Thus, technology limitations led to increased collaboration.

As Chowning labored to implement McNabb's voice synthesis approach at IRCAM, the shared sound turned Bennett and Sundberg onto his work. As Chowning recalled, "Whatever I did at one end of IRCAM, everyone would hear. All of a sudden, they [Bennett and Sundberg] heard these beautiful soprano tones coming out and they were still fumbling trying to get this. [Laughter.]"[64] Through the shared audio, Bennett, Sundberg, and Chowning became aware of one another's work. Sundberg, in turn, proved to be an important resource for Chowning's work on the voice.

On another occasion, Chowning's vocal tones attracted the attention of Pierre Boulez as he was touring the choreographer Maurice Béjart around IRCAM. As Chowning recalled:

> They heard, because of the audio switch, at seven o'clock [in the morning] these beautiful vocal tones. They came down and we had this great conversation for thirty or forty minutes that would never have happened in ordinary times. All because of this audio switch.[65]

Again, the shared sound, which resulted from equipment limitations, enabled conversations and collaborations.

Chowning's experiments with vocal synthesis resulted in his composition *Phoné* (1980–1981), in which he experiments with the various characteristics of the human voice, such as vibrato, attack, decay, and portamento. The composition leverages work on sound perception, morphing between electronic sounds and sung vowels, as Chowning varies different parameters. As he would characterize both *Phoné* and his other work on vocal synthesis, Chowning was "tending to detail"—experimenting with tiny changes in parameters to identify which ones made for convincing vocal impressions.[66] Once again, his work blended technical experimentation with musical composition.

Unfortunately, just as CCRMA seemed to emerge from the crises of 1973 and 1974, other nonmusical details would interfere with Chowning's plans: In the spring of 1979, the computer science department at Stanford, which oversaw the artificial intelligence lab, announced that the new facility nearing completion would not have room for the computer music program. In an April 1979 letter to Gordon Bell, computer pioneer and then vice president of engineering at Digital Equipment Corporation, Chowning outlined the situation:

> I was unexpectedly called back to Stanford two weeks ago to help resolve a "crise" [*sic*] which developed since my arrival in Paris in december [*sic*]. In brief, the Computer Science Department wants the A.I. Lab and CCRMA (Computer Music Project) to "divorce" because of space constraints in the new C.S. quarters which are just now being completed. Although C.S. wanted to effect this change in status more or less immediately, I held out (I believe successfully) for some reasonable time. In as much as all of our programs and NSF and NEA contracts are based upon the assumption that our association with the A.I. Lab would continue (agreed to by the Lab), it seemed only reasonable that if there must be divorce it should be effected in such a way that our work is not interrupted. This means, of course, that we must put together an independent system, which in turn means raising money.[67]

Chowning continues by noting that DEC "already has shown considerable generosity" and asks for Bell's help not through a direct donation; rather, he asks Bell to identify other "people in the computer industry to whom we can make our case and perhaps even more important to help us develop a strategy and serve as a reference/advocate within the industry."[68]

Chowning estimated the cost of the computing system at $298,000 (about $960,000 in 2014 dollars). He divided it into three phases: the first phase, which he labeled "Bootstrap," would involve acquiring a Foonly F2 and associated storage, terminals, and interfaces for $156,000. (The F2 was a mainframe computer compatible with the DEC PDP-10. Dave Poole, the tuba player and hacker who first enabled Chowning to run Mathews's Music IV program, founded Foonly.) The second phase would acquire more storage, terminals, a printer/plotter, and interfaces to achieve "independence from SAIL" for $96,000. Finally, the third phase would involve more memory, storage, and terminals for $46,000 to complete the system.[69] In essence, Chowning plotted out the minimally necessary system for continuing with CCRMA's work and the system that would allow this work to flourish. All options, however, required funds that CCRMA did not possess.

By all accounts, the AI lab separation sent CCRMA scrambling for money and again uncertain of their future. Chowning began by negotiating with the university, which agreed to have CCRMA stay at the (soon-to-be-former) AI facility in the foothills and to provide physical plant support. Later, some CCRMA graduate students would actually live at the facility. As Chowning explained:

> It was a security issue. It was Leland Smith's idea, because they had to provide security at night, nonworking hours. We were all by ourselves. ... Leland Smith said, "Why don't you let the graduate students live in the unused part? Just let them modify [it]." There were toilets and there was a sauna bath. They said, "No, we can't have that." Then they did the calculation of what it would cost to have security. [Laughter.] Then they thought it was a good idea. [Laughter.] So they let us do that. Those were interesting times.[70]

The arrangement serves as further evidence of flexible thinking among CCRMA participants.

The university also made available $100,000 for the purchase of equipment.[71] In addition, Yamaha agreed to a royalty advance to CCRMA of another $100,000 for equipment purchases, in exchange for revealing to Yamaha a means of using FM synthesis to simulate the singing voice.[72] (This technique built on Chowning's work at IRCAM on *Phoné*.) Chowning also approached Yamaha to provide a gift-in-kind of certain audio equipment.[73]

Still, Chowning and colleagues did not have enough money to replace the computing equipment necessary to continue their work. Despite CCRMA's success with NSF grants, these grants did not appear to be the best option for this shortfall—in part, because grants could not be used for teaching, musical composition, and other activities at the center. As Chowning explained in a 1979 letter to solicit funding from the Rockefeller Foundation:

> Since 1975 CCRMA has received a total of $630,000 in research support from NSF. Approximately one third of the total goes directly to the university as indirect costs. From the remainder we have supported various operating costs, two graduate students each year, a full-time system programmer, and ca ½ of the staff salaries. The shortfall has been made up from university funds and by "farming out" staff to the Institute de Recherche et Coodination Acoustique-Musique (IRCAM), the music research institute in Paris directed by Pierre Boulez.[74]

As his Rockefeller plea indicates, Chowning recognized that further NSF support alone would not solve the funding shortfall.

As early as 1969, Chowning had been compiling a list of individuals and foundations with an interest in music.[75] With the AI "divorce" on the horizon in 1979, he set to work writing letters. His work was complicated, however, by the fact that there were plans in place to build a new music department building. As a September 1979 memo on the CCRMA situation summarized frankly: "Our fundraising effort, although modest in comparison, must not conflict with the fundraising for the music building." CCRMA remained physically and, in some ways, symbolically separated from the music department, and CCRMA's financial needs played second fiddle to the department's own needs.[76]

Chowning's plan was to leverage his connections to individuals not for direct gifts, but rather for pointers and introductions to corporations and foundations that might support CCRMA's work. His targets included Tony Meier, an important Stanford benefactor with an interest in the arts; Ellen Rush, daughter of Louise Davies, who gave the naming gift for the San Francisco Symphony Hall; Jim Robertson, another San Francisco philanthropist; and Paul Hertelendy, music editor of the *Oakland Tribune*.[77] In each case, he asked for suggestions of potential foundations or organizations, which, in the words of his letter to Ellen Rush, "might find this special intersection between art and science interesting."[78]

Chowning's outreach efforts to companies and foundations themselves, however, proved difficult. In response to Chowning's letter from Paris, Gordon Bell had encouraged Chowning to contact Lewis Branscomb, vice president and chief scientist at IBM. Chowning did so in July 1979, requesting $200,000 from IBM to make up the difference between the price of an independent system and the royalty advance from Yamaha.[79] Branscomb's reply later that month thanked him for the inquiry but was not encouraging: "We have reviewed your request carefully and regret we will not be able to provide the support you seek. ... Support of this nature falls quite far outside the current scope of our program of support for higher education."[80]

The same month, Chowning wrote to Stephen White of the Sloan Foundation, at the suggestion of John Pierce. He again requested $200,000 for a computer system.[81] His letter was never received. So, Chowning followed up again with a September letter, which also went missing.[82] A third attempt reached its target, but without the hoped-for effect. White responded in October:

> Our general program is as remote as it can be from musical affairs, but under extremely favorable circumstances we might be able to wrestle it in that direction. What you propose, however, creates the least favorable circumstances of all. We are simply in no position to support the purchase of computer hardware, even for proposals squarely within program: a small proportion of the very best of those requests would exhaust our resources. We have placed such support out of bounds except in the most exceptional instances and then only when the proposal is intimately related to Foundation program [*sic*]. I wish I could be more helpful. Pierce and Boulez are powerful allies. But all I can do is hope you have better fortune elsewhere.[83]

Other appeals fared little better. Chowning wrote to the Andrew W. Mellon Foundation in October 1979 and asked for $100,000.[84] In November, the Foundation replied that they had "no program currently in operation which would enable us to assist."[85] The Rockefeller Foundation, too, turned down Chowning's request in December 1979 due to "extremely tight" funds and "[in]adequate planning time."[86]

Not to be discouraged, Chowning persisted with Rockefeller, noting in a January 1980 letter to Max Mathews that "the response from Rockefeller is hopeful for 1981 and we will work something out with them, I believe." In the same letter, he requests that Mathews send "the same letter" to another half-dozen foundations—a reference to Mathews having written supportive letters to the first group of prospects.[87] Chowning made the same request of Boulez, who responded with good wishes, "Not only do I try to hunt gold for IRCAM but for California too ... where there's more of it no doubt!"[88]

The fundraising difficulties, however, demanded changes at CCRMA. Chowning scaled back his plans for the computing system. He also put Loren Rush and John Grey, his CCRMA cofounders whose contributions were essential to CCRMA's initial success, on "temporary layoff." An April 1980 memo to Arnice Streit, who worked in finance for the Stanford School of Humanities and Sciences, adopts an air of desperation and notes that "funds would have been exhausted at the end of April had we not done so."[89]

Unfortunately, Chowning's next round of solicitations to foundations also proved disappointing. In January 1980, Chowning wrote to the L.A.W. Fund in New York.[90] They replied later that month that "While your project is a worthy one, all of the funds we have available for such purposes have already been earmarked."[91] Not to be dismayed, Chowning wrote back that he understood and requested a meeting when he was in New York in the coming March. A handwritten note at the bottom of that letter reads, "No interview unless they plan to fund. Therefore write again."[92]

The Surdna Foundation wrote in January to acknowledge Chowning's letter and to inform him that Stanford fell outside their geographic concentration.[93] The Jerome Foundation also had an incompatible geographic focus and wrote to Pierre Boulez to acknowledge his letter of support and apologize that it "is not possible for Jerome Foundation to respond favorably."[94] By contrast, the Fromm Foundation expressed strong interest in Chowning's solicitation.[95] Their capacity, however, was very limited—"a small foundation with modest funds" per their description—and they limited their support to a "one-time grant of $1,000 in the spirit of goodwill."[96]

All of this detail is to reinforce the tremendous difficulty that Chowning faced in securing financial support for CCRMA. Despite CCRMA's initial success with the NSF and NEA grants, and despite the Yamaha license and the hopes for future licensing revenue, CCRMA was on the brink of bankruptcy. Frustratingly, Chowning's strategy of appealing to individual and institutional philanthropy appeared to go nowhere.

At Stanford, the School of Humanities and Sciences (H&S) itself expressed concern and surprise that CCRMA—which had attracted such strong interest just a few years earlier—was not having success. A February 1980 memo from James Rosse, associate dean of Stanford's School of Humanities and Sciences, to Joel Smith, vice president of development, noted:

> [H&S and the provost's office] undertook a substantial obligation to John Chowning and the Computer Music group last summer. ... H&S and the Provost underwrote a

joint, net obligation of some $100,000 with the expectation that a large part of all of that amount could be raised by gifts, gifts in kind, etc. So far we are on the hook for all of it. John Chowning has not only put about $25,000 of his own into the project, but he has worked very hard to try to clear the debt. Has he had proper development support? Is the timing wrong? Is the project wrong? Is he the wrong person? What is wrong?[97]

What wasn't wrong was Chowning's tenacity. Rebuffed by Rockefeller, for example, he replied to foundation director Klein's letter in January 1980 with a notice of his intention to reapply for the next year and inquiring as to whether he could meet Klein in New York.[98] Per an April 1980 letter, that meeting happened and was followed by a proposed visit from Klein to CCRMA in June.[99] But, schedules slipped. A later April letter from Rockefeller confirmed Klein's interest in visiting in "late-June or mid-July" but handwritten notes of phone calls and phone messages show that schedule slipping farther and farther out.[100] Klein would not visit CCRMA until 1982. Again, CCRMA was not resonating with private funders.

At the same time, Chowning's luck with government grants appeared to be diminishing. For example, while grant applications submitted between 1975 and 1977 had yielded four six-figure grants (and a total of $779,000), applications submitted between 1978 and 1980 yielded only one six-figure grant (and a total of $272,000). Part of the challenge, perhaps ironically, is that some reviewers felt that the center needed more substantial support that could not be provided through smaller grants. As one reviewer wrote for a grant application titled "Auditory Distance Perception under Natural Sounding Conditions":

These people seem to be attempting to substitute a stable of relatively small grants for a center or project grant—something they probably could not get funded. ... I disapprove of this strategy on a number of grounds; primary among them is that all their time must be spent on writing new proposals, renewals, and annual reports. There must be very little time left over for work, and partial confirmation of this expectation comes from the vitas; little has apparently come from the grant money already allocated.[101]

In other words, it was one thing to support equipment and research, as the earlier NSF and NEA grants had done, but it was another thing to pay to establish an entirely new center. Moreover, Chowning was spending a tremendous amount of time attempting to find financial support, which distracted him from the real work of the center. A vicious cycle thus emerged between the search for funding and the lack of advance in research, which threatened to undermine CCRMA's existence. Indeed, the NSF turned down this grant, too.

Finally, a somewhat unlikely source would finally provide major funding for CCRMA. The nonprofit System Development Foundation (SDF) had been chief stockholder of the System Development Corporation (SDC). Upon the sale of SDC to Burroughts Corporation, SDF had an asset base of $60 million and a need to spend it. At the December 15, 1981, board meeting, the trustees of the SDF released a program statement that expressed their desire to support basic research in the information sciences.[102] Chowning and CCRMA jumped at the chance and submitted a proposal—with strong support from John Pierce, who carried significant weight in this community and who, in fact, had suggested research topics for SDF to support. (SDF hired Charles Smith as its director, who was then married to the daughter of a one-time science director at Bell Labs, Ed David. David, Pierce, and Max Mathews all knew one another, again reinforcing the role of personal networks in the nascent computer music community.[103]) In 1982, SDF awarded CCRMA a five-year grant for $2.3 million. Finally, Chowning had the lifeline he needed to maintain the center for several more years.[104]

At the same time, Yamaha was preparing to release its DX7 synthesizer, which would become the best-selling synthesizer in history and which, thirty years later, retains the number two spot in that category. At the DX7's heart: Chowning's FM synthesis technology. Stanford—and CCRMA—would receive money for each unit sold.

5 Duet for Stanford and Yamaha

The CCRMA–Yamaha relationship serves, for many observers, as a model of university technology transfer: a university-based research group and a commercial firm collaborating over many years to develop a technical breakthrough into a widespread product. Undoubtedly, the relationship has yielded enormous benefits for each organization and for computer music as a whole. Yet it also raised new questions that continue to confront university technology transfer efforts.

Relationships between universities and industry, and the broader expectations surrounding these relationships, have changed considerably over time. In a detailed study of how academic science became more market oriented, Elizabeth Popp Berman contrasts the dominant perspective of the 1960s—in which academic science was largely disconnected from concerns with economic growth—against contemporary rhetoric in which American universities serve as "engines of economic growth."[1] Consider, for example, the Obama administration's Startup America initiative, which includes a focus on "clearing the path to market for primary research in more universities, through a combination of regional ecosystem development, faculty engagement, and streamlined technology licensing" in order to spur job creation.[2] Clearly, commercialization of university research has moved to the top of economic development agendas. Berman marks the shift as occurring during the 1970s, under pressure from three trends: a perception that innovation in American industry was deteriorating; a growing body of research that pointed to the role of innovation in economic growth; and the general stagnation of the US economy.[3]

In turn, 1980 was a watershed moment in university technology transfer. That year, the US Congress passed the Patent and Trademark Law Amendments Act, better known as the Bayh–Dole Act (after the two cosponsoring senators, Evan Bayh and Bob Dole). The Bayh–Dole Act aimed to simplify the assignment of intellectual property rights for government-sponsored research and, thus, to streamline technology transfer from universities and government labs into industry. Post-1980 data indicate that university technology transfer has, indeed, experienced dramatic growth. For example, the Association of University Technology Managers (AUTM) conducts an annual survey of university technology transfer activities. Their most recent survey relays the growth in formal technology transfer offices at US universities: while only seven universities had a formal technology transfer office prior to 1970 and only 21 had such an office prior to 1980, today every major US research university has a technology transfer office. These offices have been busy, too. The AUTM survey indicates that from 1991 to 2012, invention disclosures rose from just over 6,000 to over 22,000, while new patent applications rose from less than 2,000 to over 14,000. Total licensing revenues have matched these increases.[4]

At the same time, David Mowery and colleagues, among others, have emphasized the historical origins of these activities and the active involvement of universities like Stanford well before 1980.[5] (Recall Niels Reimers's activity with the Stanford OTL in the 1960s and 1970s, as detailed in chapter 3.) In fact, in a study of Stanford, Columbia and the University of California at Berkeley, Mowery and colleagues find that although Bayh–Dole may have accelerated a trend, technology sharing with industry was well established prior to 1980.[6] Gerry George, for example, documents how the Wisconsin Alumni Research Foundation engaged in active commercialization as early as 1925.[7]

From this perspective, the CCRMA–Yamaha relationship is historically critical to understand: it involved a university that was one of the earliest to engage in technology transfer activities; it took place prior to Bayh–Dole; it "proved" Reimers's OTL model; and it shaped subsequent technology transfer policies. Moreover, a detailed analysis of the CCRMA–Yamaha relationship not only provides an important example of a particular university–industry relationship; it also shows how technology transfer activities at CCRMA were intertwined with the emergence of a new discipline (computer music), user innovation, dilemmas around open sharing, and questions about technical standards.

These relationships were made all the more complex by the fact that the aims of the two organizations—CCRMA and Yamaha—were not always aligned. As I argue throughout this book, CCRMA's ultimate emphasis lay in generating new musical compositions and their technology-development efforts proceeded in service of this goal. By contrast, Yamaha's emphasis lay in selling products, specifically, new musical instruments. Thus, Yamaha's development efforts were oriented toward profit. This contrast is not to deny Stanford's own profit-seeking (as evidenced by the Yamaha license) or Yamaha's great support of the arts. Moreover, we have already witnessed the fruits of such collaboration between commercial and academic activities, and between technical and artistic aims. Nonetheless, the complexity and, indeed, the fruitfulness of the Yamaha relationship must be understood as a function, in part, of the contrast between the organizations, with each organization latching onto the intersection of music and technology for somewhat different reasons.

As relayed in the previous chapter, Stanford and Yamaha signed the FM license in March 1975. The license marked only the beginning, however, of a long collaborative relationship. Developing FM into a commercial product would require years of further research and investment—and deep personal engagement between CCRMA and Yamaha personnel.

Scholars distinguish between knowledge of *how* to do something (*know-how*), knowledge of *why* something works as it does (*know-why*), and knowledge of *what* applications may exist (*know-what*).[8] Commercialization efforts surrounding new techniques (such as FM) depend, especially, on know-how, since it is difficult to reproduce and refine a technique if one isn't capable of performing it in the first place. In turn, inventors often possess know-how that either *cannot be* or *is not* conveyed in formal documentation such as publications and patents.[9] As such, their continued involvement is key to commercialization success.[10]

In support of this point, venture capitalist and Sun Microsystems cofounder Vinod Khosla recounts that when he tried to recruit his Sun cofounder, Andy Bechtolsheim, Bechtolsheim offered to license Khosla the technology for $10,000. Khosla replied, "Not interested. ... I want the goose that laid the golden egg, not the golden egg."[11] Yamaha, too, wanted the "goose" of CCRMA. Thus, the license specified that Stanford would provide copies of patents and "technical information for the design and manufacture of a Musical Instrument." Under a section labeled "Technical Services and Additional Know-How," however, the license agreement also stated that "the Computer Music Group [which the license defined as "John

Chowning, J. A. Moorer, John Grey and Loren Rush, and such other persons as may be agreed upon"] shall consult for [Yamaha]."[12] A March 1976 letter from Niels Reimers, the OTL director, to Yamaha describes a typical Chowning trip to Japan: Chowning would spend four days in Hamamatsu, meeting with various Yamaha engineers to assist them in the implementation of FM.[13]

Reimers's March 1976 letter also describes plans to engage Yamaha with other related Stanford inventions, including Chowning's sound localization system and an improvement to the basic FM technique developed by Andy Moorer. Thus, although the immediate focus was on Chowning's initial FM breakthrough, Stanford hoped from the beginning to provide other technologies for Yamaha's consideration.[14]

To track their development, Yamaha issued annual progress reports to Stanford. According to the March 1976 report, Yamaha's goals in 1975 were to develop a single tone synthesizer, a multichannel electronic organ and an "entirely new electronic keyboard." These products were of increasing difficulty, and Yamaha's report notes that, for the new electronic keyboard, "we have yet conceived no clear vision." The challenge Yamaha faced was that the semiconductor technology required to develop an instrument that would be both workable and obviously superior to existing offerings did not exist; in short, a new keyboard required a new chip.[15] As Mochida recalled in 1986:

> Ten years ago our IC [integrated circuit] technology was not good enough to manufacture high quality electronic musical instruments which we wanted to develop. For instance, only P-MOS IC was available then. It was slow in calculation and was not highly integrated. [More advanced chips use an "*n*-type" material, but they are more difficult to make.] Therefore we had to exert a lot of our own hard efforts in the development of IC's which had higher performance and quality.[16]

In other words, to pursue this latest generation of musical instrument, Yamaha had to get into the semiconductor business.

The technical undertaking would prove to be enormous. A 1979 letter from Chowning recalled that Yamaha had estimated three to four years for research and development of FM.[17] In fact, the licensing agreement from 1975 indicated a $25,000 penalty for Yamaha if Yamaha "is not in production of FM MOS chips for Musical Instruments by April 1, 1978" and a right to termination of the agreement by Stanford if Yamaha "is subsequently not in production by April 1, 1979."[18] Yamaha's first mass production instrument would not be marketed, however, until 1982. Since Stanford's—and CCRMA's—income was based primarily on royalties on instruments sold ($10 each per the original agreement), the delay exacerbated CCRMA's fiscal challenges—and it frustrated OTL personnel who watched the life of the Stanford patent tick away.[19] (Once Stanford's patent expired, Yamaha would no longer owe Stanford any royalties.)

Yamaha's annual reports to Stanford relayed their continued progress and challenges. For example, a March 1978 project report described an important accomplishment: Yamaha introduced "After Touch Control," which would allow a performer to manipulate a sound parameter with the amount of pressure exerted on a sustained key; even after a performer had pressed the piano-type key, she could continually alter the sustained sound by pressing more or less.[20] By contrast, existing keyboards functioned like a simple on-off switch without such control.[21] As the Yamaha report noted:

> As a trade strategy, it was required that the first TRX commercial model should have some new feature apart from its FM tone quality to make more clear distinction [*sic*] from the electronic piano type instrument which several important makers have put on the market these years.[22]

The development excited Chowning, who envisioned compositional capabilities tied to such control. Responding in April 1978 to a letter from Yohei Nagai, another Yamaha engineer and one of the few who spoke both English and French, Chowning called the progress report "very encouraging" and noted his desire to "see first hand the prototype instrument."[23]

By August 1978, Yamaha had shipped a prototype "TRX" to their US subsidiary.[24] The instrument used 55 breakthrough "LSIs" or large-scale integrated chips, each of which packed tens of thousands of transistors. Technical achievements aside, however, it still needed work. An April 1979 note to Chowning from Hiro Kato, who worked for Ishimura, shared that Yamaha featured the TRX at

> a recording session in Hollywood [earlier in 1979]. The purpose was to make Yamaha's demonstration disc for hi-fi usage. The type of music was so called "crossover" music; that is, jazz and rock on the same plate garnished with a touch of disco beat. Unfortunately for that type of music, the TRX (played by Pete Robinson) [a sound engineer and keyboard player who would go on to score several television series and films] was not outrageous enough to beat the other guy. This recording session seemed to clarify the point that the TRX definitely needs to be enriched in its timbre, especially in bass register.[25]

At the end of the day, the sounds generated by the technical marvel were not yet compelling for popular music—and thus not compelling as the basis of a new instrument. Such concerns underscored the different motivations and perspectives of CCRMA and Yamaha: Chowning developed FM in service of a composition style that was decidedly not "popular," while Yamaha labored to commercialize the technology around a frame that appealed explicitly to popular music.

Fortunately for Yamaha, the company already was developing expertise in bass sounds, which would help to address the "shortcomings" evident in the recording session: In addition to the TRX, their February 1979 progress report described work on a "manual keyboard bass instrument (MBX)." Chowning describes how, by this point, he had already encouraged them to use a particular FM arrangement, "cascade FM." This arrangement allowed one of the key parameters ("index") to be small, which in turn loaded sounds toward the low end. But, to Chowning, the bigger issue lay in the fact that Yamaha had not engaged musicians to program the synthesizer:

> They knew how I did that [the bass technique]. But, you know, if it's not in the hands and the minds of the engineer who's actually doing the voicing [programming the sounds], it doesn't matter. That was always the problem. That's why when I went [to Japan]: They took notes on everything that I did. Finally, they got David Bristow and Gary Luenberger, who were both keyboard players. They [Bristow and Luenberger] had really good intuition without much understanding of FM theory at all. They just could figure out how to make these things. They got lots of good stuff [sounds].[26]

In other words, the musician's "ear" was essential for fully developing the technology. As musicians, Bristow and Luenberger were able to coax possibilities out of the technology that eluded nonmusical engineers.

In turn, Chowning argues that sound programming or "voicing" was tied intimately to musical composition:

> The key was in voicing. You could do engineering implementation based on the article [referring to his 1973 article in the *Journal of Audio Engineering Society*]. But you couldn't make it sound good unless you had a connection to CCRMA. This is why composition was so important; it showed off voicing.[27]

In this way, CCRMA compositions served as demonstrations of the technology's potential, which Yamaha engineers could then use to inform their technical work. The direction of influence is important to note here: musical applications did not simply flow from existing technologies; instead musical applications drove further technical achievements. Such influences are important because they underscore a key point of radical interdisciplinarity—that one discipline is not inherently "favored" or "superior" to another.

At the same time, CCRMA members maintained their regular visits to Japan. The schedule from Chowning's July 1979 visit is typical: an eight-day trip with six days of work, each one filled with status reports, demonstrations, lectures, and meetings.[28] Chowning himself had to balance a desire to help Yamaha succeed with their instruments against an acknowledgment of his own interests, which were never commercial. Thus, when Yamaha sought his help with voicing, he responded:

> In regard to the requested tone parameters, I must point out the following: 1) We had no system since Nov. 1 [owing to the AI lab "divorce" described in chapter 4], although we will be able to begin work once more in the next two weeks; 2) Developing tones for these instruments and in the requested conditions is not a normal part of our work. As you know, a limited amount of FM simulation of tones has been done at CCRMA but always in the context of compositions.

Chowning continues by describing a procedure by which Yamaha engineers can analyze natural instruments and attempt to mimic them using FM. He was clear, however, that such commercial applications were removed from his own interests.[29] For Chowning, tones were developed in a musical context for the purpose of realizing specific compositions, not as generic sounds to "compete" against other instruments in pop music genres like "crossover."

Nevertheless, Chowning was contractually obligated to provide two weeks of consulting per year.[30] To Chowning, these visits, and other Yamaha engagements, carried a personal aspect. For example, Yohei Nagai requested in 1983 that Chowning send a note for the wedding of a young Yamaha employee, Teruo Nishimoto, in Japan. (Chowning enjoyed celebrity status within the company.[31]) Following up, Nagai wrote to Chowning, "Thank you very much for your telegram celebrating Nishimoto's wedding. It was very well written and safely arrived in time. As I scheduled, it was read by Mr. Hideo Yamada [another Yamaha engineer] at the climax of his wedding party, for which all forty people attended there applauded like a storm."[32]

These personal relationships also highlight how the commercialization relationship with Yamaha took on multiple facets. As John Pierce wrote in a 1983 letter to the System Development Foundation:

Another important strength of CCRMA is good relations with commercial musical technology. Chowning's relation with Yamaha through the FM Synthesis patent is an example. This goes beyond royalties. Chowning visits and helps Yamaha. They are going to lend him some of their equipment for a composition he is undertaking.[33]

In other words, part of the strength of the Yamaha–CCRMA relationship lay in the fact that it recognized intellectual property, royalties, consulting, musical composition, and personal ties simultaneously; it was (and remains) a robust and multifaceted relationship rather than a singular contractual one.

Through it all, the technical march continued. A March 1, 1981, progress report notes that the GS-1 and GS-2 (formerly called the TRX) had been previewed to a "big sensation" at NAMM in Los Angeles and at the Frankfurt Messe, the two most important musical instrument trade shows. The report also noted that the CH-3 classical organ was entering production and that another keyboard, the #1600 (later called the CE20, or Combo Ensemble), would begin production in August, thanks to Chowning's assistance with voicing.[34] At the end of 1981, Yamaha sent CCRMA a CE20 as a "Christmas gift" and shared that the instrument would be "announced as our second FM digital keyboard" at NAMM and the Frankfurt Messe, both in February 1982.[35] Thus, as Chowning returned from his February 1982 trip to Yamaha, he carried with him posters of the GS-1 and the F-70 (church organ), both of which were in production.[36] (Yamaha initially believed that the organ market would be the most lucrative market for FM—a prediction that would miss by a mile.) Seven years after signing the license with Stanford, Yamaha was finally on a roll in its commercialization of FM.

Finally, in 1983, Yamaha released the DX7 synthesizer. It was an instant blockbuster. Chowning recalled that he first heard the instrument at a bar in Palo Alto:

My wife and I had been out to see a movie and we stopped off at a local bar for a nightcap. I knew the keyboard player in the bar, and when he saw me he waved me over excitedly to come and see this "incredible new instrument" he had sitting on top of his piano. I was astonished. It was an awesome moment. I had no idea that people had been waiting in line to buy DX7s. I had no idea at all.[37]

The DX7 would be heard around the world. As Max Mathews recalled in a 2008 interview:

The DX7 brought the entry level [for digital synthesis] down to two thousand dollars, and that really expanded the field and got a lot more people and a lot more schools involved. ... Now universities all over could get into computer music or electronic music programs.[38]

In other words, Mathews argues that Yamaha's commercialization of Stanford academic research enabled a dramatic expansion of further academic research, by lowering the technical and financial barriers to entry into the new field. Thus, far from commercialization being a mere "output" of university research, Mathews highlights one way in which commercialization can spur further university research.

The DX7, however, would influence not only academic programs, but also popular music. Indeed, the DX7 quickly became the best-selling musical instrument in history, completely redefining both the synthesizer market and popular music.[39] A generation of musicians—including Madonna, Phil Collins, and Toto—relied on its shimmering digital sounds to define a new sound in music. Thus, the DX7, more so than any other instrument, marked the transposition of digital sound synthesis from the realm of academic computer music centers to popular use by individual artists.

Digital synthesis opened up new sonic possibilities that enabled these artists to develop and recreate a unique sound. In this way, their adoption reflected Chowning's motivation: to use technology to create new music. (As with Chowning's pursuit of digital synthesis, too, the success of early adoptions and of Yamaha's new digital product was anything but guaranteed.) The large number of adopters, however, also drove economies of scale around digital synthesis, as Mathews's quote indicates; suddenly, it was affordable. In turn, this affordability enabled the broad expansion of electronic music programs and of electronic music generally. Of course, CCRMA received a portion of each DX7 sale, too. As hundreds of thousands of musicians bought DX7s and other Yamaha products, these revenues enabled CCRMA itself—once on the brink of bankruptcy—to be financially viable. In short, commercialization success tied to a user-driven invention laid the foundation for an academic center, for the expansion of a new academic discipline, and for the emergence of a new brand of popular culture.

Intellectual Property Landscape

These developments unfolded against a background of patents, licenses, and other intellectual property agreements. Fundamentally, a patent provides a temporary monopoly on the use, manufacture, or sale of the patented product or process. The logic behind patents is that they provide incentives for invention: given the high uncertainty that surrounds research, the temporary monopoly provided by a patent—and, specifically, the financial reward that this monopoly provides—is necessary to incentivize an individual or organization to engage in research in the first place.[40]

As noted, the starting point for the Stanford–Yamaha relationship lay in Chowning's FM patent and the 1975 Yamaha license, which gave Yamaha the exclusive legal right to the patent and technology. As Chowning and colleagues would learn, however, contract negotiations and intellectual property arrangements could—and did—get very complicated, owing to both the uncertainty surrounding new technologies and the fundamental tension between exclusion (enforced by the patent) and openness (a hallmark of CCRMA).

The terms of the Yamaha license noted that Yamaha would "promptly inform [Stanford] of any suspected infringement of any licensed Patent by a third party." Stanford and/or Yamaha could then choose to file suit against the alleged infringer, sharing the legal costs.[41] Yamaha, as the exclusive licensee of the technology, pushed for Stanford to assert its patent rights strongly and to pursue alleged patent infringers. But for Stanford—and especially for Chowning and his colleagues at CCRMA—the practice of asserting patent rights raised a host of issues with everyone from government funders to colleagues in the field of digital music.

For example, Mochida sent a letter to Niels Reimers in August 1978, discussing alleged FM patent infringement by New England Digital (NED) and suggesting that Stanford warn NED.[42] (NED designed and manufactured the Synclavier digital synthesizer, which would be adopted by Stevie Wonder and other artists. With a list price starting at $50,000, it was aimed squarely at highly successful musicians and studios.[43]) Mochida's letter also mentions Micor Company of Arizona and their Coupland Digital Synthesizer.

Reimers's response the next month acknowledges Yamaha's complaint about NED and notes that ARP, another early synthesizer manufacturer, would likely be the next infringer. Reimers found, however, that the patent situation was putting him in a tough spot. In the same letter, he shares that he received a call in February 1978 from a lawyer with the National Science Foundation, who in turn had received a complaint from Congressman Paul Tsongas on behalf of his "constituent," ARP. The complaint was that "Stanford had given an exclusive license to Yamaha for technology that was developed under public-funded [*sic*] NSF research."[44] That claim was not exactly true since Chowning's early FM work was not supported by the NSF. (The 1975 NSF grant came several years after Chowning's breakthroughs in the 1960s and early 1970s.) Nevertheless, subsequent work on FM certainly was supported by the NSF, including an important sine summation synthesis technique that Andy Moorer developed in the late 1970s. More generally, the situation highlighted Stanford's dilemma: on one hand, Yamaha was pushing Stanford to exert Stanford's patent rights further; on the other hand, government officials were questioning Stanford's existing relationships and approaches, encouraging them to back away.

Reimers's response letter to Congressman Tsongas's office notes that Yamaha was not given an exclusive US license to sine summation, the publicly funded research, leaving them "somewhat disgruntled." (They were, however, given exclusivity for "the Japanese patent."[45]) Though there is no evidence that such an arrangement was planned to address potential NSF and congressional objections, the arrangement provided some "political cover" for Reimers and Stanford.

Struggles around the patent, however, would not go away. Just two years later, Yamaha wrote to Chowning to inform him of a US patent recently granted to Kawai for FM synthesis. Noting that "Kawai is our biggest competitor in Japan," Yamaha's letter goes on to ask about any relationship between Stanford and Kawai or between Chowning and "Mr. R. Deutsch" (the inventor on the patent).[46] Reimers's response assured Yamaha that "we have had contact neither with the Kawai company nor Mr. Deutsch."[47]

Ultimately, Yamaha pursued Kawai in a different way: under US patent law, a company must file for a patent within one year of a publication that contains the same information as the proposed patent. Since Chowning published his 1975 article more than one year before Kawai's patent application, Yamaha could use it to invalidate Kawai's patent.[48] In other words, Yamaha relied on Stanford's openness to argue that the Kawai patent was invalid since it rested on information that was already public at the time of application.

Stanford and Yamaha had other targets for patent infringement, too. A 1981 letter from the chief of Yamaha's patent department, Maki Kamiya, to Niels Reimers noted:

> We have learned from Mr. Kato of Yamaha R&D Studio that you are prepared to investigate the possibility of infringement of the FM patent by the digital synthesizer

"Synergy" made by Digital Keyboard Inc. which is the subsidiary of Crumar Corporation. We, too, are interested in this matter.[49]

Crumar, for its part, worked to build an active defense by asking CCRMA for class lists. Patte Wood, the center's administrator, refused on the grounds that sharing class lists was an invasion of students' privacy.[50] Crumar's larger point, however, certainly was correct: CCRMA shared knowledge broadly through courses, seminars, and public presentations, while Stanford still enforced a patent based on a presumption of nonpublic information at the time of application—the same technique that Yamaha had used against Kawai.[51]

In advance of 1986 license negotiations with Stanford, Yamaha's patent chief, Maki Kamiya, asked Stanford to look into possible patent infringement by another Yamaha competitor, Casio.[52] Reimers responded that a review of the Casio patent indicated that it probably did not infringe the Stanford patent.[53] The question remained open, however, as to whether Casio infringed in the product itself (versus in their patent description); though attorneys could review the patent language, determining infringement in the literal "black boxes" of equipment was difficult.[54]

All of these examples point to Stanford getting increasingly embroiled in patent disputes as a result of its active engagement in commercialization. Much of the patent-related tension arose from Yamaha's urging, of course, as they worked to protect their significant R&D investment in FM. Yet pressures came from inside Stanford, too. The growth of the OTL, the early promise of the Yamaha licensing relationship, and, especially, the blockbuster Cohen–Boyer recombinant DNA patents all raised the prominence of patents on Stanford's campus in the 1980s. (The Cohen–Boyer patents, first licensed in 1980, would go on to net Stanford and UC San Francisco $255 million.)

Reflecting these changes, the manager of patents and copyrights for Stanford's sponsored projects office, Clive Liston, circulated a memo in August 1980 asking everyone—faculty, students, consultants, visiting scientists, and nonemployees engaged in sponsored research—to sign the "SU-18" form. This form assigned patent rights for inventions made using Stanford resources to Stanford.[55] The next month, Liston's office sent a follow-up since many people still had not signed.[56] In October, a handwritten note from his office to the CCRMA administrator reads, "We need more, more, more [in reference to signed SU-18 forms] … all visitors—anyone working in anyway on the research."[57] Intellectual property—and the associated revenue—was of growing importance to Stanford, and Liston's office wished to secure it for the university. In some ways, such actions can be viewed as a likely outcome associated with Terman's vision: industry engagement and a practical orientation yielded resources, especially of the financial sort. As Stanford came to expect and even depend on these resources, however, they further emphasized intellectual property and formal technology transfer mechanisms.[58]

For his part, Chowning described how patent issues thrust him into an uncomfortable position. As he recalled in a 2008 interview when reflecting on the situation with NED, the manufacturer of the high-end Synclavier, "I encouraged them [Yamaha] just not to worry about it. ... I said, 'They're never going to make much money. They're never going to compete.' It was Jon Appleton, whom I knew."[59] Again, Chowning remarked, "That [NED] was such a small company that there would be little threat. They were a bit like colleagues since it was Dartmouth."[60] To Chowning, NED was not a corporate competitor so much as it was his three colleagues at Dartmouth who had started the company: Jon Appleton, a music professor; Sydney Alonso, a research professor in the engineering school; and Cameron Jones, an engineering student and software programmer. They bore a resemblance to CCRMA's own mixture of music and engineering talent, and asserting patent rights against their creation rubbed against CCRMA's open sharing of software and systems. But Yamaha persisted and NED acquiesced. A February 1988 letter from NED to Yamaha provides evidence that NED paid patent royalties: ten instruments sold from September through December 1987, for a total royalty to Yamaha of $494.19.[61]

Chowning's proclivity for openness got him into trouble with Yamaha at times, too. For example, a March 1980 letter from Yamaha sternly reminds Stanford not to disclose information about the FM project, following an article in the *San Jose Mercury News* in which Chowning had described the relationship:

> Honestly, we were not a little surprised with it [the article], which hurried us to reexamine the content of confidentiality keeping clause in our agreement. I do not (and will not, perhaps) say it would cause some controversy between us, but Nippon Gakki would appreciate Stanford's good understanding on the fact that, for NGK, an enterprise in trade competition, any disclosure of internal information, particularly on the newly developing project, is generally *not* favorable. We would be glad if Mr. Reimers or yourself could take care to let Stanford's related people know our such hope and reconfirm the article 5 of Amendment No. 2 of the agreement.[62]

Chowning offered a long written explanation in response, sharing how the newspaper article's author was also a fundraising target for CCRMA and how Chowning, therefore, shared information in confidence about potential revenue streams. Chowning concludes his letter with, "I made an error, but I assure you that it was not intended; and, I have also learned a lesson in regard to journalists. I am sorry if this has caused NGK any difficulties."[63] CCRMA's usual openness and sharing had rubbed up against Yamaha's desire for secrecy.

As the Yamaha letter notes, because Yamaha is "an enterprise in trade competition," it generally does not disclose information. By contrast, as a university research center, CCRMA regularly disclosed information. Partha Dasgupta and Paul David have suggested one framework for understanding these differences. They write that research activities can take place under two different institutional systems, *science* and *technology*. Under science, researchers are motivated by a desire increase their reputation among their peers, which leads them to openly disclose their contributions; under technology, by contrast, researchers are motivated by money and they keep their contributions private to as to prevent others from capitalizing on them.[64] In the Stanford–Yamaha case, collaboration across "science" and "technology" led to misunderstandings and apparent missteps.

At the same time, some members of the academic community charged that Stanford's FM patent was harmful to the field. In fact, the claims of "closedness" haunted CCRMA for years. A 2001 article in the *Computer Music Journal*, the field's leading journal, discussed open source software and contrasted it against "the protectionism begun under the Chowning years."[65] The statement drew defensive replies from two former CCRMA affiliates, but the sentiment was clear.

License Negotiations

Patents, however, were only part of the intellectual property environment that Stanford and CCRMA confronted. A major task for the groups lay in determining the licensing details: How should they structure a contract? What terms would be reasonable? Which details should be included and excluded? Here, the historic context of the licensing negotiation is critical: in the 1970s, Stanford had little experience with licensing and thus few templates and scant prior knowledge to draw upon. Moreover, their choices would have important ramifications for future licensing arrangements, including those surrounding breakthrough technologies such as recombinant DNA, DSL, fiber optic amplifiers, and cell sorters. The licensing situation was made all the more complicated by the fact that the technology itself and its perceived applications were changing in ways that neither Yamaha nor Stanford anticipated. Thus, Stanford was in uncharted territory.

The original Yamaha license is striking for its emphasis on sharing of know-how by Chowning and others.[66] In fact, the first declaration in the "Recitals" section at the beginning of the document notes that

> GRANTOR [Stanford/CCRMA] has a substantial body of Know-How necessary and useful in the design and manufacture of a Musical Instrument for improved sound production and also has the capability to synthesize various tones and presently has a library of synthesizable tones.[67]

The license agreement, in turn, specifies not only rights to manufacture under the Stanford patents, but also considerable assistance from "the computer music group [as described earlier] ... who shall act in such separate agreement as independent consultants and not as employees or representatives of GRANTOR."[68] In other words, Chowning and colleagues would establish their own contracts with Yamaha.

Stanford and Yamaha would modify this initial 1975 licensing agreement several times. In 1981, they constructed a wholly new agreement, motivated by recognition that the license and technical assistance arrangement, together with four amendments already made, had "created a complex agreement." A major reason for the growing complexity lay in the shifting technological and market landscape. As Jon Sandelin, an early employee of the Stanford OTL, described the situation:

> The challenge with Yamaha was, of course, that the product kept morphing. At first it was musical instruments. Then personal computers. No, soundcards. So there was a lot of creative renegotiation because the product identity kept changing.[69]

Even the definitions within these categories changed. For instance, Yamaha originally focused on the electronic organ market and defined "musical instrument" in the 1975 agreement as "a digital electronic organ employing a frequency modulation [FM] technique to synthesize quality electronic sound by digital techniques."[70] In the 1981 agreement, however, the definition was revised to mean "a musical instrument or device embodying techniques of Patents, and covered by claims of Patents," since Yamaha was then developing keyboards and a bass synthesizer.[71] In other words, the licensing agreement broadened from specifying a particular application—an organ—to any device embodying FM.[72]

The Stanford archives include a substantial number of handwritten notes that reflect Reimers's and Chowning's efforts to renegotiate the agreement. One set of notes, for example, sketches out comparisons to Toshiba, Texas Instruments, Dolby, and MIT in an attempt to figure out reasonable royalty rates for LSI chips.[73] The analysis revealed that different royalty rates would be appropriate for different kinds of devices, such as musical instruments versus LSI chips versus sound-making devices like video games.[74] The multiple comparisons, "talking points," and calculations evident in the notes reveal, more generally, the difficulty of negotiating contracts around a new market whose size, growth, and direction were all unknown.

It became clear, eventually, that Yamaha's biggest output would be the FM chips themselves, not musical instruments. The market for professional musical instruments such as the DX7 was relatively limited since only a small percentage of the population—professional and serious amateur keyboard players—would ever consider purchasing such an instrument. By contrast, other applications for FM chips, such as personal computers, could address a much larger market. The timing around personal computers, in particular, was ideal: the market for home computers was rapidly expanding and manufacturers foresaw a major opportunity with "multimedia PCs" that featured quality graphics and sound. (Microsoft released its Windows graphical operating system in 1985, which would come to dominate the personal computer market.) By virtue of enabling relatively inexpensive digital sound, FM chips were the favored solution to the "sound" part of this equation. Thus, as Mochida remarked in 1986:

> Our company has [now] produced a huge volume of FM synthesis chips. To the best of my knowledge, we have delivered more than 10 million pieces of FM synthesis chips to the market. Application of FM music synthesis has become so popular and diversified that there are many personal computers which incorporate the FM music synthesis in the unit. About 90 percent of the personal computers marketed in Japan adopt our FM synthesis chips.[75]

Notes from a 1987 meeting between Stanford and Yamaha elaborate on the specific applications of the LSI chip:

> Mr. Ishimura gave us a report of LSI sales. ... There were four market areas of focus as follows: 1. PC Market: Yamaha, NEC, Fujitsu, and Sharp were now using Ya-

maha chips; 2. Arcade Market: The companies Sega and Taito are now using. Yamaha is contacting Bally, Williams (Chicago), and others [in 1982, Atari, too, had approached Yamaha about a sublicense]; 3. Pachinko Market: Two million pachinko units are sold per year. [A Pachinko machine is like a vertical pinball machine, often used as a gambling device akin to the slot machine.] Yamaha has tried to penetrate this market. At present, there are no FM chips being used; and 4. Telephone Market: This is a market that Yamaha has not, but would like to penetrate. This would include music played while a line is on hold.[76]

In short, Yamaha envisioned using their LSI chips to expand the FM market far beyond musical instruments.

Figure 5.1 provides one indication of this shifting market. The figure illustrates patent applications that reference the original Chowning FM patent, along with the primary industries of the applicants. Although patent applications by musical instrument manufacturers dominated the 1980s,

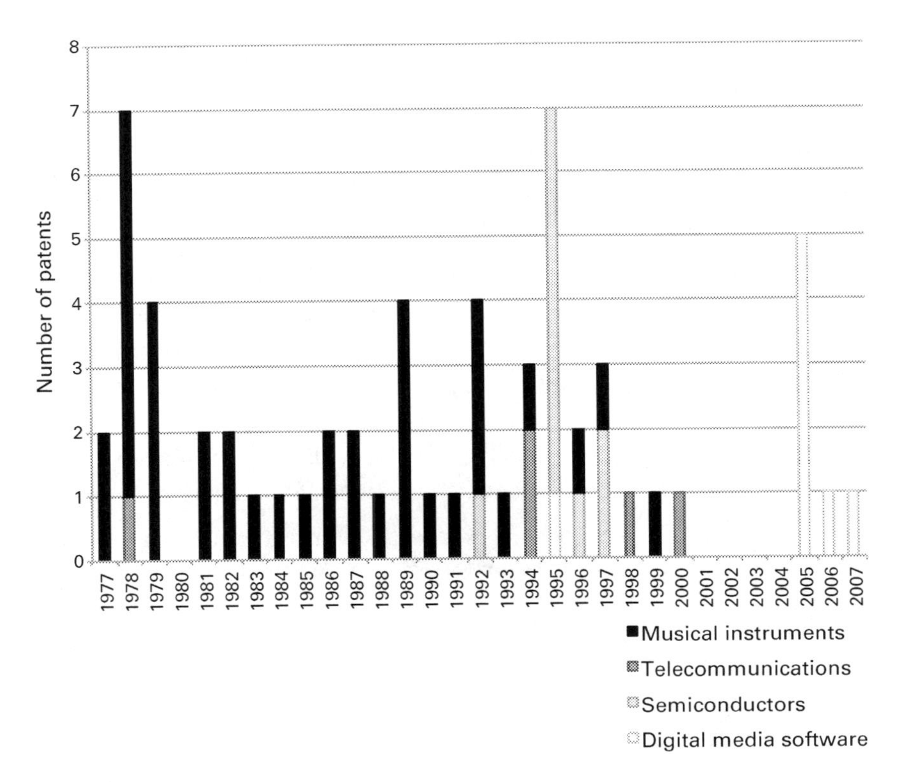

Figure 5.1
Citations to the core FM patent, by primary industry of patent applicant (university patents excluded). Source: US Patent and Trademark Office.

applications shifted predominantly to semiconductor firms in the mid-1990s and to digital media software in the most recent period.

The rise in LSI chips and applications was accompanied by a new round of license negotiations in 1986. This round proved more contentious, primarily because the apparent success of FM had raised the financial stakes substantially.[77] One important point concerned royalty arrangements on the sale of chips, which were experiencing rapid growth. Another point concerned the availability of these LSI chips to other companies who wished to sublicense from Yamaha, and the general exclusivity of the patent.[78] Despite a series of face-to-face meetings in Japan, Stanford and Yamaha did not reach an agreement.

The lack of agreement raised tensions between Stanford and Yamaha. A letter in which Stanford summarized the issues and proposed further meetings received a concerned response from Yamaha.[79] Maki Kamiya, the patent chief, wrote:

> I conveyed your suggestions to the most concerned director Mr. Hiyoshi. He even showed some anger at bringing open again what he had once settled after such elaborate negotiations. His biggest concern is the exclusivity of the FM patents. ... If exclusivity should be lost, Nippon Gakki would rather pull out from FM technology and employ some other monopolizing technology to hold priority of our products, which might even deteriorate so far lasted relation with Stanford University [*sic*].[80]

Hiro Kato, a Yamaha engineer whom Chowning had befriended, followed up with a personal letter to Chowning.[81] Kato again laid out the need for exclusivity and suggested that exclusivity was to Stanford's benefit, too—for New England Digital could not produce many instruments and only Yamaha had the critical voicing expertise. Reimers responded to the patent chief's letter that it was Yamaha, not Stanford, who was reopening the negotiations. As Chowning explained in his personal response to Hiro Kato:

> There are various facets to the agreement ... which are all to a greater or lesser degree interrelated ... after having come to an agreement, when Mr. Kamo [Kosuke Kamo, who worked in Yamaha's intellectual property group] asked that the LSI aspect be reconsidered, Mr. Reimers agreed but on the condition that the whole agreement be open, again because of the interrelation between the various aspects.[82]

Chowning concluded by noting that, "We must have 'clean air' for good relations."[83] Reimers, too, emphasized to Kamiya, "We are very anxious to reestablish the goodwill between our institutions which apparently has been disturbed by this situation."[84] Thus, the success of FM raised the stakes of the Yamaha–Stanford relationship. In turn, as Stanford attempted to engage Yamaha on the grounds of commerce—with both organizations seeking to reach an agreement that met strategic and financial goals—tensions surfaced.

Tensions also flared around the fact that Stanford was engaging with other Japanese companies, although Yamaha remained the university's primary and preferred partner. In 1984, Niels Reimers sent a letter to Yamaha. It describes in an almost apologetic tone a number of Stanford-developed music technologies under consideration by other Japanese companies, including Yamaha's major competitor, Kawai—the same company that Yamaha had inquired about just four years earlier, when Stanford assured Yamaha that it had no contact and no relationship. Reimers's letter foregrounds the importance of the Stanford–Yamaha relationship:

I [Reimers] wanted to assure you that we will continue to endeavor to consider the commercial interests of Nippon Gakki whenever possible. So, if you happen to meet an executive of Kawai, over a bottle of Santory, and he tells you of discussions with Stanford University about some important new technology, you need only smile![85]

In the face of licensing tensions, however, such assurances could be questioned.

Similarly, in 1986 Chowning worked to interest Sony in a project: a jointly designed digital recording system for research on the singing voice. His letter to Sony's President, Norio Ohga, discusses CCRMA's relationship with Yamaha:

In order that you might have some reference for our work ... there are two people in Japan who have a long acquaintance with our work and overall technical competence and with whom you can speak candidly about CCRMA. They are Mr. Kawakami Jr. and Mr. Mochida, President and Managing Director respectively of Nippon Gakki Co. (Yamaha) in Hamamatsu, Japan. It is largely because of their early insight that Yamaha successfully developed the FM synthesis technology which was discovered here at CCRMA.[86]

Thus, Chowning leveraged his success with Yamaha in an attempt to garner support from Sony.

The approach did not sit well with Yamaha. A 1986 Telex from Chowning to Mochida at Yamaha responded to Yamaha's distress over Stanford conversations with Sony:

Dear Mr. Mochida, I was distressed to receive your letter and realized that there is some unfortunate misunderstanding. I have apparently misunderstood NGK's intentions in regard to the development of certain equipment. As I am not scheduled to visit Sony until Nov 6, I hope that I can speak to you on Nov 4 or Nov 5 before my visit. I want most of all to maintain the excellent relationship that we have had with Yamaha.[87]

Chowning strove, therefore, to maintain the Yamaha relationship even as he recognized that it might not be CCRMA's only industry partner.

Ultimately, Stanford and Yamaha did settle on new licensing terms. Chip sales continued to grow, boosted by the fact that IBM adopted the Yamaha chip in the late 1980s to produce sound in its PCs. By 1990, Stanford's royalties were increasing dramatically, as illustrated in figure 5.2. In turn, CCRMA put its share of the royalties into an endowment account, leveraging the commercial success with FM to support future teaching, research, and musical composition activities at the center.

Despite the success, however, Stanford and Yamaha had not wholly resolved the issue of allowing more direct Yamaha competitors access to the technology. For example, Marquis Music contacted Reimers in 1988 because they had designed a PC sound box around the Yamaha chip. Now entering production, they needed 20,000 chips per month, but they found Yamaha unresponsive.[88] Three years later, Media Vision contacted Stanford because they, too, were having difficulty obtaining chips from Yamaha. They wrote:

We feel that Yamaha's pricing strategy will prohibit us from providing affordable audio solutions to the marketplace on a volume basis. Unfortunately, the Yamaha chip is required to provide [compatibility with the emerging soundcard standard] which

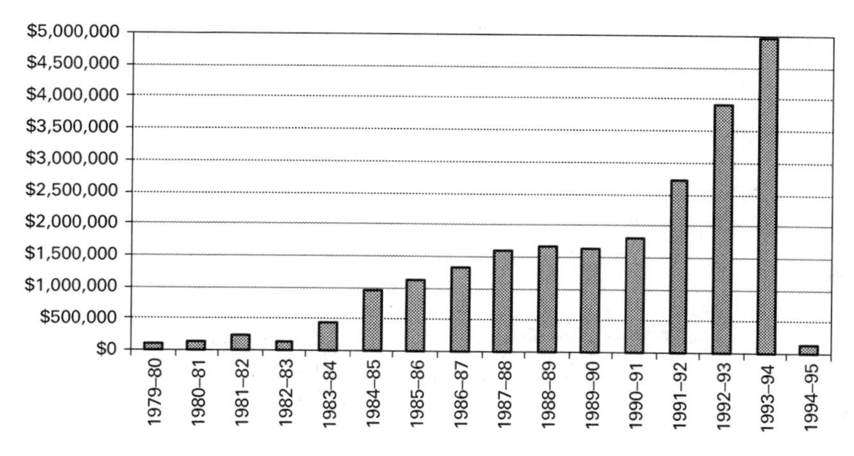

Figure 5.2
Stanford's FM synthesis licensing revenue, by year.

makes it very difficult for U.S. companies and may force an outcome deleterious to FM. We do not think it is in the best interests of U.S. personal computer manufacturers to be dependent upon technology which has been developed in the U.S. and is being employed by a Japanese company to charge U.S. customers exorbitant prices. This not only hurts the total marketplace and the end consumer, but also affects the amount of royalty dollars received by Stanford University.

Undoubtedly, Reimers remembered the contact a decade earlier from Congressman Paul Tsongas, expressing concern about the Japanese licensing relationship based on research conducted by a US university. Now, a new US company was raising similar concerns. The Media Vision letter continues:

We can certainly understand that Yamaha's purpose may simply be to protect its keyboard market. However, with the advent of personal computers and current technology, Yamaha will not be able to protect that market by restricting use of FM chips. Ironically, in the long run, Yamaha's strategy may be counterproductive to its market position. ... By restricting the sales of their FM chip, Yamaha is driving the industry to develop an alternative sound synthesis chip other than FM.[89]

The Media Vision letter demonstrates strong recognition of the relationship between commercialization, standards, intellectual property, and university royalties: Yamaha had the opportunity to make FM the de facto standard for computer soundcards, which would benefit Stanford through licensing royalties. Yet Yamaha's patent-enabled monopoly on the technology incentivized other companies to develop an alternative standard, thus threatening to hurt Stanford even as it protected Yamaha.

Reimers's subsequent letter to Yamaha parrots these key points from the Media Vision communication:

FM has the potential of being established in the field of music as a "standard," but that the present marketing strategy of Yamaha is such that market conditions will drive industry to an alternative standard. We, of course, not only would desire to see a greatly expanded sales [*sic*] of FM chips before expiration of the license, but would be proud to have FM in fact become a standard, now or later.[90]

Stanford's interest, of course, lay in sharing FM as widely as possible (and in realizing the accompanying licensing revenue); Yamaha's interest lay in protecting and growing its own business. Though the two organizations were important collaborators in bringing FM technology to market, their ultimate aims were not entirely aligned.

At the same time, Yamaha was getting assailed by other chips. A letter from Yamaha's intellectual property department to their Costa Mesa, California-based US patent counsel noted that:

> Last year, we found that copied YAMAHA chips were being sold in Taiwan. And, it has turned out that a Taiwanese LSI company named United Microelectronics Corporation (UMC) makes and sells some of these with their LSI product Nos. UM3567 and UM3566. Then, we dispatched to UMC and its distributing companies a warning letter as attached hereto. Recently, we further found that certain FM sound boards using copied FM chip [*sic*] are on the market in Taiwan, Korea, and U.S.A.[91]

On one hand, therefore, Yamaha was fighting intellectual property infringement on an international scale; on the other hand, Stanford was spurring them toward increased openness.

The situation was further complicated by the fact that Yamaha was attempting to vertically integrate computer applications of FM; ideally, they desired to control the whole sound processing environment, not just one piece of it. This perspective was most evident in Yamaha's development of a multimedia computer, built entirely by Yamaha and running a Yamaha-developed operating system and applications. If Yamaha shared chips too broadly, others could sell components of the Yamaha system, chipping away at the system's cohesiveness.[92] The Yamaha computer, however, was a major market failure. Dismayed by the experience, Yamaha pulled back from the computer market altogether, ceding the soundcard business to Creative Technology and other manufacturers and focusing on providing chips.[93]

Even this withdrawn position, however, exposed them to market threats. For example, Chromatic Research, a California-based maker of audio- and video-processing cards, hired CCRMA graduate student Avery Wang to "work around the FM patents."[94] Indeed, Wang's "solution," US Patent number 5,834,672, does not reference Chowning's patent. Similarly, Media Vision hired Perry Cook, when Cook was still a graduate research associate at CCRMA, to "engineer around all the remaining Yamaha patents on FM for the day when the Chowning patent expires."[95] For his part, Chowning stayed out of the fray. As he recalled:

> A lot of [our graduate students] were working for other companies—probably at the research level, where they [the companies] thought they could beat it [the FM patent] but they wanted help. I never asked. I never talked about the Yamaha relationship within CCRMA. I kept all that separate because I didn't want any confusion about, for example, my using the work of people here.[96]

By the mid-1990s, FM chips were no longer the primary focus of Stanford or Yamaha anyway. Instead, both groups turned attention to another CCRMA technology, waveguide physical modeling (detailed in chapter 7), as their four-decade relationship continued to evolve.

Figure 5.3
This photograph was taken in 1987 during a visit by Yamaha personnel to CCRMA. Pictured from left to right: Tsuyoshi "Goh" Futamase (Yamaha), John Chowning (CCRMA), Andy Moorer (CCRMA), Hirokazu "Hiro" Kato (Yamaha), Bernard Mont-Reynaud (CCRMA), Kanehisa Tsurumi (Yamaha), and Shigenori Oguri (Yamaha). Not pictured and presumed to be taking the photograph is Yamaha's Yozo "Steve" Iwai. Courtesy of the Stanford University Archives.

Ultimately, the commercialization of FM reveals how the two very different groups—a center within the music department of a US research university and a Japanese technology firm—came to be dependent upon one another: CCRMA enabled Yamaha to take the synthesizer world by storm, introducing one of the most radical new instruments the world had ever seen and catalyzing a shift into semiconductor manufacturing that remains important to the company today. Yamaha, in turn, provided CCRMA with critical resources—money, to be sure, and gifts of equipment, but also legitimacy and support: through the Yamaha relationship, CCRMA solidified and justified its unique blend of interdisciplinarity, open innovation, and commercialization, even as the different goals of the two organizations challenged these activities, at times. Moreover, CCRMA's and Yamaha's success enabled the broad expansion of the computer music field as a whole, seeding both further academic research and broad popular adoption. This same intertwining of activities would define CCRMA for years to come.

6 From Exposition to Development

One point of inquiry surrounding CCRMA concerns accounting for its emergence. Thus, earlier chapters have detailed how the national landscape and institutional features associated with both Stanford and the music department provided fertile ground for CCRMA to develop. We have also seen that the ability of early CCRMA advocates to assemble a diverse group of supporters—commercial interests, government agencies, artificial intelligence pioneers, composers, and others—and to repurpose existing resources enabled both the center's establishment and its sustenance in its first years, albeit with considerable challenges.

A second point of inquiry surrounding CCRMA concerns its sustenance and renewal over time. CCRMA has remained creative, innovative and cutting-edge—a difficult accomplishment for organizations as they age.[1] In turn, an exploration of CCRMA during the 1980s and 1990s sheds light on how the center continued to leverage multivocality, intertwining interdisciplinary work, open innovation, and commercialization, even as people, technologies, organizations, and resources shifted.

Bolstered by increasing royalties from Yamaha and by the $2.3 million SDF grant in 1982, Chowning and colleagues continued their efforts to build CCRMA. By most accounts, Chowning remained the central figure at CCRMA in the 1980s and into the 1990s. John Pierce, the Bell Labs engineer who had provided key support for CCRMA, spent six weeks at CCRMA in March and April 1983 and wrote a report on his visit for SDF. The bulk of the report contains descriptions of various technical projects undertaken and Pierce's frank assessment of CCRMA's personnel, strengths, and weaknesses. Pierce's overall assessment of CCRMA, however, highlights the critical role that Chowning continued to play:

CCRMA is a constellation of extremely various but remarkably able people. The predominance of musicians ... keeps CCRMA on the musical track. The electrical engineers and the computer people ... make it possible to do things. The psychoacousticians ... and an occasional psychologist, add a depth to the musical work.

CCRMA people are extremely varied in character as well as in field. ... All interact with a sense of mutual esteem and with mutual profit. CCRMA has a mixture of chaos and cooperation which is amazing as well as productive. All are very attached to CCRMA because they are doing what they want to do, individually and collectively.

What causes CCRMA to survive and flourish? John Chowning is an essential ingredient. He is on good terms with everyone, and he manages to get essential things done. This he certainly doesn't do by ordering people around; even the tractable ones are good enough so they aren't orderable. He enlists their cooperation. One day I found Julius Smith doing something he described as "work" (as opposed to his own very fine work, which he would classify as fun). I suppose he was paid for the "work," but chiefly, he knew that it was necessary to CCRMA's functioning.[2]

Chowning would be the first to insist, however, that CCRMA's functioning depended on a wide range of participants. In addition to faculty and staff, the core group consisted of doctoral candidates in both music and engineering—some of whom went on to become CCRMA-affiliated faculty themselves. For example, in 1989, CCRMA secured research faculty appointments for Bernard Mont-Reynaud, Chris Chafe, and Julius Smith. Both Chafe and Smith had first engaged with CCRMA as graduate students. As Chowning noted in a memo to the dean of the School of Humanities and Sciences, "These appointments give me considerable optimism both for the academic and funding future of CCRMA."[3]

Five years later, the university would give CCRMA two tenured faculty positions. Provost Condoleeza Rice, a talented classical pianist who would go on to become US Secretary of State, provided the drive. As Andy Moorer recalled:

The Music Department up to that point had been early music. William Bird, fifteenth-century and seventeenth-century music. We were these Johnny-come-latelies. So they were polite to us and very helpful in us seeking to get music. But the Music Department was very reluctant to allocate a professorship, one of their seats—and they kept all these professors in early music. It was Condoleeza Rice who noticed that they had twenty-six grad students in electronic and computer music and three in early music. She finally reallocated the professorships.[4]

The faculty additions bolstered Chowning's confidence in CCRMA's future. As Chowning would write in a letter to IRCAM:

Chris Chafe and Julius Smith are, therefore, now permanent, tenured faculty. These positions are in addition to the position that Jonathan Harvey [a well-known British composer who had earlier spent time at IRCAM] has been offered. CCRMA, therefore, is now secure as part of the university's future, a condition that I have not until these recent appointments felt to be the case.[5]

In a university setting, tenure-track faculty lines are both an essential resource and a symbol of institutional priorities. The addition of tenure-track faculty with strong CCRMA affiliations thus signaled that CCRMA's activities to date were yielding critical university resources and support.

Faculty, however, were only part of the story. From the beginning, CCRMA also hosted a large number of visitors (as with the visit from the IRCAM group in 1975). Even Mickey Hart, drummer with the Grateful Dead, used CCRMA as a home base in the early 1980s.[6] Other visitors participated in a popular series of summer workshops, which began in 1969.[7] These workshops brought twenty to thirty musicians, composers, scientists, and engineers to Stanford each year. In a four-week session, CCRMA personnel taught the participants basic computer programming, fundamentals of acoustics, psychoacoustics, and digital signal processing, as well as special features of the CCRMA system. Participants also had access to the facility to work on their own compositions. Although many workshop participants were private interested individuals—for example, the 1982 attendees included a private piano teacher, a synthesizer builder, several composers, a pipe organ voicer/tuner, and a harpsichord builder—faculty from other colleges and universities also attended. These faculty used the workshops as an opportunity to initiate or improve their own institutions' computer music programs. In other words, CCRMA summer workshops served as a means of spreading the emerging discipline of computer music.[8] At the same time, the workshops provided summer funding for graduate students and for recent graduates who would return to CCRMA to share their research with new groups.

Summer workshops could serve as a gateway into further studies at CCRMA, too. Paul Kirk, who was well known in commercial music circles and lived in Los Angeles at the time, participated in a workshop on a whim in 1975. As he recalled:

The idea of going to Stanford was sort of like, "What am I doing?" It felt like a step backwards. [Recall that the Stanford music department still was not widely known or respected.] [But,] I was up here [in the Bay Area] looking after my dad, who had a heart attack, so I gave Stanford a call.

... [When I reached Patte Wood, the CCRMA administrator] she said, "Yeah, it's on computer music and everything else. You learn how to generate sound using a computer and stuff." I thought, "Oh, that's curious and interesting. I'm not sure how I would use that. The computers down at UCLA are the size of bathtubs and laundry rooms."

... My wife encouraged me to go ahead and do it. ... [So] I took the workshop and we were working in the dead of night, all the time, and you'd sit there and for four seconds of sounds, you'd let this thing compute for two or three hours, and load a disk back up that was the size of this coffee table. But it was a lot of fun![9]

Kirk went on to enroll in the doctoral program through CCRMA and received his DMA degree in 1978.

CCRMA grew its course offerings beyond graduate students, too. In the late 1980s, the center expanded its formal curriculum by adding an experimental introductory computer music course for undergraduates. The offering attracted thirty students and led to calls for an undergraduate concentration in music/science/technology, which Stanford introduced in 1992.[10] That same year, Chowning proposed a new master's degree, too. The proposal was approved and master's students arrived as early as 1993.[11]

As a result of all of this activity, CCRMA grew from about twenty active faculty, staff, and students at any one time in the 1970s to about sixty starting in the 1980s. In fact, the rapid growth led to discussions on to how to optimize CCRMA's size so as to facilitate interdisciplinary interactions. As Chowning argued in a 2008 interview:

There's kind of a critical mass. It gets so big, like IRCAM [which has about 150 researchers, students, and visitors at any given time], that people wouldn't know what other people were doing. So it seemed to me that at the size that we were, it was functioning. Everyone knew what everyone else was doing. That cross-feeding was very important. Like Julius [Smith] and David Jaffe doing *Silicon Valley Breakdown* [an important composition that demonstrated a new synthesis technique]. That was great work, for music and for signal processing. ... [I did not want CCRMA] to be so big that we would lose that special character. And I think it's kind of right on the edge now. I think if we grew much more, it would kind of get lost.[12]

On one hand, CCRMA needs to be large enough that it incorporates diverse disciplines and perspectives. On the other hand, if CCRMA were too large, it might lose the mutual awareness and support that enables and encourages these diverse elements to connect and that prohibits any one of them from being large enough to form an isolated clique. Writing around the same time as CCRMA's founding, organizational scholar Peter Blau described how organizational growth is accompanied by increased differentiation and a narrower oversight by any given participant.[13] Chowning's reflections on

CCRMA's size evince an acute awareness of the need to balance the advantages and disadvantages of smaller and larger populations.

This expanding and collegial group found a new home in the mid-1980s. While CCRMA occupied the D.C. Power Lab building in the foothills away from campus, the Stanford music department had been housed at the "Knoll," an Italian Renaissance–style mansion built in 1916 that originally served as the residence for Stanford's president. When the music department moved to a new building, CCRMA planned to move from the D.C. Power facility to the Knoll; the location was closer to the campus core and provided a connection to SuNet, the Stanford University computer network. (Incidentally, Sun Microsystems took its name from the Stanford University Network.) In turn, the new location led to further growth in student involvement.[14]

CCRMA's move to the Knoll would again require substantial resources. Although the building was an improvement over the D.C. Power Lab, it remained somewhat decrepit.[15] More critically, the move coincided with a need to build new digital recording studios and to acquire equipment. The

Figure 6.1
From left to right: David A. Jaffe, John Gordon, John Chowning, and Bill Schottstaedt in the main computer room at the D.C. Power Lab in 1982. Courtesy of the Stanford University Archives. Photo by Patte Wood (© Patte Wood).

studios were necessary for emerging research projects—particularly around study of the singing voice, a longtime passion for Chowning. (Chowning would send a pair of letters in 1985 to Sherrill Milnes of the New York Metropolitan Opera requesting to record his voice for research purposes.[16]) Digital recording, however, also presented demands: cutting-edge equipment and very low background noise. Chowning, therefore, hit the fundraising trail again.

Fundraising Efforts

In many ways, CCRMA's history can be understood as an ongoing search for resources—equipment, facilities, and salaries to support faculty, staff, and students. CCRMA's initial success depended on stitching together support from government funding agencies (such as the NSF and NEA), private foundations (such as SDF), and commercial partners (such as Yamaha). The success of this approach lay in presenting the particular aspect of CCRMA's work most likely to resonate with each potential funder, a strategy that required a delicate balance: If CCRMA presented a project as *too* far outside a potential funder's comfort zone, it would be unlikely to meet success. (Recall Chowning's previous fundraising difficulties.) At the same time, much of CCRMA's differentiation lay in its work outside the mainstream—the special value it realized from combining art and technology, and academic research and commerce, in unique and powerful ways. Thus, fundraising efforts attempted to match particular aspects of CCRMA's work with the particular interests of a given donor.

The search for funding also served another role beyond the direct acquisition of resources: among individuals and organizations that were successful and high-profile in their own respective fields, it raised awareness about CCRMA, its activities, and its contributions. Fundraising efforts, in other words, served not only to acquire immediate financial resources but also to build long-term reputational resources.

One promising fundraising avenue lay in William Hewlett and David Packard, the cofounders of Hewlett-Packard (HP)—another Stanford-linked company. Hewlett and Packard had been electrical engineering students at Stanford. After graduation in 1935, they held fellowships with Fred Terman, the Stanford professor who would rise to become dean of the School of Engineering and, later still, provost. (Recall chapter 2's discussion of

Terman's efforts to restructure Stanford programs and funding relationships.) Terman encouraged Hewlett and Packard to form a company, which they did in 1939.

In November 1984, John Pierce, who was highly respected in the electrical engineering community, crafted very similar and personal letters to "Bill" Hewlett and to "Dave" Packard.[17] In his letters, Pierce references HP's launch of "a recording program in cooperation with Erato Records"—a potential signal of HP's interest in music. He then notes:

> We're not broke, and are reasonably well equipped. But we can't do many things we would like to do for lack of money. We need new computers. Above all, we need to find a source of some $400,000 for a first-rate digital recording studio, to be named after whoever supplies the funds.[18]

Bill Hewlett responded that month and described his son Walter's great interest in the "applications of computers to music."[19] The next month, December, David Packard responded, too, and requested to have his son visit CCRMA. Packard's letter reads, in part, "David Woodley, my son, is on the board of my Foundation and his recommendation would be helpful for us to consider financial support."[20] Thus, Chowning leveraged the personal connections of his great supporter, John Pierce, to pursue support for CCRMA's move to the new building.

Both Walter Hewlett and David Woodley visited CCRMA in January 1985, each of them very taken with the technical work.[21] Unfortunately, as an internal Stanford memo to Chowning noted, "Neither foundation [Hewlett or Packard] has a stated interest that could, by any stretch of interpretation, be related to your project."[22] Indeed, although Walter Hewlett did engage deeply in the technical work at CCRMA—he still holds a consulting professor position in the associated Center for Computer Assisted Research in the Humanities (CCARH) at Stanford—this assessment was correct: neither foundation had a clear interest in music and neither foundation ultimately gave financial support.

Another potential supporter was Gordon Getty, who made a "long awaited visit to campus" in December 1985.[23] (Getty is the fourth child of oil tycoon J. Paul Getty and, according to Forbes, is worth an estimated $2 billion.[24]) The fundraising team at Stanford had desired, per an internal memo, to

> develop a collegial relationship with Gordon around his fascinations for music, computers, composition, vocal pedagogy, and performance. The Center for Computer Research in Music and Acoustics appeared to be the ideal match for these interests.[25]

Getty shared an informal working lunch with various CCRMA personnel at the D.C. Power Lab—the facility in the foothills that CCRMA had inherited from the AI group. The Stanford Office of Development file notes indicate that the Stanford team intentionally tried to avoid formality. Thus, Getty

> arrived alone and on time in his shiny black Buick, and after a brief discussion about Stanford with Music Department chairman Al Cohen, he was taken to CCRMA's labs out on Arastradero [Road]. This literally rat-infested dilapidated building is where he spent the rest of the afternoon engaged in serious, animated, and laughter-filled conversation. He remarked more than once, "You guys really have something here." ... He was shown the complete setup of Yamaha frequency modulation equipment and enjoyed playing with it so much that he ordered a complete set for his own use.[26]

As with the visit from the group of famous IRCAM-affiliated composers in 1975, the emphasis was on the work itself rather than on refined amenities and star treatment.

The following February, Chowning arranged for Getty to visit with Pierre Boulez and Steve Jobs. Again, the personal ties ran thick and were essential to pulling together diverse groups: Jobs was highly interested in music and Getty was a composer; Chowning knew Jobs through Jobs's first girlfriend, whose uncle was a close friend of Chowning's. For his part, Jobs, who had left Apple at this point to start NeXT, used the meeting to encourage Boulez to acquire NeXT computers at IRCAM.[27] Despite his great interest in CCRMA, however, Getty did not make the hoped-for major gift, though he did offer important financial support for programmatic efforts.

In November 1984, Chowning sent a letter to Louise Davies, who gave the naming gift for Davies Symphony Hall in San Francisco. The letter references Chowning's time in Paris and Boulez's plans to present his composition *Repons* in San Francisco in 1986. Chowning's letter exhibits a very personal tone, even referencing Davies's and Chowning's children. The letter also addresses Chowning's intended business: a request for $400,000 to $500,000 to build a "Louise Davies Psychoacoustic Studio" in the Knoll.[28] Again, however, major support did not materialize.

Chowning focused his efforts especially on Doreen Townsend, a San Francisco philanthropist who began supporting CCRMA in the 1970s. His April 1984 letter to Townsend proposed naming CCRMA after her:

> While governments in most Western countries provide the greater part of the support for the arts, we in the United States must depend largely upon private support. While CCRMA has been able to attract both federal and private support in recent years, it is only because we have demonstrated our musical, scientific, and technical abilities.

Your "hunch," some ten years ago, that CCRMA would develop and become a leader in the development of music in the 20th century turned out to be right and allowed us to develop to the point that we were able to attract this support.[29]

Chowning's own recognition of the importance of demonstrating "musical, scientific, and technical abilities" underscores how these different activities seemed to mutually constitute CCRMA's success. After describing his plans for the new listening spaces and recording studios, and the associated singing voices project, Chowning's letter continues, "So, dear Doreen, once more I ask you for help."[30]

Chowning's courtship of Townsend continued. He invited her to a December 1985 performance of *Invisible Cities*, an important work by CCRMA composer Michael McNabb. When Townsend's driver got lost, Chowning himself traveled to San Francisco the next day to accompany her to the Saturday night performance. Thus, an internal memo from a Stanford development officer reads, "John also arranged for a small reception, and generally gave red carpet treatment for his No. 1 benefactor. This guy [Chowning] should be on the Development Office payroll. Well done, John!"[31] Ultimately, Townsend gave a $200,000 cash gift in response to Chowning's $600,000 solicitation—a generous gift, but well below Chowning's hopes.[32]

In the face of smaller gifts, Chowning had speculated how he might reduce the cost of the Knoll project. He concluded that the only way to substantially reduce costs would be to eliminate the recording studio and control room. As he wrote in a January 1985 memo: "Not having these rooms would substantially effect [*sic*] the program and it seemed therefor [*sic*] that we should go ahead with the entire project in spite of the increment in cost." To make this happen, CCRMA borrowed from the FM patent royalty account, which they had intended to save until it could serve as an endowment to cover operating expenses.[33] Chowning's overriding interest, however, lay in supporting musical composition and novel research at the intersection of music and technology. If realizing these goals required tapping the Yamaha funds, then he reasoned that it was a worthy cause.

Equipment and Standardization

Another challenge lay in acquiring equipment for the Knoll move. Underlying this pursuit was a deep interest in standardization and the benefits to be gained from standardization. As noted in the introduction, standards enable sharing through interoperability: when multiple groups use the same computer system, for example, they can share software and hardware upgrades, as CCRMA and IRCAM did in the 1970s. Standards also enable people themselves to move more seamlessly between settings, by reducing technical barriers tied to a need to learn new systems. Yet, by the very fact that they are shared standards, standards can make it difficult to customize systems for any particular user—and to the extent that customization occurs, it moves away from the benefits of the standard.[34]

In some cases, standards for CCRMA equipment were already established. The Sony PCM-1610 digital recorder, for example, was widely adopted by professional recording studios. Chowning requested and received a long-term loan of one from Sony.[35]

Computer music standards, however, were more challenging since CCRMA itself was at the forefront of motivating the design and development of systems. Indeed, a key aspect of the infrastructure at CCRMA was the computing system. CCRMA had started by mimicking the PDP-10 at Bell Labs, and Chowning knew firsthand the difficulties of moving from one system to another. (Recall how Chowning's initial work relied on David Poole to transition Mathews's Music IV program from the Bell system to the Stanford system.) Conversely, when Boulez started IRCAM, IRCAM copied CCRMA's hardware and software—with CCRMA's blessing and help—saving, per Chowning's estimate, "tens of man-years" of time and effort.[36] Stanford's Samson Box, however, again moved away from standardization. Although it was a marvelous machine for its time, Stanford had the only one in existence. Thus, they had to develop all of their own software and, once developed, this software could not be shared with other groups.

To John Pierce, this approach was troublesome. In a 1983 letter to the System Development Foundation (SDF), which had awarded CCRMA its $2.3 million lifeline in 1982, he outlined some of the challenges:

> The present music synthesis system, based on the Funely [meaning Foonly] computer and the Samson Box, is necessary for the functioning and survival of CCRMA, for it is what the composers use, with great facility and skill. Yet, it is more a vestige of the past than a wave of the future.
>
> … I heard Barrie Vercoe [at MIT] and Dick Moore [at UC San Diego] urge John Chowning to get an 1155 (because it is fast and cheap) and a VAX [a Digital Equipment Corporation computer]. I wonder. I think that the future of computer music lies with really cheap hardware, such as the 68000 [a Motorola microprocessor] and

special-purpose hardware for synthesis. ... Going to an 1155 and a VAX instead of the Funely [again, Pierce means Foonly] would require a lot of software work, including the conversion of many present compositional resources to a different language and a different operating system. And, there would be a considerable hardware and hardware maintenance cost and burden.

... Another very real concern for the future is sampling rate, and its standardization. CCRMA pieces come with almost any sampling rate. [Sampling rate refers to the number of times each second that a signal is measured. The compact disk uses a standard sampling rate of 44,100.] ... Japanese firms such as Sony are producing all sorts of very high quality digital sound equipment, and it all works at the same standard sampling rate (44,000 samples per second?) and at no other sampling rate. In supplying computer music examples for demonstration compact disks, CCRMA people face a difficult problem in high-quality conversion from one sampling rate to another. The course of computer music would be much cheaper if CCRMA and others could settle on and stick to the commercial sampling rate ... In fact, I wonder if computer music that doesn't conform to commercial digital standards has any future at all.[37]

As Pierce's letter indicates, standardization was a critical issue for the future of the field. On one hand, standardization affected the machines used to produce computer music in the first place. On the other hand, standardization also affected the ways in which this music might be distributed. Absent appropriate standardization, Pierce feared that the field of computer music itself could fragment and fizzle as each center adopted its own hardware, developed its own software, and distributed compositions using a variety of incompatible sampling rates.

Chowning himself had already been thinking about standardization and the next generation of computing technology, though his own thinking was shaped largely by his experience with the Artificial Intelligence group at Stanford. In a 1981 proposal to SDF, he described how

the Computer Science Department at Stanford is connecting its large computers via Ethernet and developing the Motorola 68000 based Sun [Microsystems] personal computing stations. CCRMA would benefit greatly by following the same direction. ... In addition to the known qualities of the Sun terminal of powerful graphics and computation, the Sun station is particularly attractive to CCRMA in two ways: (1) it is based in the C language and UNIX system which is the principle language at both UCSD and MIT (in addition to many other computer music groups) facilitating inter-laboratory communication, and (2) it is a modular architecture based on a standardized bus and card which allows peripherals and specialized inter-faces to be connected with very great ease.[38]

Chowning's vision had yet to be realized, however, and computing at CCRMA itself remained tied to the one-of-a-kind Samson Box. Characterizing this time period, Gareth Loy, a CCRMA graduate who went on to help build UC San Diego's computer music program, recalled, "There was a little war [among the centers], each proposing a different system."[39]

Concerned about this lack of standardization, SDF convened all of the major computer music research centers in the United States to figure out standardized next-generation systems for each group. The idea was that these groups could develop systems together and, therefore, share more effectively. The Stanford archives contain notes from a two-day meeting in November 1982 at MIT, attended by representatives from Stanford, UCSD, Lucasfilm, MIT, Bell Labs, Systems Concepts, and SDF.[40] This meeting was followed by another meeting in February 1983 that focused on four main topics: system design; composer environment; performance interface; and signal processing. Each topic had four to six subareas, and each subarea had a responsible lead or leads.[41] Thus, the immense complexity of the technical infrastructure for digital audio and computer music was evident even in the structure of discussions.

Finally, in May 1983, MIT, Stanford, and UCSD came together with a proposal. A number of technical aspects remained unresolved. The proposal noted general agreement, however, that "the target system probably will be some descendant of a 68000 workstation running UNIX, augmented by special interactive controls and real-time music processing hardware."[42] Thus, the group shared Pierce's and Chowning's assessments.

The choice of equipment also carried implications for funding and for the equipment suppliers themselves. For example, a 1984 memo from Rob Poor, who was serving as CCRMA's technical director at the time, describes a proposed three-way relationship between Xerox, SDF, and CCRMA:

> This morning I met with Charlie Smith [head of the SDF] to talk about Xerox Lisp machines, Bill Spencer's potential offer to give us machines [Spencer was vice president and manager of Xerox PARC], and the relationship between Xerox and SDF.
>
> Charlie Smith suggests that Bill Spencer's offer is as follows: Xerox gives DandyTigers [a Xerox computer] and printers to CCRMA. In return, CCMRA [*sic*] brings respectability to the DandyTigers. Bill Spencer is especially interested in music manuscripting as a research problem. Charlie says that "Bill Spencer enjoys theater," and accordingly would like to be wined and dined by CCRMA.
>
> What Xerox and SDF can offer CCRMA: If we can shake equipment out of Xerox, then SDF may be able to provide money for bodies (salaries for researchers). In order to shake equipment out of Xerox, CCRMA needs to demonstrate that donated machines will be used for glorious things, and won't become dusty.

... As it turns out, Don Knuth is very interested in music manuscripting, especially using MetaFont techniques, but he doesn't have the time to get involved in such a project. Charlie suggested that we could work a deal with Don Knuth whereby Don is the PI for a manuscripting project for CCRMA. The funds and the MetaFont techniques come to us, and we turn it into music manuscripting.[43]

Knuth's involvement was important given his high status: He is a 1979 recipient of the National Medal of Science, author of the TeX typesetting system and the multivolume *The Art of Computer Programming*, and a legend in the computer science community. Still, the fact that CCRMA's use would bring "respectability" to Xerox machines is itself strong evidence of CCRMA's emergent prestige: the center was only nine years old at this point, and just ten years prior to this memo, Chowning had been denied tenure; now, a major corporation hoped to leverage a partnership with CCRMA to enhance the prestige of its own offering.

This perspective also highlights how support for CCRMA could represent an exchange as much as a gift: CCRMA could leverage personal relationships to get exposure, equipment, and other resources in exchange for reputation. Moreover, to the point of standardization, this equipment also enabled CCRMA to run Lisp programs—Lisp being the standard language of the AI community and one that CCRMA had used to build its own suite of programs. In other words, personal relationships, gifts, technology development, and emergent standards were all tied up with one another.

Chowning himself shared the belief that adopting commercial technologies held several advantages. In a 1985 letter he reported on the attendance of a Yamaha representative, Mr. Hirano, at an academic computer music meeting:

I believe that Mr. Hirano was surprised at the degree of interest that was expressed by computer music composers and researchers in your "X" series products at the conference. There were many references throughout the presentation to especially the DX7. The "X" series has become the "moving technology" in computer music for several reasons which I think are perhaps worth enumerating.[44]

Chowning goes on to argue that the DX7's low cost, availability, and ability to connect with other instruments through the MIDI interface signaled that widespread commercial systems might ultimately supplant the high-end specialized machines used by leading computer music centers. (MIDI, or the Musical Instruments Digital Interface, enables instruments from different manufacturers to communicate, such that pressing a key on one instrument, for example, can trigger a sound on another instrument. Although

MIDI's origins lie in commercial systems, it became a widespread standard in both academia and industry—again, signaling how university–industry influences run both directions.)

Chowning, in fact, reveled in the fact that standardization allowed open sharing not only by high-end computer music centers, but also by everyday users who had been using analog systems up to that point. In a 2008 interview, he reflected on the DX7's introduction in 1983:

> That whole music world was DX7. They had DX7 clubs. Bars that had DX7 bands. It's all over the place. These kids would be trading voices [sounds]. Take their [sound] cartridge, stick it in, and download it. Now somebody else has it. There was this kind of community of users which had a lot to do with the success. Some voice that may have been developed in Indonesia, in the time of a plane flight was all of sudden all over Europe. That was kind of astonishing. ... The ease with which the technology could be transferred from user to user with just a cartridge, out of one [instrument] and into another, and the fact that it would be the same, which was unlike any analog synthesizer because the digital technology guaranteed that these were exact replicas of what was done elsewhere.[45]

Chowning's reflection on the ease of copying is important. Although users could openly share sounds in the context of analog synthesis, digital instruments like the DX7 facilitated vastly easier sharing—even though the underlying technology was more sophisticated. In fact, the complexity of FM programming encouraged copying and sharing since it was difficult to create a new sound from scratch—owing to both the complexity of FM synthesis and the poor user interface on the DX7. With Yamaha's support, Chowning and David Bristow wrote *FM Theory and Applications: By Musicians, For Musicians* (1987) to teach users how to program the new instrument.[46] Yet the vast majority of users relied on factory presets and other sound libraries and did not program the instrument themselves.

Chowning found his views on the benefits of commercial standards echoed by his great supporter, Pierre Boulez. In a September 1985 letter to Yamaha's Yasunori Mochida, Chowning was excited to report Boulez's adoption of Yamaha equipment:

> I would like you to know that in early August, David Bristow and I gave Pierre Boulez a detailed explanation of the YAMAHA equipment at IRCAM. He was extraordinarily attentive and interested, to the extent that he decided on the spot to use some of the equipment in his next piece. Considering that Pierre is a major composer/conductor of our century and has very demanding "ears," I was pleased indeed. It is the first time that he has been captivated by commercially available synthesis and processing equipment. ... I felt that it was a moment of some historical importance.[47]

Per Chowning's assessment, one of the most important living composers had seen promise in commercially produced and economically motivated digital equipment. It was a watershed moment.

In the late 1980s, CCRMA would make another dramatic move by adopting NeXT computers. Steve Jobs started NeXT in 1985, the same year that he departed Apple. Jobs had a long-standing interest in music and he conceived of high-quality audio as an integral part of his proposed NeXT computer. Indeed, as Julius Smith, who would work for Jobs at NeXT recalled, "Steve Jobs was extremely, extremely supportive of the music mission. He's always been extremely supportive of music. He wants to do great things and music is one of the main [things]."[48] Thus, the NeXT was the first computer with a signal-processing chip that could be dedicated to sound.[49]

In 1986, Jobs contacted Andy Moorer, who in turn recommended that Jobs hire Julius Smith to put together the audio portion of the machine.[50] Smith, who was a CCRMA Research Associate at the time, recalled what happened next:

> In '86, Steve Jobs called me up and said, "Why don't we talk? Your name keeps coming up. We need to talk." They'd decided to put a DSP 56000 chip on every motherboard, so they needed a signal processing person to deal with all that, whatever that could do. And Steve Jobs also knew that he wanted to do music in a big way. He wanted the NeXT computer to be a breakthrough computer for music.[51]

With his NeXT cofounders, Jobs traveled around the United States to meet with university representatives. At Stanford, Smith attended the meeting with Pierre Boulez, John Chowning, and Gordon Getty.

Smith, in turn, pulled other CCRMA affiliates into the NeXT music group, including David A. Jaffe. As Jaffe recalled:

> I can't tell you how exciting that was there [at NeXT] then. I can't remember if I was the 26th or the 32nd employee, but I was one of the very early employees and that was the time when everybody got interviewed by Steve [Jobs] and Steve was hanging around all the time. So it was incredibly exciting—we just thought we were going to change the world. ... I think everybody at NeXT thought that. We were going to change the world.[52]

Although the work environment was high-pressure, Smith and others found that they thrived. As Smith recalled:

> He [Jobs] used to come into my cubicle every day and just beat up on me. "What are you going to do that we can ship?" He just looked at me as this PhD guy who's going to float around and worry about MIPS [a measure of computer processor performance] and produce nothing. And he made it really clear that he thought that. And

I just stood up to him. I think he ended up liking me because I stood my ground. I knew what I was talking about. I just kept saying to him, "Steve, you know, you can fire me any time you want. But if you want music, here's what I'm planning to do. And if this is what you want, I can do it. Ask me anything, but about that." And on my turf, he really didn't know as much as me. Even if he is a genius, I can still know some things that he doesn't know! [Laughter.] So we got along well. My analogy is he wanted to come into your cubicle and hit you in the stomach as hard as he could, and he wanted to break his knuckles doing that. So if he walks out of your cubicle with broken knuckles, he's happy. [Laughter.][53]

NeXT released their first machines in 1989 and CCRMA was an early adopter. (Jobs attended one of the CCRMA concerts around the same time and Chowning publicly thanked him for creating the first computer to include music capability.[54]) The machines offered good processing power from a Motorola 68000 chip and attention to audio—exactly what Chowning, Pierce, and others had outlined as requirements a few years earlier.

Indeed, as Smith recalled the various efforts to build a music workstation at CCRMA:

The common denominator is that it was an enormous amount of work to get a music/audio workstation together. So, this NeXT opportunity just seemed like just a wonderful opportunity to make it happen on a much bigger scale commercially and with scales that would allow the price to be way lower; wouldn't it be great if we had a person at NeXT to help make sure that it could be the next music workstation? That was our point of view on the whole opportunity.[55]

Bill Schottstaedt, in turn, undertook the enormous task of translating the Samson Box algorithms to the NeXT by means of Common Lisp and a Music V dialect known as CLM or Common Lisp Music.[56] In November 1990, CCRMA announced plans to officially "retire" the Samson Box by the end of the year.[57] The memo announcing the change bore the header "The End of an Era."[58]

In turn, adoption of standardized equipment facilitated personnel exchanges (just as CCRMA and IRCAM's mutual adoption of the PDP-10 facilitated movement of composers and researchers between those two centers). For example, from 1990 to 1995, the Rockefeller Foundation funded the Intercambio Music Exchange Program between CCRMA, the Center for Research in Computing and the Arts (CRCA) at the University of California at San Diego, and the Laboratorio de Investigación y Produccion Musical (LIPM) in Buenos Aires, Argentina. Composers from each center would stay at another center for somewhere between one week and six months.

The standardization of equipment and software—NeXT computers running CLM—allowed a composer to start a piece at one center and complete it at another one. Thus, standardized technology facilitated cultural exchange.[59]

Standardization also facilitated further technical exchanges. For example, one of the LIPM participants in the program, Fernando López Lezcano, became an expert in the NeXT system while he was at CCRMA.[60] When he returned to LIPM, he recalled:

> I taught some classes and I brought back all the latest upgrades, and software packages, and everything, and I installed those in the two NeXT workstations they had at LIPM. I even carried ... upgrade boards with me, because the original [NeXT] cubes were shipped with a 68030 [processor], but they were intended actually to run a 68040.[61]

Another attraction of the NeXT machine lay in its MusicKit software—an object-oriented library used in the design of music applications for the NeXT computer.[62] MusicKit combined the synthesis flexibility of Mathews's Music V program with the control and interface parameters of MIDI. In 1992, CCRMA and NeXT agreed to have CCRMA take over the maintenance and distribution of the NeXT MusicKit. As Smith recalled:

> Steve Jobs actually was the originator of this idea. We were sitting around and he said, "Let's put it in the public domain." Those were his exact words. But, of course, he hands it off to the lawyers at NeXT and it ended up being a real pain. ... I was the go-between. I was basically representing NeXT and CCRMA in some sense, going back and forth, trying to get it done.[63]

In August 1992, Smith could finally announce good news to the MusicKit email distribution list: "Steve Jobs himself finally signed the CCRMA/NeXT agreement which enables CCRMA to distribute the Music Kit and DSP Tools along with source [code]."[64] The distribution of source code, in particular, was important. As the public announcement of the arrangement described:

> For the first time, source code (!) is available. ... This means researchers and developers may study the source or even customize the Music Kit and DSP Tools to suit their needs. Enhancements can be sent to musickit@ccrma.stanford.edu to have them considered for future CCRMA releases. Commercial NeXT software developers may freely incorporate and adapt the software to accelerate development of NeXTSTEP software products. (Free commercial use of files copyrighted by NeXT Inc. are understandably restricted to NeXTSTEP platforms.)[65]

By moving to the NeXT and by freely distributing the MusicKit software, CCRMA was again merging its interests in open innovation, through free software sharing facilitated by technical standards; in commercialization, evident in NeXT's origins and goals; and in encouraging the further diffusion of computer music as a discipline.

Composition and Technology

Of course, the ultimate point of equipment and software, from the perspective of CCRMA participants, was to facilitate musical composition. The program notes for many of these compositions, not surprisingly, elaborate upon both the artistic and technological aspects of these pieces. For example, the program notes for Richard Karpen's *ECLIPSE* (1986) describe how the piece reflects Karpen's "ongoing interest in evolutionary processes as models for musical structures." Continuing, Karpen describes how

> the programs used to generate these pitch streams were written by the composer in the Pla language. ... The synthesis techniques used include several types of Frequency Modulation, Amplitude Modulation and Additive Synthesis, but the primary "orchestration" technique involves the overlap of many iterations of "notes" to create complex dynamically changing sounds and musical textures.

The fact that the program notes included such detailed technical description underscores the interplay between technical advancements and compositional activities at CCRMA.

In a 2009 interview, Mike McNabb, too, reflected on these relationships:

> It's really hard to even separate where all the creativity came from. When you talk about one piece of music, any one piece of music, there couldn't help but be at least half a dozen people involved besides the composer because we had to write our own software, the engineers had to build their own equipment, all this stuff. It was like you'd lose track: Did Julius [Smith, an electrical engineer] come up with this special [engineering] thing and we thought, "Well, that's cool. I'm going to use it in a piece." Or the other way around: "I want to do X" and they [people like Julius Smith] would say, "Well one way you could do that is like this."[66]

Indeed, CCRMA composers developed a number of new techniques in order to serve their compositional needs. For example, the program notes for Celso Aguiar's *All Blue, I Write with a Blue Pencil, on a Blue Sky* (1996) note that:

> The piece is about sound transformation, as a metaphor to the transformation of consciousness. ... The cello transformations were obtained with SMSplus, a CLM system build on top of Xavier Serra's Spectral Modeling Synthesis and developed by the composer. A procedure for modeling the physical properties of a room via feedback-

delay-networks was employed ("Ball within a Box," developed by Italian researcher Davide Rocchesso at CCRMA, with additional enhancements by the composer).

Similarly, Juan Pampin's *Toco Madera* (1996) program notes read:

North of San Francisco, near Point Arena, the sea transforms the beach into a beautiful, constantly evolving mile long sculpture. On the beach hundreds of wood logs are washed onto the coast by the Pacific Ocean. I discovered this sculpture (or is it an installation?) while beginning work on *Toco Madera*. The dense textures created by drift wood of all sizes inspired the form and process of the piece. I realized that my compositional work had to be similar to the role of the sea. ... The spectral synthesis and transformations of the sampled percussion instruments were done using ATS, spectral modeling software programmed by me in LISP. All the digital sound processing and synthesis for the piece was performed with CLM, developed at CCRMA by Bill Schottstaedt.

Matthew Fields, who was a CCRMA graduate student in the mid-1980s, described how a walk to CCRMA's location in the foothills (prior to the 1986 move) encouraged him to refine a "granular synthesis" technique, which he used in a subsequent composition:

There's one place along the way where I had to pass over this little babbling brook. And all the way there, after passing the brook, I would contemplate, well, how do you synthesize the sound of a babbling brook? And eventually what I came up with was something that I later learned was well known to other people in the field, it was something that Xenakis had been playing with, simply taking an enormous number of little teeny events and adding them together, he was calling it granular synthesis. ...

... And so, what I figured was, "Oh, the sound of the babbling brook is basically the combination of a bunch of semi-random individual little 'Plinks' made by each droplet of the brook." And so I immediately wrote a program that generated several thousands of notes per second, and very quickly synthesized the sound of a flushing toilet. ... And I realized that I'd overdone it. [Laughter.] And so the first thing I did was I reduced the reverberation, and I reduced the number of notes to about 250 per second. And then I did have a pretty good babbling brook, and I did use that in a piece of music, and maybe I'll use that in another piece of music.[67]

These examples serve to underscore the intertwining of technical and artistic pursuits at CCRMA. Again, composers such as Aguiar, Pampin, and Fields were not merely applying existing technologies to their compositions; rather, they were developing and refining new technologies in the process of their music making. Pampin, for example, only later presented and published a technical paper on his ATS technique, thus underscoring how musical applications could precede scientific sharing.[68] Moreover, the mixture of artistic metaphors and technical descriptions in the program notes signal the diverse audiences for these pieces—music aficionados, technical professionals, and people who defined themselves at the intersection of these activities.

The 1980s and 1990s witnessed a plethora of CCRMA compositions and research projects. Although limited space regrettably precludes an adequate discussion of them, a few notable projects provide further insight into the relationships between technical, artistic, research, and commercial elements at CCRMA during this period of sustenance and renewal. Mike McNabb's *Invisible Cities*, to which Chowning accompanied donor Doreen Townsend, is one exemplar project. As McNabb described in the program notes for the December 1985 world premiere:

> I decided over two years ago to compose a large form work explicitly for dance, with several related movements around a common theme. The novel *Invisible Cities* [by Italo Calvino] has always been one of my favorite books, and its beauty, concise structure, and dream-like imagery led me to consider it as the inspiration for my music, and to suggest it as the basis for the collaborative work.[69]

The twist with McNabb's realization, however, was ingenious: With design guru Gayle Curtis, McNabb conceived of a "ballet" in which some of the dancers were actually industrial robots. The music, of course, was realized by a computer and by acoustic instruments processed through electronics. To execute the idea, McNabb and Curtis collaborated with two groups: choreographer Brenda Way and the Oberlin Dance Collective (later, ODC) of San Francisco, a leading contemporary dance group; and the Veterans Administration hospital in Palo Alto, whose Robotic Aid Project aimed to use robots to assist injured Vietnam War veterans.[70]

To support the project, Chowning engaged in his now characteristic fundraising at the intersection of technology and music, and applied and artistic motives. Thus, early on he approached Steve Jobs and Steve Wozniak, the young entrepreneurs who had just launched a major ad campaign for their company's new computer: the Apple Macintosh. Chowning's letter highlighted the marketing advantages that might be gained from Apple's support, again suggesting that financial support would benefit not only CCRMA but also the donor through reputational spillover effects. Chowning also offered a gentle reminder of the choice that consumers faced between the battling PC and Macintosh platforms. After explaining the concept of the robot ballet, Chowning's letter reads:

We believe that we can borrow the robots from Datamation but we need a PC (MacIntosh?) [*sic*] for programming the robots and a sponsor to cover the expenses. The total costs, including preparation, production, artists' fees and European tour are between $70,000 and $80,000. Might Apple be interested in such a project? In exchange for such support we would give the first performance for Apple employees in early October and a substantial amount of "interesting" press both in this country and abroad.[71]

Chowning never heard back. (Jobs, of course, would be forced from Apple a year later.)

Not to be dismayed, Chowning wrote in January 1985 to Joseph Engelberger of Unimation Incorporated, manufacturer of the PUMA robotic arms that McNabb and Curtis planned to use as dancers. This time, he positioned Unimation's support as an opportunity for the company to connect industrial R&D with artistic realization. His letter reads:

In addition to the public aspects of the piece, the development of robots for choreography and performance will result in research and usable software and hardware for the control of robots in general. Work in this area has already begun in conjunction with Stanford professor Larry Leifer and the Veterans Administration in developing voice command robotic arms to be manipulators for severely disabled people.[72]

Thus, Chowning pitched the project on the basis of its artistic, practical, and commercial bases.

Engelberger responded the next month, expressing interest in the project:

I enjoyed the video of a PUMA dancing to live accompaniment on public television. The more ambitious combination of human dancers with a couple of robot artists is intriguing and at the very least should be great fun. Computer music is the icing.

Having read a bit about the centuries-old problem of precisely recording choreography, I must conclude that the restricted flexibility of a robot should ease the notation challenge. (We already use the word choreography when programming a number of robot arms to work in close cooperation.)[73]

Both Engelberger's enthusiasm and his comment that "computer music is the icing" are indicative, again, of multivocality: Engelberger latched onto that aspect of *Invisible Cities* that most appealed to him—choreography of robotic movements—but also appreciated the integration or "value add" of the other components. Other observers, meanwhile, would appreciate *Invisible Cities* primarily for its musical or human dance elements. Different audiences, therefore, appreciated it for different reasons.

In his letter to Chowning, Engelberger also cautioned, however, that he was not in a position to support the project: "My disposition toward your project is of small import since Unimation Incorporated is now a wholly-owned subsidiary of Westinghouse Electric Corporation." Though Engelberger forwarded Chowning's request, Westinghouse did not support it.[74]

The tenacious Chowning and McNabb, however, continued their funding search and ultimately pieced together several donors: the National Endowment for the Arts, the California Arts Council, the Wallace Gerbode Foundation, Mr. and Mrs. Howard Pruzan, and, quite appropriately, Mr. and Mrs. Gordon Getty.[75]

In the end, the challenge of executing *Invisible Cities* was enormous and the production was only partially successful. The *Chicago Tribune* reported that the audience consisted of "computer buffs, music lovers and the just-plain curious who wanted to watch a dozen people dance with a robot."[76] In reviewing the premiere, the *San Jose Mercury News* wrote, "'Invisible Cities' was a noble experiment, but because of obvious technical, financial and logistical problems it was far from a finished product."[77]

Nevertheless, the same newspaper had high praise for McNabb's innovation when reflecting on the entire 1985–86 San Francisco Bay Area concert season in July 1986:

> The 1985–86 Bay Area concert season that just wound down posed questions, answered some of them and above all maintained the area's imposing position in championing the cutting edge of new music. Some of the past season's music, new and not so new, made news, and the dance world made its contribution, too. ... The year's most significant innovation was the robotic dance "Invisible Cities."[78]

As *Invisible Cities* demonstrated, CCRMA continued to push the boundaries of music, technology, and human–computer interaction.

Another CCRMA project also served to bring computer music to new audiences. Dexter Morrill, one of the project's champions, had been a Stanford music student studying orchestration under Leland Smith in the early 1960s. (He thus overlapped with Chowning.) In the early 1970s, now a faculty member at Colgate University, Morrill again spent time at Stanford and he visited CCRMA. Inspired, he decided to build a computer music system at Colgate, which he finished in 1972 with the support of Chowning and CCRMA.

Much of Morrill's work is characterized by his mixture of computer music and acoustic instruments. His 1984 work, *Getz Variations*, was composed for jazz saxophonist Stan Getz and combined tenor saxophone with computer-generated tape. The first performance took place in an outdoor program at Stanford's Frost Amphitheater, the same campus venue described in chapter 4. Another Morrill project would be even more ambitious: He proposed a twenty-eight-minute television program about the process of creating music with a computer. As described in an NEA grant application, the program would

> take place under the auspices of John Chowning ... [and would] feature Wynton Marsalis, the brilliant classical and jazz trumpet player, arranger and composer. They will be the vehicle through which the audience will learn about the relationship between the imagination of the musician and composer and the possibilities of the computer. At CCRMA, the audience will see and hear sounds and interact with a musician during performance. They will see Marsalis and Morrill discuss how to use these capabilities in a composition with trumpet, in a uniquely American blend of idioms, jazz and computer music.[79]

Although CCRMA had already reached diverse groups, as described, a television program promised to bring computer music into living rooms across the country. The NEA awarded $10,000 to Stanford to support the musical composition aspect of the project.

To George Olczak, the producer of the special, Marsalis's continued success, somewhat ironically, made the full project difficult to execute. In a July 1987 letter to Stephen Peeps, director of university relations at Stanford, Olczak wrote:

> In the three years since I conceived of this project, Wynton's career has grown and evolved in ways that have decreased his contact with projects being developed. His management now concerns itself not only with the matter of fees, rights, and ownership, but also with the question and assessment of musical risks.[80]

An objection to the program on the basis of "musical risks" was telling: CCRMA composers were accustomed to musical risks. As Bill Schottstaedt, a CCRMA composer, characterized the situation:

> For modern music composers ... there's absolutely no money in the recording and sort of concerts [you do], unless you get very lucky. ... The fact that you weren't going to make money out of it or probably never would, was not important. That wasn't the concern at the time. There was the slight fact that I was living in a house trailer illegally in Palo Alto and had $14.00 and my cello. That was basically it. [Laughter.][81]

In other words, modern music composition was far removed from concerns with commercial success. For artists such as Marsalis, however, embracing computer music could threaten a successful musical career.

Moreover, to some observers Marsalis seemed to equate CCRMA with mainstream classical music. Perry Cook was a CCRMA electrical engineering graduate student who worked with Morrill to design a computer interface for a trumpet. As Cook recalled:

> Wynton had won both Grammies [in jazz and classical music]. ... [He then said], "Jazz is the indigenous American music. Classical music is dead white European dudes. [Laughter.] It's great; they're some of the smartest people in the world. [But] they make some of the most unlistenable music I have ever heard. [Laughter.] That's not where I'm going to spend my time."[82]

Morrill himself was a jazz musician and many CCRMA composers embraced the computer as a means of realizing improvisatory styles. Yet for other people, CCRMA now signaled an association with mainstream classical music—a telling and ironic shift in light of earlier perceptions that computer music was not legitimate classical music.

In the end, funding for the film component of the project did not materialize, and Marsalis decided he did not have time in his schedule.[83] The project, however, was not lost. One important result was Cook's trumpet interface for the NeXT computer, which he disclosed to the Stanford OTL in 1989.[84] More importantly, Cook went on to use the NeXT machine to conduct some of the most important research in physical modeling synthesis.

Other projects from the 1980s focused even more directly on the issue of creating interfaces between people and computers for the purpose of making music. For example, Hugh Lusted and Ben Knapp, both CCRMA-affiliated researchers, began a project in 1987 focused on the use of bioelectric sensors to control a music synthesizer. The system used small electrodes to pick up signals from a musician's brain and from the muscles in her eye, arm, and hand. Once processed, these signals could then control an electronic instrument.[85]

Lusted and Knapp applied for various patents on the interface system, named BioMuse, and a number of companies expressed interest. Among them, of course, was Yamaha. Someone in Yamaha's "Living Division" had learned of the technology from a report that CCRMA shared with select organizations. Yamaha grew interested in using the bioelectric controller for a "better sleep environment" project, looking at relationship between sound, music, and "one's mental state." They set up a visit to CCRMA, though nothing apparently came of it.[86]

The patent never earned much money, but Lusted and Knapp were generous in applying the earnings toward further BioMuse research, including controllers for disabled people.[87] That same year, they would configure a controller to enable disabled users to play air guitar at Loma Linda Medical Center. In fact, serving disabled persons is a theme that arises repeatedly at CCRMA. Examples include McNabb's Veterans Administration collaboration in *Invisible Cities*; a 1992 proposal for a wind controller interface for quadriplegic student trumpeter; Brent Gillespie and Sile O'Modhrain's work on a powered joystick that translated graphical information into tactile format for the blind; and a student project in collaboration with player-piano maker PianoDisc that modified a piano pedal system for use by a musician with amputated legs.[88]

Max Mathews also focused on electronic music interfaces in the 1980s and 1990s. Mathews's inspiration stemmed from the inflexibility that performers experienced when following taped music accompaniment—a situation that characterized many compositions in which the synthesizer part was prerecorded and the musician then performed live alongside it. As Mathews recalled, "Pierre Boulez [IRCAM's director] wanted technology to allow him to conduct the tape—to have the accompaniment follow his solo."[89] The first iteration of Mathews's device, the Sequential Drum, employed a drumhead sensor. As the performer touched the head with a mallet, the sensor instructed the accompaniment to move forward, allowing the performer to continually control the tempo. In the next iteration, the Daton, Mathews put strain gauges at each of the four corners of a panel. By interpolating the force at all four corners, this system provided two dimensions of control (X and Y).[90]

Mathews retired from Bell Labs in 1985 and became professor of music (research) at Stanford in 1987. At the same time, one of his associates from Bell Labs, Bob Boie, suggested that the radio technology Boie had developed as sensors for robots could be useful for Mathews's device. He was right. Boie and Mathews developed a prototype of a new device, the Radio Baton, which added a third dimension of control (X, Y, and Z) and did away with all mechanical moving parts.[91] Mathews was so excited by the commercial prospects of this approach that he sent a letter to Laurie Miller at Bell Labs to suggest that CCRMA could commercialize the Boie approach.[92] On Christmas Day in 1990, Stanford received a patent on Mathews's application. That same year, Roland sent three engineers to evaluate the technology.[93]

Though Roland did not ultimately sign a license, Mathews founded his own company in 1994 to commercialize the technology. The theme of musical interests leading to commercial opportunities is now familiar.

Mathews's primary interest lay not in the commercial success of the Radio Baton, however, so much as in the possibility of controlling music in new ways. His 1991 listing of those people who received the first versions of the Radio Baton includes Jean-Claude Risset, with whom Mathews had worked at Bell Labs and whose brass tone analysis enabled Chowning's major leap with FM.[94]

As CCRMA's invention disclosures and patents on the Radio Baton, BioMuse controller, trumpet-computer interface, and other technology advances indicate, this period of renewal and growth at CCRMA was marked by a continued emphasis on the commercial development of technologies that Stanford had pioneered for musical purposes. During this same period of the 1980s and 1990s, however, the emphasis that CCRMA placed on commercial prospects shifted substantially: Although CCRMA researchers still developed core technologies for musical reasons tied to composition or performance, the emphasis placed on intellectual property, patents, licensing, and associated revenue increased, driven in part by the dramatic increase in FM revenues during these years (see figure 5.2). Although none of the particular examples highlighted in this section exhibited significant commercial success, as we'll see in the next chapter, another development held promise of being "the next big thing."

7 Plucking the Golden Gate Bridge

The April 25, 1985, edition of the *San Francisco Chronicle* featured a story on the terrific success of the Yamaha DX7. A picture alongside the story showed Niels Reimers, the Stanford OTL director, next to the CCRMA-facilitated instrument. The headline, however, read "Why U.S. Inventions Profit Foreigners."[1] Far from unabashed praise for the instrument and the CCRMA–Yamaha relationship that gave rise to it, the article questioned why a foreign company was profiting—handsomely—from a US invention.

An important part of the Bayh–Dole Act of 1980, the legislation that eased patenting of federally funded university research, is that preference is given to US-based and small companies. This preference was directly tied to US worries about technology competitiveness with the Japanese. In the 1970s and 1980s, US policy makers and businesspeople alike noted with apprehension the growing Japanese dominance in consumer electronics and other transistor- and semiconductor-related goods. Although US-based research had led to many of the initial breakthroughs in these fields, it appeared that Japanese industry was reaping the primary rewards.[2]

US observers tied Japanese business success to Japanese industrial policy. Chalmer Johnson's influential book, *MITI and the Japanese Miracle*, reflected the dominant belief that Japanese government planners and their resultant policies had positioned that country for dominance.[3] Thus, US policy needed to react, observers argued, to spur the commercialization of US research by US companies.[4]

The 1980s also witnessed the explosive growth of the biotechnology industry, which was based in large part on university-conducted research. Most notably, perhaps, Stanley Cohen at Stanford and Herb Boyer at UC San Francisco developed recombinant DNA (rDNA) in 1973. rDNA enables the connection of genetic material from different sources, and scientists have used the technique to create human insulin, human growth hormone, herbicide- and insect-resistant crops, and other products. Starting in 1980, Stanford licensed the technique on behalf of both universities and the license ultimately netted $255 million for Stanford and UCSF.[5]

Stanford's leadership and, indeed, university leaders around the country took notice of the tremendous financial success and of the booming biotechnology industry. In the face of uncertain federal funding, the potential of hundreds of millions of dollars in unrestricted cash held obvious allure. Given both international competitiveness and significant profit tied to university research, the backdrop behind technology licensing in the 1980s was rather different, therefore, from the environment that Chowning and Reimers encountered in the 1970s as they worked to commercialize FM.[6]

Against this backdrop, CCRMA researchers developed another breakthrough technology: physical modeling synthesis. Physical modeling synthesis rests on the observation that physical actions, such as the vibration of a string, can be represented as mathematical equations. In turn, an instrument such as a violin can be "broken down" into a series of equations that account for the strings, bridge, resonating body, and other characteristics.

In the early 1980s, Stanford computer science graduate students Kevin Karplus and Alexander Strong developed a simple, dynamically modified wavetable synthesis algorithm that sounded surprisingly close to a plucked or struck string. At the same time, David A. Jaffe, who had arrived at CCRMA as a graduate student in the 1970s, was working on a composition for mezzo-soprano, eight guitars, and computer-generated tape. Jaffe's composition, *May All Your Children Be Acrobats* (1981), blends text reflecting the backgrounds of a wide range of Americans (excerpted from Carl Sandburg's "The People, Yes") with music representing a wide variety of styles, including bluegrass, Irish, Jewish, and African-American music, as well as American popular and European classical styles.[7]

For the tape part, Jaffe was attempting to use Chowning's FM technique to simulate plucked strings, but with limited success. Fortunately, Jaffe played violin in a string quartet with Strong, who played viola. As Jaffe recalled:

> It was the Mozart piano quartet. ... The violist was Alex Strong, who I didn't know. We just started talking and he was kind of a technical computer science-y kind of guy. I said something about how I was trying to synthesize guitars and he said, "Oh, you know, we just discovered this really great way of synthesizing guitars and I'd

love to show it to you, but you have to sign a nondisclosure." And I said, "Okay, I'd love to do that." So, we got together and they showed me what they had done. I thought it sounded really great and I got their permission to implement it on the Samson Box.[8]

Working with Julius Smith, who quickly recognized that the Karplus–Strong algorithm could be interpreted as an extremely simplified physical model, Jaffe extended and refined the algorithm. He used it in *May All Your Children Be Acrobats*, making this composition the first piece to use physical modeling.[9]

Smith, too, had a strong interest in synthesizing string sounds. In describing his dissertation work in the late 1970s, Smith recalled:

Mostly I was aiming for violin modeling. My mission was to learn everything I could find in the world of signal processing that might be useful in making a virtual violin, a really good violin synthesizer. Or more generally, bowed strings. The reason for that was in my home studio I had some synthesizers, and you could not buy for any amount of money a good bowed string synthesizer. So that was why I chose it. It was a really important family of instruments and they could not be synthesized. I thought that was an important problem.[10]

In other words, Smith's concern with a "real world" musical problem drove his choice of a dissertation topic in electrical engineering.

At the same time, however, Smith kept his musical motivations quiet:

Having a fellowship really made it possible to work on that. But I kind of kept it quiet. For the first three years or so, you wouldn't know I was working on the violin. It looked like I was studying system identification and digital filter design, which I was. I really was studying that stuff. But I had in my mind one application.[11]

Smith's lack of public attention to the applied musical aspects of his work lay in his perception that these aspects would detract from his standing as an electrical engineer. As he explained:

I just felt like I would be a second-class citizen in my department if I made it known that I was seriously interested in music applications. I also wanted to be a full-fledged one-hundred percent through-and-through EE [electrical engineering] signal processing guy. I did not want to compromise my EE. I wanted to get a hard-core PhD in electrical engineering. And the music stuff in that context would just be an application example. Just like saying, "Let's let X be a 440 Hertz sinusoid" [the frequency of the "concert A" pitch to which orchestras tune]. It's just, I could pick any example I want. So I'll pick this music example. [Laughter] ... There was this sort of secret filtering going on where I wasn't interested in anything that [didn't] seem like it was going to be useful.[12]

Although Smith does not draw the direct comparison to Chowning's tenure denial, he nonetheless expresses acute awareness that a musically focused electrical engineer might not be perceived as a "genuine" electrical engineer; interdisciplinarity could dilute one's disciplinary standing. Moreover, as Smith notes, a focus on something "useful," like music, was not in line with the hard-core theoretical work for which electrical engineers in academia were rewarded. Smith's commentary, therefore, reminds us that CCRMA's ability to balance such activities remained unique, even within Stanford.

At the same time, Jaffe's compositions were demonstrating that physical modeling technology could prove to be *extremely* useful. Impressed with the results of *May All Your Children Be Acrobats*, Jaffe next began work on a four-channel physical modeling piece. *Silicon Valley Breakdown* (1982) would become a classic of the genre, performed in over 25 countries. The piece, in Jaffe's words,

> is a spatial multi-stylistic work scored for a symphony of imaginary plucked stringed instruments. These range from a tiny "piccolo mandolin" to an immense bass "plucked Golden Gate Bridge."[13]

The image of "plucking" the cables of the Golden Gate Bridge like a string instrument would resonate with other composers, illustrating the power of physical modeling to produce entirely new kinds of sound and music.

In reflecting on the development of physical modeling synthesis and these early compositions, Jaffe explained how:

> The refinement of the algorithm was driven by the composition. In *May All Your Children Be Acrobats*, a lot of the problems hadn't been solved yet ... for example, the tuning wasn't solved at that point—or if it was solved, it was solved using the low-pass filter rather than the all-pass filter. I know that we didn't have pick position at that point. ... There were also effects like very high notes we couldn't do.[14]

In turn, continued refinements of the algorithm, "things like up and down picking, ... the pick position and an all-pass filter for tuning," were driven by Jaffe's desire to realize compositions. As with Mike McNabb's description of "losing track" of whether engineers or musicians drove creativity, Jaffe's reflections highlight the intricate interplay between compositional and technical activities: Jaffe's musical desires suggested the specific technical refinements that he implemented.

One particular set of developments around the physical modeling algorithms would prove to be especially important. A major challenge in physical modeling lay in the computational requirements: a brute force approach of solving the equations for each sound required tremendous processing power and thus limited real-time applications of the technique. In the mid-1980s, Smith proposed another approach: using waveguides. In a "real" instrument, the waveguide is the medium along which the sound wave travels, such as the instrument bore or string. In a digital environment, these waveguides can be simulated with digital delay lines, which are computationally efficient. In short, Smith found a way to use waveguides to dramatically decrease the computational requirements of physical modeling synthesis, which in turn opened up a number of new applications for the technology.

To Stanford personnel searching for another moneymaker like FM and recombinant DNA, Smith's digital waveguide developments seemed like a future blockbuster. A 1988 memo from Joe Koepnick in Stanford's Office of Technology Licensing (OTL) to Anna Ranieri in the Office of Development summarizes Stanford's hopes for Smith's waveguide development:

> We think this technology rivals the FM synthesis technology that is exclusively licensed to Yamaha from Stanford. The FM synthesis technique is the basis of all of Yamaha's synthesizers. The FM license has been very fruitful for both Stanford and Yamaha; and we hope to conclude a similarly fruitful agreement with Yamaha regarding the DWT [Digital Waveguide Technology]. By the way, the FM patent will expire in the early 1990s [and revenues to Stanford will cease].[15]

One looming concern for Stanford, as Koepnick's memo indicates, was the approaching end of FM patent royalties. Yet Stanford foresaw an even larger "fiscal cliff," to use contemporary parlance: The lucrative rDNA patents, which ultimately netted ten times the revenue of FM, would expire in 1997.[16] Thus, two major revenue streams were due to disappear within a few years of one another. Technology licensing revenue was very much on the minds of Stanford administrators.

Stanford's initial plan was to sign an agreement with Yamaha for DWT that was similar to the FM agreement. As the licensing associate, Joe Koepnick, noted:

> It's a classic case of 90 percent of the cases that we license are repeat customers. Yamaha's already had great success with the FM. We get something in the music department, we send it to them: "What do you think?" They were interested.[17]

But Yamaha still had reservations. They took an "option" to DWT—basically, a right to investigate it further and then to take a license if they desired—that would expire at the end of 1988. In an August 1988 letter to Yamaha, Koepnick inquired whether they intended to take a license.[18] Yamaha responded that they intended to do so, subject to royalty conditions, but they also conceived of DWT as a different kind of technology:

> We consider DWT is not so basic or principal technology as the FM tone synthesis. For example, FM is capable of producing tones of every tone color while DWT is applicable to a specific tone color or colors. Therefore an electronic musical instrument can not [*sic*] be implemented by DWT only.[19]

Though no one at Stanford recognized it at the time, DWT would not prove to be simply another FM.[20]

In early 1989, a contingent from Stanford traveled to Japan to negotiate licensing terms with Yamaha.[21] A key feature of the FM license was worldwide exclusivity for Yamaha. This exclusivity motivated Yamaha to dedicate significant resources to the development of FM. As discussed in chapter 5, however, this exclusivity also presented challenges for Stanford, as other companies desired to access a Stanford-invented technology that Yamaha controlled. Sandelin, the licensing associate who worked closely with FM, recalled that

> there was a lot of bickering with US companies. How come Yamaha has this exclusive right and it's developed by a US university? That shaped some provisions. ... The big change was that we would not grant Yamaha [an] exclusive [license]. ... There were a number of adaptations that were made ... to make sure that North American companies had access.[22]

Thus, Stanford's DWT licensing strategy responded to criticisms of its FM license strategy.

In the DWT case, Stanford agreed to give Yamaha an exclusive license outside of North America; but, companies within North America could still license the technology from Stanford. In addition to insulating the university from the political objections that accompanied FM, Stanford's hope was that this arrangement would develop interest among more companies—in turn, further establishing the technology and ultimately increasing Stanford's royalties on related products. By 1993, the OTL had signed Sierra Semiconductor, Crystal Semiconductor, Media Vision, and Atari as licensees, bringing the total number of licensees to five.[23]

The nonexclusive license was structured to allow companies to experiment with potential applications of the DWT technology. The license terms clearly draw from Stanford's rDNA experience. With rDNA, Stanford took a wholly nonexclusive approach. In turn, initial rDNA adopters ranged from breweries to cosmetic companies, until the specific drug development applications of the technique grew clear.[24] In the DWT case, Stanford personnel themselves seemed a bit unclear as to all of the potential applications. As a 1992 OTL newsletter relayed:

> The waveguide technology's most immediate applications are in electronic synthesizers and personal computers. But Koepnick and these companies are also looking forward to what they predict will be the next consumer electronics boom: multi-media. Koepnick envisions a 4′ × 4′ × 3′ flat panel display on the living room wall, controlled by computer and synthesizer keyboards. The owner will be able to compose music using a myriad of sounds and also have access to everything from music to movies to banking and groceries. "It would be your video phone and answering machine as well," Koepnick adds. The multi-media system would also be educational, he says, making education "interactive, so it's fun for kids to learn."[25]

Koepnick's vision was prescient, though perhaps twenty years too early. But the role of DWT in this system was less than clear. As Stanford would discover, there were other ways to produce sound for multimedia systems.

In other ways, too, Stanford shaped its approach to DWT in response to their experiences and "lessons learned" from FM. One of their primary lessons lay in the limited patent life—and, therefore, the limited revenue timespan. As figure 5.2 (chapter 5) illustrates, Stanford's FM patent expired in 1994, just as revenues were accelerating. As an experiment, in 1993 the OTL thus proposed a trademark plan designed around DWT. Reimers had contemplated trademarks as early as 1983. In a Telex to Yamaha that year, he inquired:

> Have you considered strategy of Dolby (noise reduction technology)? That is, to develop FM as industry sound synthesis "standard." This would involve FM trademark license to permit buyer to advertise that his product uses "FM" sound synthesis. If FM of highest quality, and that becomes known to buyers, a new market entrant for an alternative sound synthesis technology to FM will have greater marketing difficulty.[26]

Dolby had experienced great success with its trademark that signaled a special noise reduction technology. Even consumers with no understanding of signal-to-noise ratios and various technical schemes for improving them were willing to pay more for tape recorders that featured the Dolby trademark. Yamaha, however, did not pursue the strategy, reasoning that a trademark was unnecessary since most synthesizer purchasers either judged on the basis of sound alone or were technically savvy enough to understand which products featured FM, regardless of the presence of a trademark. The trademark idea, however, stuck around the OTL.

The OTL modeled its 1993 trademark plan explicitly on Dolby's program. As the introduction of the plan states:

> While the same FM patent licensing strategy could be applied [to DWT], cumulative royalty revenues can be increased dramatically by licensing the patents together with a trademark and software as a complete package. The Plan proposed herein will allow the worldwide licensing of waveguide indefinitely. The model for this Trademark Plan is based on Dolby Laboratories' licensing program, whereby several consumer electronic technologies are licensed internationally along with Dolby trademarks. Dolby's program generates around $15 million annually in royalty income at an annual expense of about $2 million. It is anticipated that the waveguide program will have a similar income-to-expense ratio.[27]

Stanford settled on the name "Sondius" for the trademark.

To add value to the trademark, Stanford needed patents tied to sound technologies. Thus, the trademark program was associated with a flurry of patenting activity. Julius Smith alone filed eight patents between 1992 and 1994. As he described the motivation:

> The flurry of additional patents that I did was in the spirit of "Let's fill up the boat as big as we can." There was sort of this, "Yamaha had taken out a big license. Music was on a roll. Let's just, anything we can think of, let's just throw it in there and make our patent portfolio big and strong. Get the students involved. Every CCRMA student in my group should graduate with a PhD and a patent!" [Laughter.] That was just kind of the thinking of the time.[28]

While commercial interests had long played a role at CCRMA, patenting in connection with the Sondius program dramatically raised its profile and marked an increased emphasis on formal patent-linked technology transfer efforts managed through the OTL.

The patent flurry focused on quantity more than strategy. Thus, it collected a number of unrelated patents under a single umbrella. As Smith noted:

> All of the Stanford music technology people were sucked into the Sondius program. It lumped together irrelevant patents, such as clipped signal restoration that has nothing to do with synthesis. [Clipped signal restoration fixes recordings in which the signal level was too high and caused a harsh audio artifact known as "clipping."] Stanford took out lots of patents—invested in them due to the big buzz. The trademark program wanted to have as many patents as possible.[29]

While the Sondius trademark represented a means to extend Stanford's revenue indefinitely, the university also worked to reduce the time-to-market for waveguide technology. The seven-year commercial development period for FM—from the 1975 license to the 1982 product release—was simply too long from the university's perspective. As Mary Watanabe, the licensing associate who managed the Sondius program, noted, "Looking at FM is what caused us to try this experiment because we saw that the revenue hit its peak when the patent expired. So we thought we'd try to address the situation by setting up this program."[30]

The plan was to build on the NeXT MusicKit software—the same software that CCRMA maintained and distributed with Steve Jobs's permission, as relayed in chapter 6—to make it easy for potential licensees to implement DWT. In 1989, Michael Minnick, a NeXT employee, developed an application to create MusicKit patches graphically, by arranging and connecting modules on a computer screen. He called the prototype SynthEdit and presented a paper at the 1990 International Computer Music Conference.[31] In 1992, Princeton University student Eric Jordan created a similar application called GraSP (Graphical Synth Patch), with assistance from David A. Jaffe. (Recall that Jaffe was the physical modeling whiz and *Silicon Valley Breakdown* composer. He was teaching at Princeton at the time of Jordan's work.[32])

Nick Porcaro, a visiting scholar at CCRMA, continued work on GraSP, with assistance from Jaffe and Julius Smith, and he started integrating it more deeply with the NeXT's Draw program and the MusicKit. In September 1993, Porcaro and Smith obtained funding from the Stanford OTL for Porcaro to further develop the application, which eventually became known as SynthBuilder.

SynthBuilder, was a core element in Stanford's plan to develop waveguide sounds in order to increase the value of the trademark. The program also represented a major shift for the Stanford OTL in that they invested directly in technology development, alongside CCRMA. Thus, CCRMA ultimately invested $1.35 million from the FM royalty account, using it to hire two developers to work on DWT: Jaffe and Porcaro.[33] One year later, Porcaro contacted his colleague Pat Scandalis and Scandalis joined the development team.[34]

Jaffe, Porcaro, and Scandalis were paid an hourly wage and took up positions alongside regular university researchers—professors and graduate students—at CCRMA. Their mission was to "increase the value of the university's patents" in order to attract additional licensees. Much of the effort was put into the development of SynthBuilder, which was a first step toward creating a sound library to demonstrate DWT technology.

In turn, the sound library itself was another goal. As Pat Scandalis, one of the developers, recalled, "The original charter was to deliver a whole General MIDI set done with physical modeling, which was an extremely ambitious goal."[35] (General MIDI is a set of 128 standardized patches.) To assist with creating the sound library, two CCRMA graduate students, Tim Stilson and Scott Van Duyne, joined the development team as paid employees.

The OTL supported these efforts, in part, through funds that the OTL had earned from previous licenses and that it administered as research grants. For example, the OTL awarded Chowning $23,500 for a related project in 1991; they awarded another $25,000 to Chowning and Smith in June 1992; and in February 1994, the OTL officially turned down a CCRMA-wide funding proposal, but still offered the group $20,000 from another set of funds.[36] An important point concerns the justification for these research proposals. As Chowning explained in applying for the 1991 grant:

> This [project] is an outgrowth of Professor Julius Smith's work in closed waveguide networks for which a patent has been issued. Yamaha has licensed the waveguide work and this research would not only increase its value to them but may attract other interests in speech-related activities as well.[37]

Again, the 1992 funding application notes:

> CCRMA is approaching the end of the patent life in 1994 of the FM synthesis patent. Our future rests upon our ability to produce continuing income. This collection of interdependent projects is one that has real prospects for both intellectual and financial payoff.[38]

Thus, the OTL's research grants were clearly tied to projects that might yield financial benefits for Stanford. In turn, CCRMA worked to position its proposals accordingly.

The SynthBuilder project, however, raised a number of issues for CCRMA tied to open innovation. Since SynthBuilder was related to the MusicKit, which was freely distributed (recall the announcement from the previous chapter), one core issue concerned whether the development team would share sounds they had created with SynthBuilder. The issue came to a head in 1996, as developer Pat Scandalis outlined in an email to Mary Watanabe:

The Sondius voices could be ported to CLM [the sound synthesis package in use at CCRMA and freely distributed around the world]. That is what Bill [Schottstaedt] is asking for.

[In original email from Watanabe]: What are some of the issues here?

[Reply]: Sondius instruments ported to CLM will drift through the academic community around the world. The algorithms that we use will be freely available (but in a very cryptic form, CLM Lisp). One question would be, what does Sondius define as its intellectual property. Is it purely patents, or is it also the expertise that we build into the algorithms? Do we have the concept of trade secrets as well as patents? I feel that since the Sondius program is a trademark program, the value of the mark is drived [*sic*] both from the patent portfolio, and the expertise archived in the program, in the form of algorithms.

Scandalis's email raises genuine questions about the extent to which the fruits of commercially oriented labor in an academic environment should be shared, and the ways in which intellectual property considerations may shape the group's approach. Continuing, he writes:

One could argue that everyone should get the algorithms, just give them away, because any commercial product would have to come to Stanford to license the patents. But what about companies in countries that have been historically bad about recognizing and paying for patents? They could have free access to the technology though [*sic*] the algorithms. So one perspective might be that the Sondius instruments should not be freely available to the whole world.

One middle ground position that Bill S. talked to me about was to port the Sondius instruments, but only as precomiled [*sic*] instruments, so that composers could use them, but not see their implementation. [Such an approach is akin to giving a painter new premixed colors, but not sharing how the colors were created or enabling them to be changed.] It raises hard questions.[39]

In other words, the Sondius development effort rubbed against the open sharing that had characterized CCRMA. As Bill Schottstaedt, the CCRMA researcher referenced in Scandalis's email, recalled the situation:

There was one time here at CCRMA where the Sondius group was working on sound synthesis. I wanted to take part of the physical modeling of this research, but they felt they couldn't tell anyone outside of their group. It pissed me off.[40]

To be sure, academic pursuits, too, can result in secrecy; as academic researchers race to be the first to discover something new, they can withhold information tied to intermediate steps.[41] The difference in the Sondius case, however, is that the relative secrecy was motivated by commercial considerations rather than academic desires. In turn, that motivation reordered sharing relationships, since protecting commercial interests suggested secrecy even within CCRMA.

The Sondius effort also raised conflict-of-interest issues. Specifically, because Julius Smith had a financial interest in waveguide physical modeling, Stanford's Conflict of Interest policy prevented him from overseeing the work of the developers who were hired into CCRMA to further develop the technology. The rationale of the policy is that a professor should not be able to leverage university resources to his or her direct financial benefit. Since Smith would receive royalties from licenses related to the development effort, the university reasoned that he should not simultaneously oversee the university's investment in this effort. The result, as noted by Scott Van Duyne, one of the graduate students on the project, was that, "The guy with the knowledge, the best résumé, for overseeing our work [Smith] wasn't allowed to oversee our work."[42] In turn, the project sometimes suffered from a lack of engineering leadership and from a lack of integration between marketing and engineering, since the licensing associate in charge of marketing had limited technical understanding.

Graduate students also faced conflicts between their academic work and their commercial development work through Sondius. As Koepnick recalled:

> We had a couple of conflict things that we had to be careful about. ... You want to make sure that the student is not distracted from his research and that he's not doing research that's not benefiting him, that's benefiting the university or the company. In this case, if you weren't careful, somebody could argue that we were distracting Tim [Stilson, another graduate student] from getting his thesis. Tim is there three years and his advisor's going, "You should be out of here." And Tim says, "Well, I'm spending all this time on Sondius."

Thus, the situation of these student-developers in the university context meant that they were placed at the nexus of two competing demands—personal academic achievement and development for the sake of commercial gain. While CCRMA had earlier leveraged such differences to generate novelty and acquire resources, the enhanced emphasis placed on commercial activities appeared to throw these intertwined relationships out of balance.

At the same time, Stanford grew concerned about other companies infringing the DWT patents. For example, in 1995, Perry Cook sent an email to Watanabe and Smith to alert them that Invision, a Palo Alto-based music software company, was introducing a new product called CyberSynth. Cook wrote:

> It's a software-only synthesizer, like Seer Systems' synthesizer. [Seer was a Sondius licensee.] I've seen mock-ups of the boxes and they clearly state the types of synthe-

sis used, including Physical Modeling. The chief architect on this project is Steve O'Connell (Yep, the author of the SynthKit patent), ex-Korg, ex-Yamaha, DSP guy who arguably knows the most about physical modeling of anyone outside of Stanford or Yamaha.

In the same email, Cook shares that

Steve gave a pretty negative talk at the S.F. AES [Audio Engineering Society] meeting, basically saying that physical modeling has been around so long that no patents on this topic were valid. Julius [Smith] was at that talk as well.[43]

As Cook's email highlights, Stanford's desire to enforce its intellectual property around DWT in order to generate revenue placed it in conflict with firms that did not necessarily respect Stanford's claims.

Stanford also had a conflict with Korg, which had received a patent on waveguide synthesis and which was developing its own graphical system based on O'Connell's work.[44] Financial records show that Stanford paid more than $5,000 to law firm Flehr Hohbach for an analysis of the Korg patent.[45] A preliminary working memo from the firm indicated that many of Korg's claims appeared to be covered by prior art and would not withstand a legal challenge.[46] A legal challenge, however, would be expensive. Moreover, it could be bad press. Ultimately, Yamaha—a major Korg partner—stepped in to resolve the conflict and Korg signed as a Sondius licensee.[47]

As the Stanford team worked to develop the Sondius trademark by building example sounds through SynthBuilder, Yamaha also had a large engineering staff—around a hundred people—dedicated to developing the technology. In 1994, they released their first commercial product based on DWT: the Yamaha VL1 synthesizer. The instrument received significant press attention in outlets ranging from *Business Week* to *Wired* to trade magazines like *Keyboard* and *Electronic Musician*. Smith received interviews from the *Wall Street Journal*, the *Washington Post*, *Billboard*, and NPR's "All Things Considered."[48]

The VL1 is a beautiful instrument, with gold hardware and a burr-Walnut veneer panel "similar to a Jag's dashboard," according to one reviewer.[49] Its sounds were phenomenal, too—particularly for string and woodwind instruments. The same reviewer noted, "NOTHING in the synth world produces rock guitars like a VL1."[50] Such praise was particularly nice for Smith, a talented guitarist.

Whereas the DX7's introduction, however, marked a period of rapid sales, the VL1 was not a commercial success. First, it was expensive, with a list price of $5,000 amid a more common $2,500 price point for professional synthesizers. Second, the VL1 could produce only two notes at a time, owing to the significant computational requirements and complexity of DWT. Thus, it could be used for "leads" and solos, but it was not useful as an all-around keyboard to mimic pianos, organs, and other instruments that play several notes at once. As such, it was a specialty instrument.

Perhaps the most significant challenge to the VL1, however, was that DWT required a new type of interface to realize its potential. Thus, although the VL1 looked like a traditional keyboard, it required the simultaneous use of various foot and mouth controllers, too. Yamaha bundled the instrument with a breath controller that looks like a microphone attached to a headset and that uses the performer's breath to control a selected synthesis parameter. As one music guide summarized the situation, "[The VL1 is] undoubtedly expressive beyond any normal synth's wildest dreams but, like a 'real instrument,' it takes time to master."[51] For the vast majority of keyboard players who had already mastered the piano-type key system, the need to learn additional interfaces stymied adoption. Put slightly differently, the VL1 moved away from one of the longest-established standards in the music-making world—black-and-white piano-style keys—and it ran into severe resistance as a result. As noted, CCRMA participants had long encountered the benefits and costs of technical standards. (Recall the move from specialized to widely available computers, for example.) In the commercial realm, Yamaha and CCRMA found that moving away from a standard—even when such moves offered musical benefits—could dramatically quell adoption.

Though the VL1's lack of commercial success may have been a bad omen, the Stanford team continued to develop DWT. By the end of 1996, the team had completed SynthBuilder and several demonstration sounds. To their dismay, however, the years of effort—and the large financial investment—yielded only two additional licensees.

Rather than watch the development team disband, OTL licensing associate Koepnick took the unusual step in late 1996 of leaving Stanford to start a company that would continue DWT commercialization efforts. He and the other cofounders—essentially, the CCRMA development team—named the company Staccato Systems. Staccato received licenses to the Sondius technologies in exchange for an equity stake by Stanford.

Stanford, indeed, had high hopes for the company. A January 1998 article in the *Stanford Magazine* described the frantic efforts at the university to identify a successor to the highly lucrative Cohen–Boyer rDNA patents, which expired in 1997. As the article notes:

As they sift through the Cohen/Boyer wannabes, [OTL Director Kathy] Ku and her OTL colleagues have settled on an unlikely group of Stanford grads as the heir apparent with the most potential. Until recently, Staccato Systems, Inc., ran its "worldwide headquarters" from a two-car garage in Mountain View, complete with a washer-dryer and cement floor carpeted by dust bunnies. A complicated array of desktop computers and electronic synthesizers was jammed into the center of the room and along the walls. If you looked carefully, you could see the garage door behind a pile of sound-absorbing sponge.

... Staccato is a classic Silicon Valley paradigm—a group of musicians, engineers, computer nerds and a director who left his full-time job at OTL to run them in this ordered chaos.[52]

Staccato presented a tricky situation, however, for both Stanford and Yamaha: Yamaha's collaborator in the OTL, Koepnick, was suddenly leading a potential competitor. Kathy Ku (the OTL director), Jon Sandelin, and Mary Watanabe (Koepnick's replacement on the Sondius docket) were nervous, therefore, as they traveled to Japan in January 1997 to meet with Yamaha.

Yamaha had plans of its own. A number of musical instrument manufacturers had agreed to the General MIDI standard in 1991, which specified

Figure 7.1
Staccato Systems cofounders (pictured from left to right) Scott Van Duyne, Nick Porcaro, and Pat Scandalis in 1997 in the Mountain View garage that first housed the start-up. Courtesy of the Stanford News Service. Photo by Linda Cicero.

certain standard instruments or sounds that a compliant device would produce. The general idea was that if a standard MIDI file specified a part to be played by sound number 41 on an instrument, a user could be assured that sound 41 would correspond to a violin—and that the device contained a violin sound in the first place. Different manufacturers, however, then extended the General MIDI standard in different ways—still adhering to the core sound bank but offering additional standard sounds as an attempted competitive advantage. Yamaha, for example, introduced the XG standard in 1994, which raised the number of sounds from 128 to 600 and included a number of additional control parameters. Of course, such manufacturer-specific efforts failed to yield additional benefits from standardization, precisely because they were not shared across manufacturers.

In the January meeting with Stanford, Yamaha proposed that the two groups combine forces under a new trademark, "Sondius XG," which combined Stanford's Sondius program with Yamaha's XG program. The new trademark, to many observers, marked a new era in university technology licensing. As the then president of the Association of University Technology Managers, Marvin Guthrie, commented in 1998, "I can't think of a technology where a university has become so closely associated with the product as Stanford appears to be with this. ... They had a special technology and they saw a way to build a relationship."[53] Traditionally, universities licensed intellectual property to companies, and the university association was not obvious in the final product, except to industry insiders who understood the technology and the intellectual property landscape. With Sondius, however, Stanford attempted to leverage the Stanford name itself to "brand" products. In turn, Sondius XG publicly branded the alliance between Stanford and Yamaha. In light of the earlier criticism that had been leveled for Stanford's close relationship with Yamaha (recall the critiques from Media Vision and ARP, along with the *San Francisco Chronicle* article), the overt shift to cobranding music technologies is itself evidence of the dramatic shift in perceptions around university–industry engagement: activities that had raised suspicion and concern just a decade earlier were now unabashedly publicized.

Stanford and Yamaha announced the partnership at a joint press conference in July 1997. In turn, Staccato Systems became the first Sondius-XG licensee[54] and Yamaha offered to invest $1 million in Staccato in order to align the interests of Stanford, Yamaha, and Staccato. Staccato raised another $3.2 million from Allegis Capital and Chase Capital Partners.

The Staccato team continued development efforts begun at CCRMA, redirecting this work toward the computer games market, where they met with considerable success. In 2001, Staccato Systems sold to Analog Devices for $30 million.

The Sondius XG trademark, however, never had much traction. Only Korg signed as a licensee, under pressure from Yamaha and in the shadow of the patent dispute with Stanford. Part of this lackluster performance may be attributed to a lack of marketing: neither CCRMA nor the OTL put any money into marketing the Sondius trademark. In fact, although the Sondius plan includes a number of royalty comparisons and projections, it is striking for the lack of attention to marketing: nowhere does the forty-seven-page plan address how consumers will come to learn about and value Sondius. The only reference to marketing at all is a note accompanying one phase of the plan to "begin promoting the trademark informally through use and develop a plan for promoting the mark formally." The idea seems to have been that products would display the trademark, and as these products were successful, the trademark would increase in value. This approach, however, introduced a "chicken–egg" challenge: with no immediate brand value to end users, companies had less motivation to license the trademark; but, without companies licensing the trademark and using it on successful products, end users did not understand its value. As Koepnick later reflected:

> Sondius was very ambitious. ... What we didn't realize is that creating value as a brand is an incredibly long process and it's very intensive. That was when the dot-com things came out. Everybody's investing in these small companies. The brands are going to win. ... Brand is very powerful. Sony's brand is very powerful, but it took hundreds of years to get to this point. That was where we just didn't have the resources.[55]

The difficulty and expense of developing a brand caught the Sondius team by surprise—in part, because it was composed of technical experts with a strong musical orientation but little experience in purposefully generating a substantial new market.

To many observers of the Sondius XG trademark program, however, the program was never intended to gain traction. As Smith described the situation, Yamaha had agreed to exclusivity but for North American companies because that agreement kept Creative Technology, a Singapore-based company, from accessing the technology. (Yamaha had lost to Creative Technology in the PC soundcards market, as discussed at the end of chapter 5.) In 1996, however, Creative Technology established a distribution agreement with US-based Seer Systems, which already had a Sondius license. Suddenly, Creative Technology effectively had a license, too, through Seer Systems. As Smith recalled:

> [The Creative–Seer Systems relationship] caused some real upheavals. That caused the Sondius XG program. It triggered the pooling of IP. They basically shifted, a big turn at sea, they shifted the model from exclusive patent licensing to "Let's build up our own trademark, the XG trademark, and let's put all of our patents into this XG trademark. And if you want to use these patents, you've got to use our trademark."[56]

Thus, Sondius XG was as much a competitive reaction as it was a proactive development program.

The problem, of course, was that few companies had a desire to advertise a Yamaha trademark on their own products. As Pat Scandalis saw it:

> When you added the XG, it polarized the other vendors because we couldn't really go to Roland and say, "Hey would you like to license this technology? It's really cool. You can make way cool products." They wouldn't have anything to do with it if it had XG [since XG was a Yamaha trademark].[57]

Similarly, Joe Bryan, a Korg engineer, argued:

> There's a barrier to widespread adoption of physical modeling (PM) synths. Anyone who wants to develop one has to pay Yamaha/Stanford for the Sondius license and co-brand their work with it. If you haven't read the Sondius agreement, it's pretty interesting. Suffice to say no one's rushing out to develop PM synths anymore.[58]

The close branding association between Yamaha and Sondius XG effectively killed the adoption of Sondius XG by other companies.

Progress in complementary technologies also threatened the DWT program. Specifically, a major advantage of DWT lies in its very low memory requirements. As the price of computer memory fell through the 1980s, it eroded DWT's advantage. As Scandalis recalled, "Originally, people were thinking that physical modeling was going to solve the memory problem. But in the end, memory wasn't a problem." Continued improvement in wavetable synthesis, an alternative technology, also presented challenges. Scandalis remembered, "It was becoming apparent that wavetable was really better for a lot of things and that physical modeling was really good for just a few things."[59] Moreover, the technical implementation was difficult—even for the CCRMA engineers who were among the most skilled in the world. As Watanabe, the licensing associate, characterized the situation: "The technology was much more difficult from a technical standpoint than we originally thought. ... Much more difficult for people to assimilate into their programs."[60] Indeed, it was one thing for highly skilled CCRMA personnel to use and develop DWT in their own research and compositions; it was another thing for them to develop it in a way that enabled *others* to easily do so.

Ultimately, the experiment of placing developers within CCRMA in order to increase intellectual property revenue met with mixed success: on one hand, their work facilitated the emergence of Staccato Systems and, thus, its subsequent sale; in this way, the university may have incubated the technology during a critical early period. On the other hand, the program fell far short of expectations. Moreover, there is some evidence that university development efforts were actually *harmful* to the technology's diffusion. Again, Stanford's primary goal in the development project was to increase the value of the patent portfolio, which would allow the university to earn more money from the licenses. Presumably, therefore, further development drove higher licensing fees. The Sondius licensing fee was $50,000 up front, with a $25,000 annual "maintenance fee" and a negotiated percentage of royalties on product sales. To Smith, "They priced it out of reach of small companies. It's extremely expensive. ... There have been lots of people over the years who want to do something, but are locked out."[61] Ironically, Stanford's own development efforts may have prevented others from engaging in development as a result of the high licensing fees. In turn, these actions may have limited the diffusion of the technology.

Stanford's technology development efforts also raised new questions about sharing, as with the dilemma over sounds and Schottstaedt's CLM program. Smith, too, recalled questions about sharing research results in academic seminars: "What if someone from the outside attends? You could argue that's disclosure and lose the patent."[62] Whereas traditional university environments may value and reward such disclosure, commercial interests inject new concerns into sharing conversations—critically, spilling over into long-standing academic traditions such as seminars. In other words, emergent tensions were not limited to the commercial activities themselves, but instead implicated existing academic activities.

In turn, the sale of Staccato Systems to Analog Devices effectively shut down most avenues of information sharing; Analog Devices did not openly share information about further developments in the tools. Moreover, the academics were left with little incentive to continue research with their current version of the tool since intellectual property rights to any discoveries would be tied to Analog Devices, which now owned the tool; academic researchers would be pursuing projects legally bound to a commercial entity with which they had no formal ties. As Smith noted in 2004, "This was not good for the lab. When Staccato went, so did the intellectual property, so did the software tools. We would have to start all over without the tools. It's never going to happen."[63] Smith went on to describe several potential and valuable extensions of the technology that could not be executed because of these restrictions. (Interestingly, however, Smith, Scandalis, and Porcaro released an iPhone/iPad electric guitar based on DWT—the MoForte Guitar—in 2014, after the key patents had expired.)

Ultimately, these observations highlight how the importation of commercial development activities into an academic lab served not merely to extend or accelerate technology development, as the instigators hoped, but also affected intellectual production at CCRMA by reorienting the activities of faculty and students and by altering open sharing practices. In turn, the Sondius experiment may serve as a counterexample around the coevolution of academic disciplines, technological discoveries, and commercial activities: When CCRMA emphasized the academic aims—but, critically, with openness to commercial potential as an *outgrowth* of these aims—they realized success. Conversely, when CCRMA consciously emphasized commercial aims, these activities threatened to displace academic activities. In other words, Sondius illustrates that interdisciplinarity, open innovation, and commercialization are not only intertwined, but also that the particular shape of these relationships—game-changing novelty, as with CCRMA's emergence and renewal, or unrealized expectations and commercially tied tensions, as with Sondius—depend on the prioritization and balance between these activities.

Sondius yielded another important lesson, too, in that it was tied to a particularistic model of commercialization: the licensing of patents. As CCRMA would emphasize in the 2000s, however, there were other ways to spur commercialization and to realize financial benefits while maintaining an emphasis on artistic and academic aims.

8 Recapitulation and Variations

If the 1990s were marked, in part, by concern with hands-on commercialization and intellectual property, then a resurgence of free and open sharing have characterized the new millennium at CCRMA. To be clear, open innovation never disappeared at CCRMA. Faculty, staff, and students alike always supported the free and open sharing of resources, research, music, and software. As Bill Schottstaedt recalled, it was assumed that all code at the Stanford Artificial Intelligence Lab was open to anyone, apparently a long-standing tradition in the Lisp computer language community.[1] (Lisp became the preferred language for AI.) As discussed in chapter 4, CCRMA shared the Music 10 program with a number of other centers, including IRCAM. Similarly, Rick Taube's Common Music composition software, which he started writing while serving as a guest composer at CCRMA, and Bill Schottstaedt's Common Lisp Music (CLM) sound synthesis package, Common Music Notation (CMN) music notation package, and Snd sound-editing software have always been open.[2] Thus, when a 2001 review in the *Computer Music Journal* alleged that CCRMA had been "closed" in the Chowning FM era, Johannes Goebel, a CCRMA affiliate who now serves as director of the Experimental Media and Performing Arts Center at Rensselaer Polytechnic Institute, argued in his response letter, "One should not forget that open-source is not a development of the 1980s and 1990s but stems from the 1960s and 1970s."[3]

At the same time, the influence of commercial interests on sharing practices is undeniable. As the original provocateurs argued in response to Goebel's letter, "Currently, music software is among the most copy-protected of any genre."[4] Chowning himself noted, in reference to activity outside of CCRMA, "The whole patent thing kind of went nuts after FM. Everybody was trying to patent everything. Musicians instead of doing music started doing inventions, most of which amounted to nothing."[5] Even within CCRMA, the commercial development period around Sondius clearly highlighted tensions around sharing, along with subtle questions about the distribution of resources, people, and priorities between commercially motivated technology development and other activities core to CCRMA. For example, Perry Cook, a CCRMA graduate who later served as CCRMA's Technical Director, cited the commercialization emphasis of the 1990s as one reason that he left CCRMA for Princeton in 1996:

> I had also grown weary of the OTL [Office of Technology Licensing] way of life. ... We got to the point where the graduate students and the faculty were thinking about what they're going to invent or patent and turn into companies. ... I was really tired of that. ... The SU-18 [the intellectual property agreement form at Stanford] was just too much.[6]

At Princeton, in fact, Cook conducted an "experiment" of sharing all of his work openly: "That was my social experiment: What would life be like without [the] OTL? As a result, I generated a shitload of great grad students who are world famous. ... [and] I still got paid. I still got hired as a consultant. I still got to do all the cool stuff I wanted to do."[7] Cook's experience was not one of eschewing commercial engagement; rather, it was one of influencing commercial development in ways that did not rely primarily on patents and licenses.

Against this backdrop, it is interesting to note that in 1996, as the Sondius development work reached its finale, CCRMA also began using Linux, a Unix-like, free, and open source operating system. As Fernando López-Lezcano, a Lecturer and systems administrator at CCRMA, would later recall, "It was an interesting experiment that proved Linux was becoming a viable platform for our work."[8] Initially, concerns centered on whether soundcards, which provided a necessary audio interface, would work with the platform. Another issue concerned the platform's latency—the delay between when an audio signal enters a system and when it emerges from it. As López-Lezcano described, matter-of-factly:

> Patches became available for the Linux kernel that enabled it to start working at the low latencies suitable for realtime reliable audio work, so I started building custom monolithic kernels that incorporated those patches and all the drivers I needed for the hardware included in our machines.[9]

In translation, López-Lezcano signals that he both built on and contributed to the Linux open source effort.

With a growing set of machines at CCRMA—twenty-six or twenty-seven, by López-Lezcano's count—one of López-Lezcano's primary goals lay in keeping software and systems standardized; he, too, recognized the tremendous benefits of standardization.[10] Toward this goal, López-Lezcano put a number of the software programs into packages. Soon, CCRMA users wanted the same packages available on their home machines, too. So, López-Lezcano wrote up instructions on how to download the packages and configure a standard machine running Linux.[11]

In time, López-Lezcano's packages moved from a network-accessible directory, to a simple website for CCRMA users, to a website "publicly" announced, to a computer music email list in September 2001. As López-Lezcano noted, the collection of programs, which would be named Planet CCRMA, provided access "to all of the open source sound, midi and music software that we routinely used in research, music making and teaching [at CCRMA]. ... The same software we were using at CCRMA was now available for anyone in the world to download and install."[12] Thus, anyone in the world could reproduce the CCRMA technical environment, for free.

In addition, Planet CCRMA provided a forum for other contributors to distribute their software. Indeed, as the package went public, López-Lezcano received more and more requests for additional music software to be included. Soon, the project took on a life of its own: Planet CCRMA, according to López-Lezcano, "was never an 'official' project, it was a side effect of me packaging stuff to install at CCRMA." Yet he later wrote, "I have created a monster :-)."[13] By 2005, there were more than 600 individual packages.[14]

López-Lezcano argues that the free and open nature of Planet CCRMA benefits all parties. Outside users gain free access to cutting-edge music and audio software. At the same time, the openness allowed projects like CLM (Bill Schottstaedt's sound synthesis package) to expand beyond limited academic circles and to draw in new talent. Thus, as López-Lezcano summarized in 2009, "Everyone benefited from the freedom and wide access made possible by the Internet."[15] In a 2012 interview, he elaborated:

> Planet CCRMA also changed the face of CCRMA. ... I had a mailing list and people would subscribe and download, ask questions, and they would also ask for packages for software. They would say, "Oh, well, there's this very neat drum machine that I would love to see in Planet CCRMA." I would say, "Okay, let me see what can be done," and I would package it and I would release it [to Planet CCRMA], but I would also install it in all the machines at CCRMA.

We became part of a global network of people that wanted to use Linux for music that didn't necessarily have the same background, desires, and goals as the people who were working at CCRMA. That meant that there was cross-pollination with the world at large—anyone, anywhere. They [e.g., outsiders] could install Planet CCRMA and they would get all the applications that I compile for it ... and maybe they'd never use them and they'd use something else, but they'd have things that they would never have thought about. And the other side of the coin was also true ... we also have a lot of stuff here that we wouldn't have otherwise. ...

There's something very interesting in ... the fact that we put this on a little website and we just gave it a little push—and it pushed back.[16]

López-Lezcano's observations are critical and bear restatement: Although many observers focus on technology transfer from universities to firms or, perhaps, to end users, López-Lezcano's image is of a community in which people from a wide array of backgrounds and environments contribute to a shared resource, thereby enriching universities. Unlike a linear model, from basic research to applied research to development, CCRMA's embrace of a wide range of backgrounds again shows how "downstream" applications and users can influence "upstream" research at places like CCRMA.[17]

Moreover, the combination of free and open source software with the standardization that underlies such software also facilitates commercialization. Julius Smith explained:

[Free, open source software, or FOSS] provides a vast, free, powerful infrastructure that anyone can use. This jump-starts all sorts of new commercial efforts. ... FOSS greatly facilitates engineers migrating from one job to the next, and starting new companies, without having to "rewrite the wheel" every time.[18]

In turn, as more and more people use the same software infrastructure, the benefits continue to grow: applications increase, company demand for people with knowledge of how to work in the environment increases, and new insights arise from the expanding size and diversity of the community.

At the same time, CCRMA reinvigorated and revamped other programs for outside engagement. For example, CCRMA had started an "industrial affiliates program" in 1987, modeled after similar programs at other Stanford departments. Member companies paid an annual fee, historically ranging from $5,000 to $30,000, in exchange for the opportunity to attend CCRMA conferences, workshops, and informal presentations, and to receive research reports. Aside from providing financial support for CCRMA, a major aim of the program was to increase the employment prospects of CCRMA graduates. Thus, at an annual meeting, each graduate student would present his or her work. Member companies represented the musical instrument, audio equipment, and computer industries, among others.

In 2005, CCRMA revamped the industrial affiliates' arrangement and added a new program, "Open Questions." As the CCRMA website describes the program:

> [Member companies participate] by formulating research questions that can be used in CCRMA teaching. Communication directly between company engineers and students is encouraged. For CCRMA's part, student instruction gains a valuable experiential component driven by problems relevant to today's industries, and for the companies tough questions get aired in a new way. All results are shared completely and openly.[19]

Thus, CCRMA pursued a new model of industry engagement in which real-world questions formed the basis of classroom instruction. For companies, focusing CCRMA students and faculty on perplexing issues holds obvious research benefits. But the relationship also allows companies to "vet" potential future employees, developing close research relationships with students under the auspices of the program. For students, the program is beneficial in that it helps them connect their classroom education with current problems in industry, and it gives them a "leg up" in their job search.

The industrial affiliates program also features a visitors program, under which visiting engineers from member companies come to CCRMA for an extended period. These visitors join existing projects and spur new ones; they coauthor research papers with CCRMA students and faculty; they take part in courses and colloquia; and some industrial affiliates visitors even enroll as CCRMA master's degree students.

The idea of the program is not to transfer from university to industry, but rather to cocreate with industry for the benefit of firms, CCRMA, and students alike. Thus, CCRMA emphasizes that anyone who would like to access the center's existing research can do so online, free of charge. Instead, the motivation behind the Industrial Affiliates program is to "expand the forces for problem-solving."[20] Of course, this approach builds on the vision of industry engagement elaborated by Stanford provost Frederick Terman in the years following World War II: recall from chapter 2 that Terman brought in industry experts to teach courses and to collaborate on Stanford research projects; thus, his vision was not of one-way flows from universities to industry, but rather of collaborative relationships in which researchers from diverse origins contributed to projects of collective interest.

CCRMA's free and open sharing—and their combining of these efforts with summer short courses and continued research collaborations with industry partners—marks a novel approach to technology development and commercialization: as management scholars would phrase it, the center has come to focus on its "core competency" of research and education, rather than licensing and product development. In so doing, CCRMA has defined a field of play in which it does not compete with commercial firms, but instead encourages them to engage with the center. In a 2008 interview, Julius Smith explained how this revised business model benefits CCRMA:

> Our business model has shifted to simply teaching. That's our business model. We get the sporadic grant here and there. But we're not getting new patent revenues at all. The OTL model has been dead here for a long time. Even though we have some residual [licensing revenue], it's waning and it'll probably just dry up altogether in a few years. It just isn't working anymore. But the teaching model is doing great. We're getting more applicants, better students. We have a nice new building now. The renovation finally happened. [The Knoll, CCRMA's building, underwent renovation in 2005, financed, in part, through donations.] So we have all the success we can handle, pretty much. It's just plain old departmental programs that are drawing great students and putting out great people, who then get into industry, who we then know. They then hire our next wave of students. Relationships form. Who knows what might come of it?

Smith thus links the renewed emphasis on teaching with CCRMA's network of supporters. Continuing, he ties CCRMA's embrace of free, open source software to the center's ability to connect with industry and to place graduates:

> We have a lot of friends in the industry now. It's just this organic growing thing. And it's nice to have no patents. It's nice that they [students, alumni, and others] can just use anything we've done. They can just go to our website and we can say, "Hey, try this out."
>
> Just yesterday, I saw Roger Linn of Linn Design—he's the inventor of the drum machine—I saw him over the weekend and I told him about Faust [a programming language designed for real-time signal processing and synthesis]. I told him about my electric guitars. And he told me about the AdrenaLinn 3 [a guitar effects pedal that Linn designed] and what's in it. [Then] I wrote a little Faust program to implement it and emailed him. It's all free. He can download our whole system and he can download Faust. Everything's free, and you can get all the code. He's actually thinking about using that in his products, and that's great.
>
> What do we get? Well, I don't know. We know Roger Linn and he likes us. Maybe we helped him. And if he's wildly successful, he'll probably want to give back in one

way or another. In my opinion, hiring our students, either as summer interns or after they graduate, is more than repayment enough.[21]

Thus, technology commercialization continues to play a central role at CCRMA, both reinforcing and resulting from interdisciplinary efforts and open innovation. The shape of commercialization has changed in recent years, however, as intellectual property–focused direct commercialization efforts in the 1990s gave way to free and open-source-oriented efforts in the 2000s. In turn, CCRMA has found that the most fruitful commercialization approaches may lie not in "formal" technology transfer, but rather in informal and free sharing that builds long-term personal relationships—the same kinds of relationships, as with Mathews, Pierce, Boulez, and others, that proved critical to CCRMA's emergence in the first place.[22]

MoPhOs and Accidental Entrepreneurs

This relationship between university-based research, education, and firm-based technology development has continued to play out in other recent CCRMA activities, too. For example, Ge Wang, director of the Stanford Mobile Phone Orchestra (MoPhO) described in chapter 1, served for several years both as assistant professor at CCRMA and as chief technology officer and cofounder at Smule, a maker of musical instrument applications for smart phones. The fact that he held both positions simultaneously is itself commentary on the linkages between industry and academia at CCRMA. These linkages, however, extend beyond Wang. For example, the coinstructors for an August 2012 CCRMA summer workshop on music and mobile computing were Spencer Salazar and Mark Cerqueira. Salazar was a PhD student at CCRMA, advised by Wang. He has composed music for the MoPhO and has developed applications for Smule. Cerqueira is a graduate of Princeton, where Wang completed his PhD, and a software developer for Smule. In short, the ties between the start-up and CCRMA are thick, and they span educational activities alongside commercial development.

In fact, Wang's own history reinforces the dense network that connects individual participants in the computer music community, cross-cutting commercial and academic organizations and activities. Wang's PhD advisor at Princeton was Perry Cook—the same Perry Cook who completed his PhD at CCRMA and served as its technical director before leaving for Princeton in the 1990s.[23] As a PhD student Wang tried to implement digital signal processing and synthesis techniques that he was learning, but he came to realize that the programming language that he was using (C++) did not permit the flexibility, expressivity, and "flow" that he sought. As Wang tells the story:

> I started working backwards. ... [If] we had a new programming language to do some tasks, what would that look like? So I started scribbling things out and one day I showed up in Perry's office. I said, "Perry, I think we should do yet another programming language for computer music." He said, "Okay." And I started drawing; like in this language, what if you could do A, B, and C? And I started with the ChucK operator. ... Perry looked at it and said, "You know. That looks fairly insane. Go for it."[24]

The mailing list for ChucK users now includes hundreds of people, and Wang guesses that the number of users "is probably at least that much, if not half an order of magnitude bigger."[25]

A free and open source approach underlies both the adoption and continued development of ChucK. Wang notes that he looked to Cook's own practice of releasing the Synthesis Toolkit, a software package to facilitate the development of physical modeling, as free and open source software. As Wang explained:

> I think there's no better feeling than to make something and have someone actually use it and maybe even do things that you don't expect. So, I think in 2003, I thought "Let's put this [ChucK] out there." I think it's a way to get more people to try it. In the end, it's cool because there are people using it, hopefully, and two, I think it's a way to improve the language.[26]

Wang's motivation is notable: free and open sharing enables both diffusion and subsequent improvements by others. The fact that he took a cue about free and open sharing from Cook, whose own perspective was shaped by his experience at CCRMA, reinforces how both people and practices in computer music transcend organizational boundaries.

As with Cook, too, Wang's engagement in free and open sharing is not to suggest that he was blind to the commercial potential of his creations. Quite the contrary, in fact: Wang's audio programming language, ChucK, is the same one used by Smule, Wang's mobile-phone music app start-up. Yet the path from ChucK to Smule reveals a far more complex picture than that of an academic seeking financial profit from his research work: at Princeton, Cook and Dan Trueman (an associate professor of music) pitched Wang on the idea of a "laptop orchestra" that would use ChucK. Wang loved the idea. In 2005, he helped start the Princeton Laptop Orchestra, or PLOrk.

When Stanford hired Wang as a professor in 2007, he transposed the laptop orchestra idea to CCRMA, founding the Stanford Laptop Orchestra, or SLOrk. Both efforts, as Wang describes them, were highly experimental. Paraphrasing CCRMA's director, Chris Chafe, Wang claims:

> [Like Chafe says,] "If we knew what we were doing, then it wouldn't be research." This is all about taking the ill-defined into the realm of the well-defined.[27]

At Stanford, the group cut holes in IKEA salad bowls and inserted car stereo amplifiers and speakers. The result is a custom half-spherical speaker that resembles the head of R2D2. Each SLOrk performer has one hooked up to his or her laptop.

Wang soon expanded his attention, however, from laptops to mobile phones. Shortly after arriving at CCRMA, he met Henri Penttinen, a visiting researcher, and Georg Essl, who was at Deutsch Telecom at the time. Inspired by the laptop orchestra and realizing that modern mobile phones possess computing power comparable to early desktop computers, the three researchers together proposed the idea of a mobile phone orchestra. (They would lovingly abbreviate the ensemble as the Stanford MoPhO.) To get

Figure 8.1
Members of the Stanford Laptop Orchestra (SLOrk) perform at the 2008 Pan-Asian Music Festival. Courtesy of the Stanford University Archives. Photo by Enrique Aguiree.

them started, Nokia, one of CCRMA's industrial affiliates, donated twenty smartphones.

Wang found that laptop and mobile phone orchestras demanded and developed new skills in programming, musical composition, and performance. In turn, his curiosity about scalability grew. To answer questions around scalability, however, he needed to reach beyond the small ensembles at Princeton and Stanford. In a 2012 interview, he explained:

> To really study this well [referring to large-scale collaboration around music making], we need to study a large mass of people. It's [i.e., a smartphone is] inherently a very personal computer and inherently a very social thing. Somehow, Smule really spun out of this spiritual side of the laptop orchestra and the mobile phone orchestra.[28]

Later in the same interview, Wang falls back on his role as an educator to explain his goals: "[I think] that our first, and maybe last, order of business as educators in computer music is to bring people in, get them excited, get them inspired, and make sure that they leave even more so."[29] In other words, Wang's claimed motivation for Smule is based on academic research questions and a desire to bring music-making to the masses. In fact, in an interview with the *San Francisco Business Times*, Wang said, "I'm very much an accidental entrepreneur. I had no intention to start a company."[30] The fact that he identified a start-up as the best way to achieve his goal is itself commentary on the intertwining of commercial, technical, and artistic aims. Indeed, Smule's commercial orientation is undeniable: the company counts leading Silicon Valley venture capitalists among its funders. To CCRMA researchers such as Wang, however, commercial activities are not separate from academic aims but instead, in some ways, are inseparable from them. In fact, Smule has been at the forefront of experimenting with alternative business models for apps, giving away the core apps for free and then charging for upgrades and additional features—an approach that balances Wang's desire for broad distribution (via free downloads) with Smule's desire to make money (via charges for upgrades and additional features).

Revisiting Radical Interdisciplinarity

These activities underscore how CCRMA's pursuit of radical interdisciplinarity has moved beyond the intertwining of music, science, and engineering to ensnare a growing range of activities and disciplines that serve to reinforce one another. Recent work by Chris Chafe, the current CCRMA director, provides further examples of these relationships. Chafe has long been attracted to the idea of collaborating across distances: Imagine a jazz saxophonist in Oakland jamming with a pianist in Portland, a drummer in New York, and a bass player in Minneapolis. The primary challenge, Chafe realized, lay in audio latency—the slight but meaningful delays between sound transmission, processing, and reception.

In turn, Chafe initiated the SoundWIRE project in 2000 and set about working on next-generation networking techniques that reduced latency. His collaborators include the Banff Centre in Alberta, Canada; Rensselaer Polytechnic Institute (RPI) in Troy, New York; Sonic Arts Research Centre (SARC) in Belfast, Northern Ireland; and the University of California at Santa Cruz (UCSC).

SoundWIRE is not simply a research project. In fact, when asked about it, Chafe immediately jumps to the numerous musical performances enabled by the technology. For example, the 2007 concert *100 Meeting Places* took place simultaneously at Stanford, RPI, UCSC, and Loyola University in Chicago, with performances and audiences in each location (and additional audience members who viewed a live stream on the Internet). The concert featured open improvisations along with compositions by Chafe and by Pauline Oliveros (the former San Francisco Tape Music Center director) that were designed to take advantage of the unique geographically distributed ensemble.

Nevertheless, the technical achievements are important to recognize. For example, Chafe developed a new method for evaluating the quality of service of a digital network connection and later patented a distributed acoustic reverberator for audio collaboration.[31] The underlying system that enables multimachine network performance over the Internet, JackTrip, is—perhaps not surprisingly—available via open source.

Related work by Chafe explores *sonification,* or the translation of data into audio signals.[32] For Chafe, a natural application lay in sonifying network delays. As the *New York Times* reported in a 2002 feature on his research:

> Listen carefully to the sound of the network, and you will hear the difference between congestion and the seamless flow of data. ... [Chafe's] musical detection service translates the behavior of data packets into a range of sounds worthy of John Cage: a packet that loses information along its route emits staccato hiccups. Delayed packets sound at a lower pitch than packets zipping along more quickly, which give a clear, high tone. Dr. Chafe, who says that listening is a neglected skill in the world of computer diagnostics, hopes his new tool will come in handy in future interac-

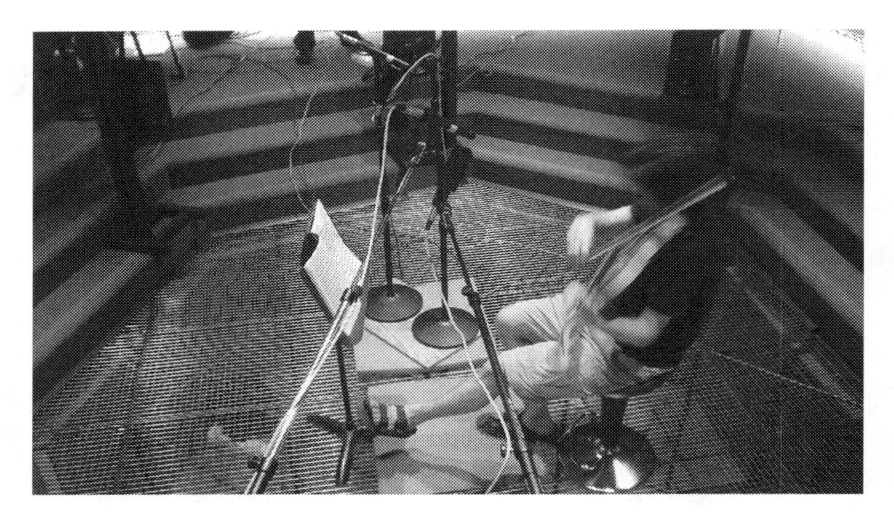

Figure 8.2
Barry Shiffman performs at CCRMA as part of a geographically distributed string quintet, facilitated by the SoundWIRE project. The other four members of the quintet are located at the Banff Centre in Canada. Microphones on each instrument picked up the direct sound, with individual speakers surrounding Shiffman dedicated to each of the four remote instruments (two violins, a viola, and a violoncello). Additional microphones picked up the acoustics of the space at the Banff Centre and reproduced them in the CCRMA space. Photo by Juan-Carlos Caceres.

tive Internet technologies that rely on tight, uninterrupted connections, like high-quality video teleconferencing. "Our musical senses can be useful, intuitive tools for understanding how a network is behaving at a given instance," he said.[33]

More recently, Chafe has composed music from data stemming from medical seizures; from real-time data on the levels of CO_2, noise, temperature, humidity, light, and volatile organic compounds in a number of cities, through a project titled *Smog Music*; and even from data on the CO_2 emitted as a tomato ripens, reported by the *Los Angeles Times* with the headline, "Music of the (Delicious Reddish) Spheres."[34]

Chafe's sonification activities serve to further advance the radical interdisciplinarity that has characterized CCRMA from its origins—not simply the application of technology to music but also the application of musical insights and musical "senses" to bleeding-edge technical challenges, such that these diverse disciplines contribute to and change one another in mutually beneficial ways. Thus, these activities advance musical *and* technical aims. In fact, Chafe views sonification as a means of using the emotional connection inherent in musical composition to encourage people to engage with otherwise "dry" data. As Chafe remarked in a *Wired* magazine article on the *Smog Music* project, "Our intent is to [travel] under the source of these fluxes in a way that is somewhat emotionally meaningful."[35] Chafe's collaborator, Greg Niemeyer at the University of California at Berkeley's Center for New Media, elaborated, in turn, on how such connection could serve to encourage engagement, moving beyond passive perception to instead shape active behaviors:

> We think we found a way to make air quality a personal issue. ... What we're doing is not so much about sound and music and art—it's more about getting people to take interest in changing their behavior.[36]

Thus, the activity has spread, in a sense, beyond the labels of "music" versus "research," or "artistic activity" versus "technical activity," to emphasize how music and digital audio tools can facilitate emotional engagement with real-world problems. And, perhaps not surprisingly, there's a commercial aspect to the project as well: Niemeyer formed a partnership with Aclima Labs to commercialize the air-quality sensor.

Other recent CCRMA projects, too, have pushed beyond the boundaries of music and technology to engage other humanities and social science disciplines. For example, the Chavín de Huántar Archaeological Acoustics Project is a collaboration between archeology, acoustics, and electrical engineering. Its origins can be traced to Chowning's composition *Voices*, which was inspired by Pythia, the Oracle at Delphi, Greece. As Chowning writes in the program notes for *Voices*, "The oracles were often associated with caves and chasms and at Delphi it may have been that volatile vapors, at times emanating from an opening in the rock, enhanced the ecstatic state of the Pythia."[37] In preparing for the 2005 premier of *Voices*, Chowning searched the Internet for ancient sites having interesting acoustics. He came across an article in the *Stanford* magazine about Professor John Rick's 2001 discovery of twenty ceremonial Strombus shell trumpets at the Chavín de Huántar site in Peru.

Chowning arranged a meeting with Rick, graduate student Patte Huang, and Jonathan Abel, a CCRMA consulting professor who has been involved with several audio companies and is an expert on digital signal processing and acoustics. The group met in a seminar room at CCRMA where graduate student Miriam Kolar happened to be doing some work. Kolar's background, perhaps not surprisingly, includes an MFA degree and experience as a recording engineer in Los Angeles, prior to joining the CCRMA PhD program. In the seminar room, Kolar asked if she could listen in on the conversation. She quickly moved from observer to lead investigator for what would become the Chavín de Huántar Archaeological Acoustics Project.

Rick, the anthropologist, had the hunch that acoustics were a big part of the Chavín site; archeologist Luis Lumbreras had described acoustic features of the site in the 1970s. Neither Rick not Lumbreras, however, had the technical knowledge to measure and analyze these acoustic properties. Thus, as Abel tells the story, when Chowning approached Rick, Rick's response was, "Oh, my god, a real-life acoustic scientist!"[38]

Beginning in 2008, the team (which would eventually include Chris Chafe, Perry Cook, Julius Smith, and other CCRMA faculty and students) began to visit the site to make detailed acoustic measurements. Their work was supported by both academic and commercial sources: The Stanford Institute for Creativity and the Arts provided equipment and travel funds, while Meyer Sound, Countryman Associates, Sennheiser, and Network-Sound provided both equipment and consulting expertise.

The Chavín collaboration is particularly notable in that it has helped to ferment a new interdisciplinary field of acoustic archaeology. In the Chavín case, the team has demonstrated how the physical structure of the site enabled certain acoustic phenomena that were used for ritualistic purposes. In other cases, different teams of researchers have examined the acoustic properties of archeological sites ranging from Stonehenge to the canyons of Utah.[39]

CCRMA researchers have used similar techniques to collaborate with art historians. Bissera Pentcheva, an associate professor of art and art history at Stanford, has long studied the Hagia Sophia, the grand and glittering sixth-century Great Church of Constantinople (now Istanbul). One of Pentcheva's goals has been to convey the experience of actually being in the church, which is intimately tied to both the building's art and use. As the website for the Icons of Sound project, the formal name of the collaboration, states:

> At sunrise and sunset the marble and gold visually simulate the quiver of water as light streaming through the windows animates the polished surfaces. This sensation of moving water, achieved through the visual animacy of shimmering surfaces, was simultaneously enhanced by the wet acoustics of the space. With echoes lasting slightly over 10 seconds, human breath emptied in the form of chanting was transformed into the sound of water splashing against the walls.

Hagia Sophia challenges our contemporary expectation of the intelligibility of language. We are accustomed to hear the spoken or sung word clearly in dry, non-reverberant spaces in order to decode the encoded message. By contrast, the wet acoustics of Hagia Sophia blur the intelligibility of the message, making words sound like emanation, emerging from the depth of the sea. Not surprisingly, much of the ritual in Hagia Sophia involved chanting and not recitative speech.[40]

Jonathan Abel, the electrical engineer and acoustics expert, is a collaborator on the Icons of Sound project, as well. In a 2012 interview, he explained how the acoustic environment shaped both the experience and construction:

The Hagia Sophia is a super-reverberant space. People sing differently in it. How the performance and the space interact is something that directly relates to the experience you have in the space, that directly relates to how these spaces were built and came about and were refined. [41]

Thus, the opportunity lies in understanding how the acoustic features of the Hagia Sophia shape the experience of the space itself and the performance of music originally composed with the space in mind.

The challenge lies in measuring the Hagia Sophia. Part of this challenge is cultural, owing to the site's continued religious significance, and part of the challenge is technical, given the unique acoustics of the space. As Abel explains:

There are all of these problems that come up that you won't think about until you have an application. We wanted to reproduce the acoustics of Hagia Sophia. You can't just show up [at Hagia Sophia] with a bunch of loudspeakers and recording equipment [owing to the building's continued religious and cultural significance] and make the usual acoustics measurements. So we devised a way to get what we needed from a balloon pop recording. We never would have done that if it weren't for the project.

The team ultimately convinced a guard at the site to pop a balloon so that they could measure the sound. Abel describes what happened next:

Just as the museum was closing, Bissera [Pentcheva, the art and art history professor] got a guard to pop a balloon. After two, three seconds, someone starts making a little bit of noise. After five seconds, everybody starts talking, even though you can still hear the balloon pop fading—the place has an eleven-second-long reverb. Back at CCRMA, we started looking at how to extrapolate room responses through noise and below the noise floor, another thing we wouldn't have studied had it not been for the application. It turns out that what we came up with is also useful for cleaning up impulse responses used in convolution reverbs.[42]

As Abel's commentary indicates, the attempt to measure the Hagia Sophia for the purpose of art history and musical performance immediately implicated broader cultural issues and it suggested new technical challenges that inspired further contributions. Abel, incidentally, also served as cofounder and chief technology officer of Universal Audio, which makes high-end audio equipment for recording studios.

Later in the interview, Abel returns to the Hagia Sophia example to reflect on how his interactions with art history have shaped his technical work:

> I am definitely learning about acoustics. ... I am starting to think about issues like the interaction of a space with a musical performance, the notion that these guys will get in there [the Hagia Sophia] and sing a drone and they will shift their frequency by like a few cents to find the resonance; or, the way a singer will prolong the sound to accommodate a reverb that is really long lasting; or, the way that someone will glide between notes a little bit differently because the room is making it sound weird when they're at an intermediate note. ... I think the things I've learned really more have to do with perspective. There's work that I wouldn't have been doing [had I not engaged with the humanities]. But beyond that, I think I listen from a different perspective, which is kind of interesting. It is totally fun.[43]

Today, in fact, Abel is taking the insights developed from the study of Chavín de Huántar and the Hagia Sophia and is applying them toward understanding the geometry of the subterranean cracks created by petroleum fracking operations.

Forty years ago, when first proposing CCRMA to the NEA, Chowning wrote:

> The extraordinary results already obtained [in computer music] have occurred in those few instances where scientists and musicians have taken the opportunity to bring their respective skills to bear on problems of common interest in a rich interdisciplinary environment. It is an example of cooperation, but more, an expression of the freedom of intellect and invention, where creative minds from diverse disciplines have joined in a common goal to produce fundamental knowledge which must be the source for new music, and to produce works of art which reflect the scientific-technological riches of the present.[44]

Today, CCRMA continues to leverage the multivocality of technologies, such as the signal processing techniques that Abel develops, to intertwine interdisciplinary pursuits with commercial endeavors against a backdrop of open innovation. Far from resting on past accomplishments, this approach has led CCRMA participants to engage an ever expanding range of disciplines and activities, generating novelty at diverse intersections.

9 Coda

Today, digital music is widespread: Our phones function as musical instruments and media players, electronic keyboards fill shelves at Target and Walmart, and entry-level Apple computers carry far more processing power and more sophisticated music software than CCRMA's $87,500 Samson Box. As we reflect on the surge of digital music into everyday life, CCRMA deserves much of the credit: the center's faculty, staff, and students invented and commercialized key technologies; they populate academic programs and commercial firms around the world; and, perhaps most important, their success with crossing disciplinary boundaries, engaging in open innovation, and commercializing their research added legitimacy to these activities, facilitating the emergence of other computer music groups and encouraging other explorations at the boundaries of technical and artistic, commercial and academic.

At the same time, it would be a mistake to view this progression simply as another story tied to the inexorable march of technology: CCRMA's history reveals that the center's role in the computer music revolution was neither inevitable nor predetermined. Indeed, there were many junctures where the center could easily have failed—or failed even to begin. For instance, absent Mathews's generosity in sharing the Music IV program or Poole's assistance in running Music IV at Stanford, Chowning might have left Stanford as a graduate student; absent Stanford's remarkable reversal on Chowning's tenure case, his experiments in computer music might have served as a warning rather than an inspiration for others who would pursue novel programs as assistant professors; absent Yamaha's gamble in developing FM or the System Development Foundation's $2.3 million lifeline in 1982, the center might have run out of operating funds.

Critically, the same activities that spelled opportunity for the center—integrating diverse disciplines, engaging in invention alongside composition, and tuning in to commercial aims—also presented its greatest challenges. For example, Chowning's novel engagement of artificial intelligence and audio engineering, his development of technologies for use in composition, and his unusual consideration of the diffusion of these technologies beyond the confines of Stanford all raised early questions among administrators and funders alike. The CCRMA account, therefore, is not one in which interdisciplinarity, open innovation, and commercialization simply yield success; rather, it is an account in which CCRMA's specific approach to and leveraging of these activities enabled it to emerge and to become a sustaining site for computer music and digital audio.

Most pointedly, CCRMA's history also provides a detailed appreciation of how these difference activities are fully intertwined and coevolve. For example, successful technology commercialization, as with the Yamaha DX7, can provide both resources and legitimacy for an emergent academic field such as computer music. As Chowning remarked in a 2008 interview, "We [CCRMA] would not have existed but for that [FM] patent. We would have been gone."[1] In fact, even the *potential* of resources can lure in reluctant participants. For instance, in the same interview, Chowning argued, "[The fact] that this happened [the FM patent and CCRMA's associated success] and that a musician with no training [did it] was used by lots of people at other universities to get support from the university ... 'Look, it can happen here as well.'" At the same time, these effects are not unidirectional; rather, commercialization efforts can simultaneously restructure or reorder priorities in these fields in different ways, as evident in both the FM and Sondius cases.[2]

Similarly, open innovation and open sharing can facilitate interdisciplinarity at the same time that they facilitate commercialization. Recall, for example, Chowning's early boundary crossing between music and computer science, which was made possible by Mathews's sharing, and Smule's use of open source software for its iPhone apps. The point is that the activities associated with these different themes—interdisciplinarity, open innovation, and commercialization—influence and reinforce one another.

In turn, this perspective points to a need to broaden and reconsider existing literatures that touch on only limited aspects of this relationship. The existing literature on university technology transfer and research commercialization, for instance, has offered detailed attention to how and why faculty engage in technology transfer; to the role of university technology-transfer offices; and to the role of university and government policies.[3] It has largely overlooked, however, how interdisciplinary work can both undergird and result from commercialization efforts. Moreover, this literature has offered little attention to the ways in which commercial firms can serve roles beyond that of "downstream recipient" of university research.[4]

Similarly, the coevolutionary perspective advanced by the CCRMA account broadens the literature on open innovation. This literature has focused on the motivations for individuals and organizations to engage in open and user innovation, and the strategic dilemmas that can accompany such activity.[5] It has largely overlooked, however, the ways in which academic inventors may be conceptualized as "user innovators," how university technology transfer efforts may shape user communities, and how emergent academic disciplines may both depend on and contribute to open innovation efforts that involve diverse participants with widely varying motivations.[6]

Finally, work on interdisciplinarity has focused on the history of interdisciplinary work and on barriers to its execution. This literature has given scant attention, however, to commercialization and technology transfer as important influences on interdisciplinary collaboration and the emergence of new disciplines.[7] In turn, as CCRMA's history makes clear, a more complete understanding of any of these literatures independently requires consideration of all of them collectively.

Multivocality

CCRMA's intertwining of these diverse activities signals the crucial role of multivocality in the center's history. Multivocality, as discussed, is the tactical capacity of an individual or organization to sustain multiple attributions to its activities.[8] At the intersection of interdisciplinarity, open innovation, and commercialization, CCRMA personnel continually leveraged the fact that the same activities could be interpreted differently by different groups, and thus valued on different grounds. For example, the National Science Foundation, the Office of Naval Research, and the California Arts Council might all value a research project on new digital signal processing techniques, but for very different reasons: where the NSF may see scientific advancement, the US Navy may see sonar applications, and the California Arts Council may see new musical compositions. Thus, multivocality enabled CCRMA to operate across boundaries, be they between academic and commercial interests, artistic versus scientific pursuits, or basic versus applied research. Moreover, CCRMA leveraged multivocality to build relationships with, and to draw critical support from, a wide range of people and organizations. In other words, CCRMA's skill at multivocality enabled them not only to work across boundaries, but also to find success precisely as a result of this work.

One of the most critical underlying skills of the CCRMA group lies, therefore, in the ability to reinterpret—to transpose a tool or a concept from one context to another and to generate novelty in the process.[9] Paul Kirk, the composer who took a CCRMA summer workshop in the 1970s and subsequently enrolled as a graduate student, offers a poignant example of such transposition when he describes how early interactions with the artificial intelligence (AI) group forced musicians to reconceptualize music in AI terms, and simultaneously highlighted to AI researchers the similarities between their field and music:

> [The AI researchers were] interested in discrete pattern matching and getting their robots to work and recognize things ... [So, then] I told them that I was trying to do compositional systems: I was looking for the same type of pattern recognition and if I could then expand [a musical] pattern or contract that pattern, but [show that] it was still a pattern. Whether I could rotate the pattern or compress the pattern, but [show that] it was still a recognizable [musical] pattern. Then, they got interested because they said, "Well that's our field and now we can talk to you." I said, "Okay, great, great." Then they dropped into English. [Laughter.][10]

Kirk found that reinterpreting a melody as a general pattern, and thus reframing a musical problem as a pattern-matching problem, allowed him to connect with AI researchers and to apply their AI insights to issues in musical composition.

The similarity between musical composition and software coding, in fact, is a repeating theme at CCRMA. As Chowning explained in a 2005 *Mix Magazine* interview:

> Music is a symbolic art ... musicians are used to writing things on paper and hearing them later. So they have to deal with symbols, things that are some distance away from where they are at the sensory level. It might be why music was the first of the arts to make so much artistic use of the computer.[11]

Chowning sees symmetry between composition and software coding because both activities rely on symbolic representations that are removed from the ultimate execution or performance.

Ge Wang, the CCRMA assistant professor and Smule cofounder, made a similar point in a 2012 interview, while focusing on the aesthetic components of music and software and on the writing process itself:

> The feeling is very similar. In both approaches [music composition and software coding], I think there is a heavy aesthetic component to it. ... You have something [e.g., a goal] in mind, but you also have something in mind of how you want to achieve that [goal] and how you actually negotiate this openness. ...
>
> Also, in both cases, building the gears and putting them next to each other and watching them spin in some kind of machination or synchrony can be pretty magical. I like setting processes in motion, and in that [way], writing music and writing software are very much alike. They both, for me at least, involve a lot of tinkering ... You have to try a lot of different things. ...
>
> Then, there are all these little rewards along the way when you get a passage working or you get a little feature or something working in the software and then that allows you to see more of what the final product is going to be. When that happens, I want to keep going.[12]

Although music and software may seem far apart—and certainly seemed worlds apart as Mathews, Chowning, and other pioneers engaged in their early work—the processes behind them can be very similar.

In fact, Paul Kirk expanded on the analogy, describing how he later applied musical composition to his work in designing enterprise software systems:

> [I moved] into enterprise architecture, which is understanding "How does your business actually flow, how is that aided in terms of information, [and] how is that put together – the entities, the attributes." Actually, that is the same style of thinking of, "How do you write a symphony?" And it's the same style of thinking of, "How do you write a theater piece?" ... It's just now, instead of thinking about writing a ballet, plus the story and the film and everything else, I'm thinking about what's the business about. It's the same method of thinking. It's just about something else. ... Every skill that I ever learned from thinking about music translates over. The beautiful thing [is that] everything that I learned at CCRMA translates over.[13]

These reflections serve to unearth the key to the puzzle of CCRMA's emergence and sustenance: CCRMA succeeds through its multivocality. Its participants envision abstract connections that facilitate multiple interpretations of the same activity; they sing the same tune differently to different audiences, engaging diverse groups with diverse aims in diverse activities by highlighting the commonalities among them.

Technological Underpinnings

This analysis of CCRMA also extends work on multivocality by foregrounding the role of technologies and technological artifacts. Thus, whereas research on multivocality has emphasized different interpretations of individuals' and organizations' actions and statements, the CCRMA case highlights how technologies and technological artifacts can facilitate and undergird these multiple interpretations.

Scholars have long acknowledged how technologies are embedded in social systems and how technologies afford flexibility in interpretation and use.[14] Building on these ideas, and speaking directly to differences in technology interpretation across groups, sociologists have proposed that technologies can serve as *boundary objects*.[15] Susan Leigh Star notes that a boundary object possesses three attributes. The first attribute is "interpretive flexibility," which refers to how different social groups can have different interpretations of the same technological artifact.[16] This first attribute supports a second one: boundary objects allow different groups to work together without consensus, drawing upon their unique interpretations.[17] Finally, boundary objects are most useful at the organizational level.[18]

Many of the technologies used and developed by CCRMA personnel exhibit these same features. The computer, as used by CCRMA, is one obvious example. In their 1974 NEA grant application, Chowning, Leland Smith, and Al Cohen referenced the different applications of the computer at Bell Labs and noted their intention to maintain the technology attributes that facilitated such diversity: "Based on this past experience, the proposed [CCRMA] facility will maintain those attributes of generality, flexibility, and precision which have been of utmost importance in the research performed to date."[19] Similarly, CCRMA alumnus Dick Moore, who went on to operate UC San Diego's computer music center, wrote in 1979, "The computer may be viewed as a general purpose tool with the unprecedented function of extending our power of mind, as other tools extend our muscular or sensorial powers."[20] Generality and flexibility are important because they afford different interpretations by different groups.

Other CCRMA technologies, too, exhibited these features. For example, the acoustic analysis techniques described in chapter 8 could be applied to archeological explorations or to the design of concert halls. The haptic feedback mechanisms that graduate student Brent Gillespie developed could enable a single keyboard to emulate the action of a piano, organ, or harpsichord, or they could serve as aids for disabled people. Thus, by virtue of their flexibility, these technologies appealed to multiple groups and could, therefore, bring these groups together. Indeed, as Pierce would write in a letter of recommendation for Chowning: "Starting from essentially nothing, he has brought diverse talents together into a field of common general interest."[21]

At the same time, the different uses and interpretations of CCRMA technologies extend conceptualizations of boundary objects in useful ways. For example, boundary object researchers have focused primarily on bringing together different groups that each adhere to their own perspective.[22] In the CCRMA case, however, these groups—such as musicians and engineers—permanently *shift* their perceptions as a result of interactions facilitated by boundary objects.[23] As a result, the emphasis at CCRMA is not on mediation, but rather on creation—on recombination and novelty as a result of bringing diverse groups together.

In considering these different groups, it is worth emphasizing, too, that CCRMA's use and development of technologies brought together not just diverse academic fields, but also diverse elements of society—military and National Security Agency personnel with hippie band members; well-heeled businessmen with avant-garde composers; high-society philanthropists with struggling graduate students; and Latin American and French musicians with artificial intelligence pioneers. Much more than simply "lying between," therefore, CCRMA's use of boundary objects emphasizes the creation of novelty at diverse intersections.

In turn, the CCRMA case also shows how boundary objects facilitate what might be termed *instrumental ambiguity*. Thus, technologies not only facilitate multiple interpretations, as the literature emphasizes, but also enable this ambiguity to be used strategically. Julius Smith, for example, described how the ambiguity of digital signal processing (DSP) enabled him to pursue musical interests while working on Cold War–era national security projects:

I graduated [and] got a job, a nice postdoc at Systems Control Technology, doing the same kinds of things I was doing at ESL [Electromagnetic Systems Laboratories, a Sunnyvale, California company started by former Secretary of Defense William Perry]—basically, signal processing for esoteric government agencies. They needed a lot of signal processing in those days, during the Cold War. [Laughter.] It was a great way to learn signal processing. Once again, I had audio signal processing in my mind. But for my day job, I did high-frequency radio communications signal processing, or I did underwater acoustics signal processing. But the math was the same, so in my mind I was working on stuff I was going to use for music.[24]

In other words, Smith leveraged the ambiguity of DSP to pursue multiple interests under the radar of his employer. In this way, boundary objects like DSP not only enable music and defense applications to connect, but also enable individuals and groups to pursue different interests simultaneously. Herein lies the connection between technologies and multivocality: CCRMA participants leverage the flexibility of technologies that they use and develop to facilitate multiple interpretations of their actions and activities more generally. Rather than seeking "closure," or the dominance of one interpretation, they work to maintain ambiguity that can be strategically leveraged to maintain diverse relationships, activities, and goals.[25]

Music: The Cantus Firmus

In music, a *cantus firmus* is a melody that forms the foundation of a composition. In turn, music itself is the cantus firmus of CCRMA's people and activities. Music was a shared love of both John Pierce and Max Mathews, the Bell Labs pioneers who were so instrumental in facilitating Chowning's early activity.[26] Chowning's own motivations were musical, despite his significant commercial success with FM. Similarly, Chris Chafe, who currently serves as CCRMA's director, described music as the common bond among CCRMA's diverse participants:

Everyone has in common a musical foundation. Whether they're a composer or a player or one of these people that make their music in the studio. ... It's interesting. You know, composition is very broad—defining it you have all varieties. ... But it's the glue.[27]

Chafe, in fact, argues that CCRMA's close affiliation with the Stanford Department of Music is important for maintaining its accessibility:

Imagine the facility being located in a more technical department what the barrier would be for musicians approaching: would they feel that they're free to come join the project if it were headed towards engineering?[28]

Chafe's point is that music is widely accessible: Musicians and engineers alike—and, indeed, peoples of all stripes and types—can be drawn to it.[29]

At CCRMA, the accessibility of music is tied to an emphasis on music, not technology, as the end goal. In turn, engineers value musicians as musicians, not simply as "musical engineers." Here, MIT's Media Lab provides an instructive contrast. As Stewart Brand described in his 1987 book on the Media Lab:

> There are a number of artists working in the Media Lab itself, especially in music and in the Visible Language Workshop run by Muriel Cooper, but most of the legions of artists that would like to get in and play with Lab goodies are turned away. "This is not an advanced art school, we don't have an art curriculum," explains [Nicholas] Negroponte [the Media Lab Director]. "It's a highly technical environment. If people with some art background prepare themselves academically to participate directly in technical innovation, then they're welcome."[30]

To be clear, MIT's Media Lab has been enormously influential and collaborative, including several exchanges with both CCRMA and IRCAM.[31] Nevertheless, CCRMA's location in the music school has proven critical to its own success. At CCRMA, a musician with no technical knowledge is *not* turned away. In fact, CCRMA finds value in such individuals because they bring new perspectives—encouraging, for example, CCRMA software programmers to reconsider user interfaces and usability from the perspective of "non-techies." Thus, music is what Ge Wang calls a "gateway drug": it lures a diverse set of participants into the intersection of artistic creativity and technology, welcoming them with familiarity even as it suggests new possibilities.

Of course, musicians and musical concerns also lead to the creation of new technologies. Sometimes, composers themselves engage in such innovation. Chowning provides a marquee example: his tenacity coupled with his compositional aims led to one of the most celebrated digital music inventions of all time (FM synthesis). David A. Jaffe's work on physical modeling synthesis, Juan Pampin's work on spectral modeling software, and Bill Schottstaedt's work on CLM all provide further examples of composer-led innovation.

In other cases, musical needs suggest technical challenges for composers and engineers to pursue in collaboration with one another. As Andy Moorer, CCRMA alumnus and celebrated electrical engineer, explained:

> [Musical] composition was just a fountain of ideas and technical challenges. You know what engineers do: We like to find problems and solve them. And [in] this

richness and boiling of [musical] ideas, so many technical issues and technical problems came up—a few of which, a very, very few of which, we could actually look at and solve.[32]

Thus, even for engineers, musical goals serve to orient problem solving.

The point is that despite CCRMA's many technological and commercial contributions, music is the ultimate aim and the ultimate barometer by which value is judged. As Moorer continued:

I would say the role of composition was that it provided a context and a framework and a way to value the technological contributions. A technological contribution was valuable or good if it made one step more progress to some of the things that the composers wanted to do. That's how I felt about it.[33]

John Grey, the CCRMA cofounder, similarly argued, "Compared to other places ... we [CCRMA] were actually interested in ... creating beautiful sound as opposed to just waveforms. At the root of the whole adventure was, 'How do you create a beautiful sound?'"[34]

Music, therefore, serves multiple roles at CCRMA. First, it entices participation by a wide range of participants. Second, it suggests research and technology-development directions. Third, it highlights applications. (Recall how CCRMA industrial affiliates reflected on musical performances as "proofs of concept" that showed the potential of emerging technologies.) Finally, music provides "meaning" to technical pursuits. In 1999, Andy Moorer received an Academy Award for his technical achievements. As he shared with all of Hollywood—and the world—in his acceptance speech:

I thank John Chowning, for showing me that there is music in mathematics. ... that beautiful technology does not necessarily make beautiful music. That technology, scientific knowledge, is meaningless without being applied to human issues, human problems. And what could be more human than the arts itself and the nobility of applying the most detailed of our scientific knowledge to the questions of making and understanding and appreciating music itself?[35]

A Final Flourish

Today, a new generation of musicians, engineers, composers, scientists, product designers, and humanists is taking hold at CCRMA. Their phones carry far more computational power than did early computers at Stanford and Bell Labs. Their laptops carry more music software than Mathews, Chowning, and others might have imagined in the 1960s. High-speed wireless networks connect them to a wide range of computer music enthusiasts scattered, literally, around the world—all of whom can access the same free and open source software.

The environment in which they practice their art has changed, too: university administrators and national organizations alike now extol the virtues of interdisciplinarity; the popular and academic literatures alike now emphasize the role of open innovation in technology development efforts; and economic development groups around the world now praise universities as fountains of innovation. Yet the underlying driver at CCRMA—an intense curiosity about the relationships between music and technology, and a strong desire to engage a broad community in this intersection—remains unchanged.

Ge Wang, the young CCRMA professor whose work with the Stanford Mobile Phone Orchestra opened this book, may capture the sentiment best:

> I asked [my advisor, CCRMA alum Perry Cook], "What do you expect of me as a grad student?" This was towards the end as I was almost graduating. His answer was, "Really all I expect of my grad students is that they do fun interesting things that have an impact." That pretty much captures it. ... At the end of the day, we're here because of the music and because of people. Those are the two things. Technology is just the conduit. I think a good metric to think about [whether we're] on the right track is "let's try to make a lot of music" and "let's try to measure how and if we are changing people's lives."[36]

Clearly, CCRMA has succeeded on both counts.

Appendix: Interviews Conducted by Author

Interviewee Name	Date	Location
Jonathan Abel	6/28/12	Palo Alto, CA
Rene Causse	3/17/11	Paris, FR
Chris Chafe	3/1/02	Palo Alto, CA
John Chowning	7/27/05	Palo Alto, CA
John Chowning	3/25/08	Palo Alto, CA
John Chowning	4/18/08	Palo Alto, CA
John Chowning	5/13/08	Palo Alto, CA
Perry Cook	3/17/14	Applegate, OR
Michael Fingerhut	3/22/11	Paris, FR
Andrew Gerszo	3/25/11	Paris, FR
John Grey	3/18/14	Sebastopol, CA
David A. Jaffe	4/1/09	Berkeley, CA
Paul Kirk	10/9/07	San Jose, CA
Joe Koepnick	8/13/04	Palo Alto, CA
Fernando López-Lezcano	12/7/12	Palo Alto, CA
Gareth Loy	10/23/12	Palo Alto, CA
Max Mathews	5/21/08	Palo Alto, CA
Mike McNabb	4/17/09	San Francisco, CA
Andy Moorer	4/1/09	(via telephone)
Nick Porcaro	8/17/04	(via telephone)
Niels Reimers	6/25/12	Carmel, CA
Xavier Rodet	3/22/11	Paris, FR
Fred Rousseau	3/21/11	Paris, FR
Jon Sandelin	2/8/05	Palo Alto, CA
Pat Scandalis	8/12/04	Redwood City, CA

Bill Schottstaedt	6/28/12	Palo Alto, CA
Julius Smith	7/28/04	Palo Alto, CA
Julius Smith	3/1/07	Palo Alto, CA
Julius Smith	4/17/08	Palo Alto, CA
Julius Smith	5/13/08	Palo Alto, CA
Leland Smith	5/22/08	Palo Alto, CA
John Strawn	6/11/13	San Francisco, CA
Scott Van Duyne	9/1/04	Palo Alto, CA
Hugues Vinet	3/21/11	Paris, FR
Avery Wang	5/3/06	Palo Alto, CA
Ge Wang	6/29/12	Palo Alto, CA
Mary Watanabe	7/29/04	Palo Alto, CA

Notes

Chapter 1

1. To the question of what constitutes a musical instrument, Ge Wang, the MoPhO's director, is fond of noting that a Stradivarius violin in his hands may not be an instrument—for Wang does not play a string instrument—while a bucket and two sticks in the hands of a talented percussionist most certainly constitute an instrument. Interview with Ge Wang conducted by Andrew Nelson on June 29, 2012, in Palo Alto, California. In subsequent notes, unless another interviewer is named, the interviewer is Andrew Nelson and the date and location of the interview are listed in the appendix.

2. See, e.g., Levitt and March 1988, Levinthal and March 1993.

3. Klein 1990, 11. Scholars have proposed various terms with subtle differences in meaning for work that engages multiple disciplines, including *interdisciplinary, transdisciplinary, multidisciplinary,* and *cross-disciplinary*. These different terms reflect concerns with the composition of a team versus the focus of a research project; with the inclusion of multiple scientific disciplines or multiple disciplines in general; and with the mixing versus fusion of disciplines. See Barry and Born 2013; Frodeman, Klein, and Mitcham 2010; Jantsch 1947; Lawrence and Després 2004.

4. Rhoten and Parker 2004. See also Derrick, Falk-Krzesinski, and Roberts 2011; Jacobs and Frickel 2009; Lattuca 2001; Salter and Hearn 1996.

5. Mody and Nelson 2013. Radical interdisciplinarity thus borrows elements from the concepts of transdisciplinary, multidisciplinary, and cross-disciplinary research, emphasizing an equal (nonhierarchical) partnership between diverse disciplines and the generation of new knowledge as a result of this partnership.

6. Barry and Born 2013; Jacobs and Frickel 2009; Rhoten and Parker 2004.

7. Chesbrough 2003. See also Chesbrough, Vanhaverbeke, and West 2008; Dahlander and Gann 2010; Perkmann and West 2013; West et al. 2014.

8. Oudshoorn and Pinch 2003, Kline and Pinch 1996.

9. Von Hippel 2005. See also Franke and Shah 2003; Morrison, Roberts, and von Hippel 2000; Shah and Tripsas 2007.

10. Ferraro and O'Mahony 2012; Lakhani and von Hippel 2003; Murray and O'Mahony 2007; O'Mahony 2003; West 2003; West and Gallagher 2006.

11. David and Greenstein 1990; Farrell and Saloner 1985; Katz and Shapiro 1985.

12. Sterne 2012.

13. David 1985. Composer Wendy Carlos uses the QWERTY analogy to describe how Western music seems to be locked in to a particular tuning standard: "[As] with Dvorak replacing QWERTY, it's difficult to challenge any sort of standard, once that standard has persisted for more than one generation. We all tend to forget the precariousness with which all standards are birthed, and grant those that come before us a sacrosanct status which is likely unjustifiable, and which the original designers might, if alive today, find quite laughable." Wendy Carlos, quoted in Haken, Tellman, and Wolfe 1998. See also Besen and Farrell 1994; David 1987; David and Greenstein 1990; Farrell and Saloner 1985.

14. Berman 2012; "Innovation's Golden Goose" 2002; Press and Washburn 2000; Wright, Birley, and Mosey 2004.

15. For an overview of this literature, see Rothaermel, Agung, and Jiang 2007; Perkmann and West 2013.

16. For examples of work on faculty involvement and perceptions, see Jensen and Thursby 2001; Link, Siegel, and Bozeman 2007; Owen-Smith and Powell 2001a,b. For examples of work on the role of technology transfer offices, see Siegel, Waldman, and Link 2003; Friedman and Silberman 2003. For examples of work on the role of policies, see Audretsch, Grilo, and Thurik 2007; Bozeman 2000; Kenney and Patton 2009, 2011; Lockett et al. 2005. For examples of work on processes and mechanisms, see Autio and Laamanen 1995; Harmon et al. 1997; Perkmann and Walsh 2007.

17. Mowery et al. 1999, 2001, 2004; Mowery and Sampat 2005. For a broader treatise on how market considerations came to infuse university research, see Berman 2012.

18. Link, Siegel, and Bozeman 2007; Grimpe and Fier 2010. Indeed, recent research indicates that consulting agreements, hiring of recent graduates, publications, and industrial affiliate programs are far more important and influential than patents and licenses alone. See Agrawal and Henderson 2002; Cohen, Nelson, and Walsh 2002; Nelson 2012.

19. Powell et al. 2005, 1138. See also Burt 1992; Padgett and Ansell 1993; Padgett and Powell 2012; Suthers et al. 2013; White 1985, 1992.

20. Powell et al. 2005.

21. Padgett and Ansell 1993, 1263. See also Ferraro, Etzion, and Gehman 2014.

22. As quoted in Hertelendy 1975.

Chapter 2

1. This chapter draws heavily on Mody and Nelson 2013. Terman's papers in the Stanford University Archives include correspondence and reports that detail his work at the lab: Stanford University Archives, SC0160. For further commentary on the Radio Research Laboratory, see Brown 1999; Blank 2009; Lécuyer 2006.

2. Hughes 1989; Leslie 1993.

3. Geiger and Sá 2008; Lenoir et al. 2004; Rosenberg and Nelson 1994.

4. Rosenberg and Nelson 1994.

5. Ibid., 326.

6. Rosenberg and Steinmueller 2013.

7. Elliott [1937] 1977, 24.

8. Berman 2012.

9. Gillmor 2004.

10. Terman, quoted in Lowen 1997, 96.

11. The National Science Foundation's "Survey of Federal Funds for Research and Development" tracks these trends. In an analysis, Paula Stephan (2010) notes that the amount of money spent by the US government on colleges and universities grew by a factor of 6 from 1955 to 1967.

12. Lenoir et al. 2004.

13. See Leslie 1993, chap. 6; See Lécuyer 2006, chap. 3.

14. Mody and Nelson 2013.

15. Terman, quoted in Leslie 1993, 54.

16. Leslie 1987.

17. See Mody 2012; Leslie 1993; Wisnioski 2003. At the same time, some policy makers proposed punishing universities that let campus unrest go too far, tying funding to an absence of student disruptions or to on-campus military recruitment. Berman 2012, 36.

18. Huggins, quoted in Leslie 1993, 232.

19. Ashley 1971.

20. Mody 2012.

21. Mody and Nelson 2013.

22. Kline 1971.

23. Scholars use the term *Mode 2 science* to refer to science that is driven by problems of the lay population. In turn, a common perception, as Zierhofer and Burger (2007, 51) write, is that "scientifically coping with urgent life-world problems calls for interdisciplinary participatory research." See also Gibbons et al. 1994; Nowotny, Scott, and Gibbons 2001.

24. Lyman 1971.

25. Mody and Nelson 2013. To be sure, interdisciplinary research has a long history, as documented by Balsiger (2004), Klein (1990), and others. Moreover, the Manhattan Project and other initiatives clearly demonstrated government support for such research. My point is that both public perceptions and federal funding priorities changed during this time period to emphasize it further.

26. Nelson 2005.

27. Elliott [1937] 1977, 198–199.

28. Davis and Nilan 1989, 44.

29. Mody and Nelson 2013.

30. Roose and Andersen 1970, 48.

Chapter 3

1. As Chowning recalled, "There were lots of good musicians in the service," and he had the chance to meet many of them, including famed jazz saxophonist Cannonball Adderley. Interview with John Chowning conducted by Vincent Plush on May 31, 1983, in Palo Alto, California. Nelson (2005) contains a significantly compressed version of the history reported in this chapter.

2. Plush 1983.

3. Supported by the Radiodiffusion Télévision Française (RTF) in Paris, Schaeffer switched to tape recorders in the early 1950s.

4. Holmes 2008; Manning 2004.

5. Ross 2007.

6. Manning 2004.

7. Ibid., 40.

8. Holmes 2008; Manning 2004.

9. Manning 2004.

10. Plush 1983.

11. Ibid.

12. Ibid.

13. Ibid.

14. Ibid.

15. Interview with Chowning, March 25, 2008. See also Bernstein 2008.

16. Although the organizational shift was accompanied by the departure of the original participants, the CCM continues to serve as an important center for electronic music (Bernstein 2008).

17. Bailie 1982.

18. Chowning, quoted in Jungleib 1987.

19. Plush 1983.

20. Mathews 1963.

21. The first computer to play music was the CSIRAC in Australia (Doornbusch 2005).

22. Means 2005b.

23. Ibid.

24. See Sterne 2012. Of course, as Sterne argues, there are many intermediate steps between the desire for telephonic message compression and perceptual audio coding.

25. Means 2005b.

26. Ibid. Mathews recounts the same story in Park 2009.

27. The sampling rate is tied to the bandwidth or frequency range. Thus, Mathews's 10,000 numbers per second yielded a bandwidth of 5,000 cycles per second or hertz (Hz). Generally, humans can hear the frequency range from 20 to 20,000 Hz. The compact disc standard uses a sampling rate of 44,100 numbers per second, yielding an upper frequency limit of 22,050 Hz.

28. Mathews 1963, 554.

29. Reid 2001.

30. Wisnioski (2012, 2013) traces the various motivations for corporate and government engagement with art in this period, offering special attention to the group E.A.T. (Experiments in Art and Technology). A former Bell Labs electrical engineer, Billy Klüver, formed E.A.T. to establish partnerships between engineers and musicians.

31. Chadabe 2000.

32. Interview with Chowning, May 13, 2008.

33. Chowning, quoted in Jungleib 1987.

34. Means 2005a.

35. Interview with Mathews.

36. Mathews et al. 1969.

37. Park 2009, 12.

38. Buchanan 1983; Earnest 1973. In her account of IRCAM, Georgina Born (1995) also notes links between early computer music and the defense sector, since the defense sector had precious computing resources.

39. Chowning 1993. The AI Project used a PDP-1 with an IBM 1301 disk drive until 1966. The IBM 7090 was the computer center's mainframe. It was used to run Mathews's Music IV program but, with the exception of the disk drive, was not used by SAIL. In 1966, a PDP-6 replaced the PDP-1, followed by a PDP-10 in 1967. David Poole wrote a version of Music IV in DEC assembly language for the PDP-6(10), the core of which was used until the Samson Box arrived in 1977.

40. Interview with L. Smith.

41. Ibid.

42. Plush 1983.

43. Interview with Chowning, March 25, 2008.

44. Ibid. See also Chowning 1993.

45. Padgett and Powell 2012; Scott 2001, 2003.

46. Farjoun 2002; Holm 1995; Meyer 2003.

47. Interview with Chowning, May 13, 2008.

48. Ibid.

49. Kockelmans 2003; Organization for Economic Cooperation and Development 1972; Weingart and Stehr 2000.

50. Nelson 2005.

51. Interview with L. Smith.

52. Ibid.

53. Smith's professional history is detailed in an appendix in John Chowning, Leland Smith, and Al Cohen, "The Computer Music Facility: A New Musical Medium," Proposal to the National Endowment for the Arts, June 18, 1974, Stanford University Archives, SC0634.

54. Interview with L. Smith.

55. Similar faculty–student relationships remain the norm at CCRMA. In a 2012 interview, Jonathan Abel, a consulting professor at CCRMA, shared: "[In some programs, students are] pointed in a certain direction. They are basically being mentored and sort of watched over and guided by the professor who has a target ... in mind. Well, at CCRMA, *I* am following the *students*. What happens is we admit two PhD students a year, and they have a full ride. They work on what they are interested in. The professor follows the interest of the students." Interview with Abel.

56. Interview with L. Smith.

57. Stanford University Department of Music 1982.

58. Milne 1979.

59. Interview with McNabb.

60. Allen 2007.

61. Seelig 2012. See also Kristensen 2004.

62. ABC News, "The Deep Dive," *Nightline*, aired 13 July 1999.

63. Apple Inc.'s new campus emphasizes many of these same design features, down to the glass-clad spaceship-like ring structure nestled in the foothills off of Interstate 280 (about 10 miles south of where the D.C. Power facility stood). Vanhemert 2013. In a study of a contemporary audio engineering group, Joseph Klett illustrates how even small features of a physical environment, such as whether windows are open, can shape how audio engineers go about their work and engage with sound. Klett 2014.

64. Interview with Schottstaedt.

65. Interview with Moorer.

66. Dayal 2011.

67. Interview with Chowning, May 13, 2008.

68. Interview with McNabb.

69. Interview with Strawn.

70. Later, the computer music group installed an "audio switch" that enabled each speaker to be turned off or to select different sources. As Bill Schottstaedt described it, however, even the possibility that others were listening shaped one's work process: "We had a thing called the audio switch. You could just switch to the various places and hear exactly what this person is doing. You knew that while you were doing some music, everyone else could hear what you were doing. That made you concentrate, that was a great thing. ... You couldn't just sit there and strum and hum and make yourself happy [laughter], you had to actually think, 'I'm writing a piece of music that other people are going to listen to. I'm not just here to screw around.'" In fact, most early users shared that they simply left their speakers turned on at almost all times. Interview with Schottstaedt.

71. Ibid.

72. Interview with Moorer.

73. Moorer would go on to design and lead the SoundDroid project at Lucasfilm, developing a large-scale digital signal processor used for the sounds in *Return of the Jedi*, *Indiana Jones and the Temple of Doom*, and other films. He would later cofound the firm Sonic Solutions, whose NoNOISE process is used to restore vintage recordings. Moorer won a Grammy Award in 1999 for his contributions to audio editing for films. Interview with Moorer. See also Rubin 2006.

74. Interview with Moorer.

75. Interview with Schottstaedt.

76. Means 2005a.

77. Chowning 1973; Terman 1947.

78. Chowning 1973. Peter Manning (2004, 193–195) offers a good description of FM.

79. Means 2005a. David Poole made an on-the-spot change to the synthesis code for Chowning that allowed for negative increments to the sin table. Later, at a summer workshop in 1969, engineer George Gucker gave a thorough analysis of FM when Mathews introduced his book, *The Technology of Computer Music* (Mathews et al. 1969).

80. Plush 1983.

81. Jean-Claude Risset, email message to the author, January 31, 2014. Risset, too, had been inspired by Mathews's 1963 *Science* article. As a physics graduate student at the École Normale Supérieure de Paris, Risset persuaded his advisor to send him to Bell Labs to work with Mathews. Risset stayed at Bell for more than two years, shifting his emphasis from physics to computer music and making a number of important contributions to the field. His composition *Mutations* (1969) is one of the first to use FM. Park 2009.

82. Interview with Chowning, March 25, 2008. Risset recalled that during the 1967 visit to Bell Labs, Chowning also discussed FM with distinguished mathematician Stephen Rice. Jean-Claude Risset, email to author, January 31, 2014.

83. Risset and Mathews 1969, 23.

84. Means 2005a.

85. Plush 1983.

86. Interview with John Chowning conducted by Alison Chaiken on April 13, 2006, at the KFJC studios in Los Altos Hills, California.

87. Program for the Audio Engineering Society 34th Convention, April 29–May 2, 1968, Hollywood, California, Stanford University Archives, SC0634.

88. Ibid.

89. The use of electronic music in radio and television commercials in this period also played a critical role in exposing large numbers of people to new electronic sounds (Taylor 2012).

90. Interview with Chowning, March 25, 2008.

91. Plush 1983.

92. Ibid.

93. Plush 1983; see also Bernstein 2008.

94. Interview with Moorer.

95. University of California at San Diego 1969.

96. Rubin 1994.

97. Plush 1983.

98. "Turenas" is an anagram of "natures." Chowning wrote in his 1973 article about FM, "Perhaps the most surprising aspect of the FM technique is the seemingly limited control imposed by 'nature' over the evolution of the individual spectral components, proves to be no limitation at all as far as subjective impression is concerned" (Chowning 1973, 533–534). Thus, he gives a subtle nod to his musical composition in an engineering article. It is worth noting that Loren Rush's composition from the same period, *A Little Traveling Music* (1971/1973), also simulated moving sound sources and featured evolving sounds.

99. Rubin 1994.

100. At an outdoor CCRMA concert in 2012, I heard one attendee remark to his neighbor, "If a UFO landed here right now, that would be least weird thing."

101. Jackson 2013; Pinch and Bijsterveld 2003.

102. In fact, Paul Théberge (1997) adopts this phrase as the title of his book on music technology.

103. Interview with Loy.

104. Morrison, Roberts, and von Hippel 2000; Shah and Tripsas 2007; von Hippel 2005.

105. Interview with L. Smith.

106. Oppenheimer 1984.

107. Interview with Chowning, March 25, 2008. The technology is described in US Patent 3,665,105.

108. Interview with Reimers. See also Mowery and Sampat 2001.

109. Interview with Reimers. Reimers also notes, "[Of course], there were notable exceptions, where the company patent officer was central to a partnership," but his point is that an emphasis on patent rights could overshadow collaboration.

110. Wiesendanger 2000; interview with Reimers.

111. Interview with Reimers.

112. Interview with Moorer.

113. Interview with Reimers.

114. See the following canonical texts: Bijker, Hughes, and Pinch 1987; Hughes 1993; Latour and Woolgar 1986. In turn, Hargadon and Douglas (2001) develop the role of institutional influences in these processes.

115. Option and Exclusive License Agreement between Stanford University and GRT Corporation, September 24, 1969, Stanford Office of Technology Licensing files. "GRT" is an acronym for "General Recorded Tape." Their interest was based on taped examples of moving sound sources that had been generated on the PDP-10. GRT, in turn, built the real-time hardware prototype that Moorer mentioned. When they dropped the license option, they gave the prototype to Stanford.

116. Bertil Nordin, letter to Neils [*sic*] Reimers, December 3, 1971. Stanford Office of Technology Licensing files.

117. Interview with Chowning, March 25, 2008.

118. Interview with Chowning, May 13, 2008.

119. Interview with Moorer.

120. Johnstone 1994.

121. Stanford University Office of Technology Licensing 1992.

122. In fact, Niels Reimers later noted that the Hammond evaluation team included an organ performance artist, who later shared that he had argued strongly for Hammond to partner with Stanford. His view did not prevail. Niels Reimers, email message to the author, February 3, 2014.

123. Stanford University 1993.

124. Plush 1983.

125. Ibid.

126. Ibid.

Chapter 4

1. Rhoten and Parker 2004. See also Derrick, Falk-Krzesinski, and Roberts 2011; Jacobs and Frickel 2009.

2. Chowning 1971.

3. Chowning 1973. It is notable, too, that Chowning lists his affiliation on this article as the Stanford Artificial Intelligence Laboratory, not the Stanford Department of Music (though his biographical sketch at the end does describe his position in the music department).

4. John Pierce papers, Huntington Library, Box 5, Folder Misc. Correspondence H–Z 1973–79.

5. Interview with Moorer.

6. Plush 1983. Incidentally, Tcherepnin, who had studied with Boulez in Europe and held teaching positions at the San Francisco Conservatory of Music and at Stanford, met similar skepticism when he moved to Harvard in 1972. As the *Harvard Magazine* reported in a 2013 retrospective on 1973: "Assistant professor Ivan Tcherepnin proposes a new course, Music 159: 'Composition with the Electronic Medium.' Though he anticipates resistance from his department—which is inherently distrustful of the new technology—his course is approved for the following year. The concern is raised, however, that offering credit for 'tinkering with electronics' could set the stage for credit courses in such topics as basket-weaving and woodworking." Yesterday's News 2013.

7. Padgett and Ansell 1993; Powell et al. 2005; Obstfeld 2005; Burt 1992.

8. Rhoten and Parker 2004. See also Becher and Trowler 2001; Jacobs 2014.

9. Interview with L. Smith.

10. As Grey recalled in a 2014 interview, he first encountered the use of the computer for music cognition research through Walter Dowling, who was then a new

faculty member at UCLA. Grey, who had been using analog synthesizers, realized, "Holy crap, you can create a waveform here that's stable compared to electronic synthesis ... [and] you can start to explore things like how the brain processes music." Interview with Grey.

11. Grey worked with Roger Shepard at Stanford. Prior to joining the Stanford psychology faculty, Shepard himself worked at Bell Labs.

12. Grey 1975, 16.

13. As one 2007 master's thesis summarizes Grey's contributions: "[Grey's] use of multidimensional scaling [a statistical approach] and electronically manipulated test tones foreshadowed the direction that timbral research would take." Mintz 2007, 29.

14. Leland Smith and John Chowning, "Computer Simulation of Music Instrument Tones in Reverberant Spaces," Proposal to the National Science Foundation (1974), Stanford University Archives, SC0634. Tenure letter for Chowning, from John Pierce papers, Huntington Library, Box 5, Folder Misc. Correspondence H–Z 1973–99. Unless otherwise noted, all letters, memos, invention disclosures, grant proposals, and miscellaneous documents cited in this chapter can be found in the Stanford University Archives, SC0634.

15. John Chowning, Leland Smith, and Albert Cohen, "The Computer Music Facility: A New Musical Medium," proposal to the National Endowment for the Arts, June 18, 1974.

16. Ibid.

17. Interview with Chowning, March 25, 2008.

18. Lehrman 2005a.

19. The Stanford University Archives contain two undated proposals, each of which makes reference to an NSF/NEA proposal "in preparation." Stanford University Archives, SC0634, Box 1.

20. March 2010.

21. Pierre Boulez, letter to Albert Cohen, July 26, 1974.

22. Albert Cohen, email to author, July 1, 2003.

23. Albert Cohen, letter to Pierre Boulez, August 23, 1974.

24. Nicholas Snowman, letter to Albert Cohen, October 23, 1974.

25. Tircuit 1975, 32.

26. Interview with Mathews.

27. Yasunori Mochida, letter to John Chowning, December 13, 1974.

28. Invention disclosure by C. F. Quate for "Electronic Device for Converting Written Music to Audible Sound," Stanford Docket No. S74-09.

29. Invention disclosure by James Andy Moorer for "The All-Pass Digital Reverberator," Stanford Docket No. S74-33.

30. Yasunori Mochida, remarks at an assembly in honor of John Chowning, June 1986, mimeograph.

31. License and Technical Assistance Agreement between Stanford University and Nippon Gakki, March 19, 1975.

32. Plush 1983. John Grey also reflected on the high status of the IRCAM visitors: "These were idols. ... It was amazing. These guys were mammoth heroes—and they turned out to be delightful people. It was incredible. ... Berio was such a charming, gracious, hilarious, creative spirit. My God. And Pierre Boulez was ... maybe the biggest genius I've ever met. ... How he could think so musically? It was unbelievable. But, similarly, he was so personable at the same time—so warm and even grateful. What a beautiful man. It was amazing to just have these encounters with these guys." Interview with Grey.

33. Nicholas Snowman, letter to Albert Cohen, October 23, 1974.

34. John Chowning, letter to Howard Klein, October 31, 1979. Born (1995) also documents some of the linkages between CCRMA and IRCAM.

35. "Using the Stanford-IRCAM MUSIC Program," memo, November 15, 1977.

36. John Chowning, letter to Howard Klein, October 31, 1979.

37. "Proposal to Stanford University for a Digital Synthesizer," December 17, 1975; "Some of the History of Hardware at CCRMA," accessed April 22, 2014, https://ccrma.stanford.edu/guides/planetccrma/Some.html. Gareth Loy (2013) provides an excellent overview of the Samson Box.

38. Invention disclosure by John Chowning for "Software for Systems Concepts Digital Synthesizer," Stanford Docket No. S75-49. Peter Samson, letter to John Poitras, February 6, 1976.

39. Interview with Chowning, March 25, 2008.

40. Interview with Schottstaedt.

41. Interview with Mathews.

42. Interview with J. Smith, April 17, 2008.

43. Ibid.

44. Interview with McNabb.

45. Interview with McNabb. Jan Mattox, a composer active at CCRMA around the same time, made a similar point in a 1984 *Smithsonian Magazine* article: "It isn't that computers make it easier to compose. It can be just the opposite, in fact. I remember sitting here for a whole day, trying to adjust just a few milliseconds of a tone that wasn't sounding right" (Rich 1984).

46. Michael McNabb, "Musical and Electronic Media Compositions," accessed April 22, 2014, http://www.mcnabb.com/music/.

47. The film and soundtrack were re-released in 2012 as a 3D Blu-ray disk: AIX 86067 (2013), AIX Records, 2050 Granville Avenue, Los Angeles, California (Antonucci 2013).

48. Michael McNabb, "Musical and Electronic Media Compositions."

49. Interview with Loy.

50. Chowning as quoted in Ziegler and Gross 2005. See also interview of John Chowning conducted by Allison Chaiken on April 13, 2006, in San Jose, California (aired live on radio station KSJC).

51. Tom Roberts, "Algorithm My Rhythm: John Chowning's 'Stria' and the Discovery of FM Synthesis," January 25, 2012, accessed April, 22, 2014, http://herecomesthesounduk.blogspot.com/2012/01/algorithm-my-rhythm-john-chownings.html.

52. Serra and Wood 1988; Sommer 1982. This publicity also attracted new CCRMA participants. For example, Perry Cook read a detailed description of a CCRMA concert in *db Magazine*, prompting him to think, "This sounds like a really cool place." He subsequently enrolled as a Stanford PhD student in electrical engineering, based at CCRMA. Interview with Cook.

53. Maisel 2011.

54. Patte Wood to comp.music mailing list, October 5, 1992, https://groups.google.com/forum/#!msg/comp.music/mlsdE4d4StQ/RNUi6LnIxWEJ.

55. Interview with Chowning, May 13, 2008.

56. Of course, as Fred Turner (2010) points out, these groups were not entirely separate either.

57. Interview with López Lezcano.

58. Performance issues persist with electronic music. In a 2009 interview, composer David A. Jaffe argued, "[In performances], it's really important to have a clear cause-and-effect relationship. Otherwise, you could be up there, as Andy [Moorer] likes to say, 'Doing your taxes'—you know, typing on your laptop and nobody notices. And there's just a bunch of sound coming out and it's the most boring thing possible. ... I think it's more dramatic if you see a taiko drummer or something to see the cause-

and-effect relationship." Interview with Jaffe. Katz (2004) offers an extended discussion on the ways in which recording technologies intersect with the experience of a performance. See also Pinch and Bijsterveld 2003.

59. Review of National Science Foundation grant proposal BNS-7722385, "Experiments in Timbre Perception." The NSF, not surprisingly, awarded the grant. George Lynch, letter to Richard Lyman, April 25, 1978.

60. John Chowning, letter to Yasunori Mochida, April 25, 1978. See also Means 2005a.

61. John Pierce papers, Huntington Library, Box 5, Folder Misc. Correspondence H–Z 1973–79.

62. Interview with Gerszo.

63. Interview with Rodet.

64. Interview with Chowning, May 13, 2008.

65. Ibid.

66. Roads 1982.

67. John Chowning, letter to Gordon Bell, April 24, 1979.

68. Ibid.

69. "Summary of CCRMA hardware needs," June 14, 1979.

70. Interview with Chowning, April 18, 2008.

71. John Chowning, letter to Howard Klein, October 31, 1979.

72. John Chowning, memo to Arnice Streit, April 21, 1980.

73. John Chowning, letter to Mr. Kawakami, November 2, 1979.

74. John Chowning, letter to Howard Klein, October 31, 1979.

75. "Foundations with Music Interest," January 23, 1969.

76. "Plan for Funding System for CCRMA," memo, September 16, 1979. As potential fundraising targets, the memo lists individuals, corporations (Bell, Xerox, and Intel), and foundations (Sloan, IBM, Hewlett, Stauffer, Fletcher Jones, and Rockefeller).

77. John Chowning, letter to Anthony Meier, April 23, 1979; John Chowning, letter to Ellen Rush, September 19, 1979; John Chowning, letter to James Robertson, September 19, 1979; John Chowning, letter to Paul Hertelendy, September 17, 1979.

78. John Chowning, letter to Ellen Rush, September 19, 1979.

79. John Chowning, letter to Lewis Branscomb, July 3, 1979.

80. Lewis Branscomb, letter to John Chowning, July 16, 1979.

81. John Chowning, letter to Stephen White, July 3, 1979.

82. John Chowning, letter to Stephen White, September 14, 1979.

83. Stephen White, letter to John Chowning, October 17, 1979.

84. John Chowning, letter to John Sawyer, October 28, 1979.

85. James Morris, letter to John Chowning, November 14, 1979.

86. Howard Klein, letter to John Chowning, December 19, 1979; John Chowning, letter to Howard Klein, October 31, 1979; John Chowning, letter to Howard Klein, October 28, 1979.

87. John Chowning, letter to Max Mathews, January 4, 1980.

88. John Chowning, letter to Pierre Boulez, January 4, 1980; Pierre Boulez, letter to John Chowning, January 22, 1980.

89. John Chowning, memo to Arnice Streit, April 21, 1980, Stanford University Archives, SC0634. Grey would remain disconnected from CCRMA. In a 2014 interview, Grey noted that an experience in Bali in the mid-1970s had invigorated an interest in culturally based musical perceptions and in "the things that happen transitionally between notes in any particular instrument." In his 1979 NSF grant application, he proposed to study these phenomena by using the computer. When the NSF failed to support the project, a decision that Grey found "discouraging," he moved back into acoustic music. Interview with Grey.

90. John Chowning, letter to William McHenry, January 3, 1980. The L.A.W. Fund managed some of the charitable assets of Lila Acheson Wallace, a *Readers Digest* cofounder. The fund later merged with other Wallace foundations to become The Wallace Foundation, which focuses on learning and the arts.

91. Barnabas McHenry, letter to John Chowning, January 11, 1980.

92. John Chowning, letter to Barnabas McHenry, January 25, 1980.

93. Marguerite Ryan, letter to John Chowning, January 24, 1980.

94. John Chowning, letter to A. A. Heckman, January 3, 1980; Cynthia Gehrig, letter to Pierre Boulez, January 29, 1980.

95. John Chowning, letter to Paul Fromm, March 31, 1980.

96. Paul Fromm, letter to John Chowning, April 8, 1980; Paul Fromm, letter to John Chowning, May 2, 1980.

97. James Rosse, memo to Joel Smith, February 6, 1980.

98. John Chowning, letter to Howard Klein, January 24, 1980.

99. John Chowning, letter to Howard Klein, April 16, 1980.

100. Orneata Prawl, letter to John Chowning, April 28, 1980.

101. Richard Louttit, letter to John Chowning, October 17, 1980.

102. John Chowning, memo to Henry Organ, June 1, 1982.

103. Interview with Chowning, April 18, 2008.

104. Gareth Loy, who completed his DMA through CCRMA and later helped to build UC San Diego's computer music center, recalled his reaction when UCSD, too, was awarded a grant from SDF: "It was like we won a lottery that we did not even know we had entered!" As Loy remembered, SDF had preselected several institutions to receive funding, including Stanford and UCSD. Interview with Loy.

Chapter 5

1. Berman 2012; Geiger and Sá 2008.

2. "Fact Sheet: White House launches 'Startup America' initiative," accessed April 22, 2014, http://www.whitehouse.gov/startup-america-fact-sheet.

3. Berman 2012.

4. Association of University Technology Managers (AUTM) 2014.

5. Mowery et al. 2004; Colyvas et al. 2002.

6. Mowery et al. 2001.

7. George 2005.

8. Garud 1997.

9. Cowan, David, and Foray 2000.

10. Marie Thursby and colleagues have attempted to measure this contribution, finding that inventor involvement was critical in 40 to 70 percent of cases. See Rothaermel and Thursby 2005; Thursby and Thursby 2004. Fiona Murray emphasizes the ways in which licensing, consulting, advising, and other activities comingle (Murray 2002), and how inventors also can contribute social capital to commercialization efforts (Murray 2004).

11. Vinod Khosla, Stanford Entrepreneurial Thought Leaders seminar, April 24, 2002, accessed April 22, 2014, http://ecorner.stanford.edu/authorMaterialInfo.html?mid=30.

12. License and Technical Assistance Agreement between Stanford University and Nippon Gakki, March 19, 1975, Stanford University Archives, SC0634. Unless other-

wise noted, all letters, memos, reports, and miscellaneous documents cited in this chapter can be found in the Stanford University Archives, SC0634.

13. Niels Reimers, letter to Yasunori Mochida, March 18, 1976.

14. Ibid.

15. "Progress Report on the Development of the FM-type Musical Instrument," March 20, 1976.

16. Remarks by Yasunori Mochida at an assembly in honor of John Chowning, June 1986.

17. John Chowning, letter to Howard Klein, October 31, 1979.

18. License and Technical Assistance Agreement between Stanford University and Nippon Gakki, March 19, 1975.

19. Ibid.; John Chowning, letter to Howard Klein, October 31, 1979.

20. "Progress Report on the Development of the FM-type Musical Instrument," March 15, 1978.

21. As instrument designer Keith McMillen (1994) characterized the situation, "[With traditional keyboards], the greatest creative choice left to the musician is when to release it [the key]."

22. "Progress Report on the Development of the FM-type Musical Instrument," March 15, 1978.

23. John Chowning, letter to Yohei Nagai, April 18, 1978.

24. Yasunori Mochida, letter to Niels Reimers, August 30, 1978.

25. John Chowning, letter to Hiro Kato, April 12, 1979.

26. Interview with Chowning, March 25, 2008.

27. Interview with Chowning, July 27, 2005.

28. Schedule for July 1979 visit of John Chowning at Yamaha.

29. John Chowning, Telex to Yohei Nagai, April 29, 1980.

30. License Agreement between Stanford University and Nippon Gakki, May 1, 1981.

31. Yohei Nagai, letter to John Chowning, December 15, 1983.

32. Yohei Nagai, letter to John Chowning, January 18, 1984.

33. John Pierce, letter to Charles Smith, April 23, 1983.

34. "Progress Report on the Development of the FM-type Musical Instrument," March 1, 1981.

35. K. Hirano, letter to Niels Reimers, December 19, 1981.

36. Vic Amano, letter to Niels Reimers, March 3, 1982.

37. Chowning, quoted in Colbeck 1996, 135.

38. Interview with Mathews.

39. Yamaha sold over 160,000 DX7s. The Korg M1 eventually eclipsed the DX7's sales, though the DX7 remains the second-best-selling instrument in history. Holmes 2008, 257.

40. Mansfield 1986; Nordhaus 1969. Of course, debate is vigorous as to extent to which patents are necessary to serve this role and whether the inherent cost of such monopolies is worth the benefit. See, e.g., Gallini and Scotchmer 2002; Heller and Eisenberg 1998; Lessig 1999. Murray and Stern (2007) offer a novel evaluation of the extent to which intellectual property rights hinder the flow of knowledge.

41. License and Technical Assistance Agreement between Stanford University and Nippon Gakki, March 19, 1975.

42. Yasunori Mochida, letter to Niels Reimers, August 30, 1978.

43. Colbeck 1996.

44. Niels Reimers, memo to Al Test and Mike Hudnall, September 27, 1978.

45. Ibid.

46. Yohei Nagai, letter to John Chowning, February 13, 1980.

47. Niels Reimers, letter to Yohei Nagai, February 29, 1980. Reimers then contacted attorney Al Test to inquire as to whether Kawai could legally practice FM in light of the Stanford patent. Niels Reimers, letter to Aldo Test, March 6, 1980.

48. The idea surfaced in a March 1982 letter from Yamaha, which noted that a 1975 publication by Chowning "would be quite useful and strong evidence to invalidate the KAWAI's patent application about a digital reverberation circuit." In turn, Patte Wood, the CCRMA administrator, sent a letter to Yamaha to confirm that the article had been requested by and shared with a researcher at the University of Pennsylvania. The Stanford Math and Computer Science Library also replied, confirming that the article was publicly available in the library. Hiroyuki Ohba, letter to John Chowning, March 26, 1982; Patte Wood, letter to Hiroyuki Ohba, June 14, 1982; Richard Manuck, declaration, May 12, 1982.

49. The letter goes on to inquire about anticipated legal fees, which Yamaha was contractually obligated to share. Maki Kamiya, letter to Niels Reimers, August 4, 1981.

50. Memo to the file, October 28, 1981.

51. As Stanford personnel would learn, patents were not cut and dried. In 1979, Yamaha commissioned an attorney to look into the validity of the core Stanford FM patent. The analysis concluded that there was a "significant probability that the patent would be declared invalid in a court in the United States ... probably on the order of thirty percent." The largest issue, the attorney reasoned, concerned Chowning's early publications on the FM technique. Of course, the report was marked "Confidential" and neither Yamaha nor Stanford wished for competitors to see an opportunity. Yohei Nagai, letter to John Chowning, June 20, 1979.

52. Maki Kamiya, Telex to Niels Reimers, October 2, 1986.

53. Niels Reimers, letter to Maki Kamiya, October 15, 1986.

54. Yamaha chose an alternative route to pursue Casio: potential action through the US International Trade Commission, a quasi-judicial federal agency that can block unfair practices in import trade. In a memo to the file, Niels Reimers reported on an October 1987 license negotiation with Yamaha in Japan: "The possibility of Casio infringement was discussed. Casio uses a phase distortion method and has had a U.S. patent recently issued. What was not clear to us was whether the Casio instruments employ the teaching of the Casio patent or another technology, such as FM. Mr. Hiyoshi, in particular, was quite anxious that we aggressively investigate an infringement or ITC action vs. Casio. They believe, because of the Japanese patent system, it would be unlikely that a successful action could be brought against Casio in Japan because the Japanese system does not have the U.S. doctrine of equivalents. [The doctrine of equivalents allows a court to find patent infringement as long as the device in question is "equivalent" to the patented invention—even if the device falls outside the literal scope of the patent claim.] It was believed that although the phase distortion patent of Casio differs from FM, that we have a basis under the U.S. doctrine of equivalents to bring at least an ITC action." As Reimers would later report to Yamaha, however, ITC action hinged on the extent of manufacturing done in the United States by Yamaha versus Casio. Since Yamaha manufactured its products in Japan, the ITC would not support its claims. Thus, Reimers concludes his letter to Yamaha with the words, "I'm sorry this news is not more favorable." Niels Reimers, memo to Stanford Docket File S71-017, Stanford University Archives, SC0634; Niels Reimers, letter to Maki Kamiya, February 8, 1988.

55. Clive Liston, memo to Deans, Department Heads, Principal Investigators, and Sponsored Projects Administrators, August 18, 1980; Earl Cilley, memo, June 18, 1980.

56. "Barbara," memo to Patte Wood, September 16, 1980.

57. "Barbara," memo to Patte Wood, October 28, 1980.

58. Colyvas 2007; Sampat and Nelson 2002.

59. Interview with Chowning, March 25, 2008.

60. Interview with Chowning, April 18, 2008.

61. Allen Malcolm, letter to Maki Kamiya, February 23, 1988.

62. Yasunori Mochida, letter to John Chowning, March 18, 1980.

63. John Chowning, letter to Yasunori Mochida, April 16, 1980.

64. Dasgupta and David 1994. Dasgupta and David's description of science draws heavily upon Merton 1973. Subsequent work uses the labels *public science* and *private science* to refer to Dasgupta and David's categories of *science* and *technology*, respectively. See, e.g., Colyvas and Powell 2006; Owen-Smith 2003.

65. Edwards et al. 2001.

66. License and Technical Assistance Agreement between Stanford University and Nippon Gakki, March 19, 1975.

67. Ibid.

68. Ibid.

69. Interview with Sandelin.

70. License and Technical Assistance Agreement between Stanford University and Nippon Gakki, March 19, 1975.

71. License Agreement between Stanford University and Nippon Gakki, May 1, 1981.

72. Stanford and Yamaha changed the royalty arrangement, too, from $10 per instrument to one-half of 1 percent "of the selling price [wholesale] of a musical instrument that is made, used, sold or otherwise disposed of by [Yamaha] of its Subsidiaries." License Agreement between Stanford University and Nippon Gakki, May 1, 1981.

73. David Lovejoy, notes, December 2, 1983.

74. Maki Kamiya, Telex to Niels Reimers, October 19, 1983.

75. Remarks by Yasunori Mochida at an assembly in honor of John Chowning, June 1986.

76. Niels Reimers, memo to Stanford Docket File S71-017, November 4, 1987. Atari's overture to Yamaha is evident in Hiro Kato's letter to Niels Reimers, February 9, 1982.

77. Handwritten notes for Stanford's use in license negotiations, November 1986.

78. Niels Reimers, letter to Maki Kamiya, November 14, 1986.

79. Ibid.

80. Maki Kamiya, letter to Niels Reimers, November 17, 1986.

81. Hiro Kato, letter to John Chowning, November 18, 1986.

82. John Chowning, letter to Hiro Kato, November 26, 1986.

83. Ibid.

84. Niels Reimers, letter to Maki Kamiya, November 20, 1986.

85. Niels Reimers, letter to Yasunori Mochida, December 10, 1984.

86. John Chowning, letter to Norio Ohga, October 12, 1986.

87. John Chowning, Telex to Yasunori Mochida, October 31, 1986.

88. Niels Reimers, letter to Kazukiyo Ishimura, February 26, 1988.

89. Paul Jain, letter to Niels Reimers, January 23, 1991.

90. Niels Reimers, letter to Maki Kamiya, February 6, 1991.

91. Kosuke Kamo, letter to David Fehrman, July 10, 1991.

92. The Yamaha computer was model CX5M.

93. Johnstone 1994 and 1999.

94. Wang would go on to cofound the online music service Shazaam. Interview with Wang.

95. Interview with Cook. Media Vision itself would soon run into trouble. In May 1994, the company acknowledged that the Securities and Exchange Commission and the FBI were investigating it for securities fraud. The company subsequently filed for bankruptcy. Rebello and Hof 1994; Greenberg 1996.

96. Interview with Chowning, April 18, 2008.

Chapter 6

1. March and Simon 1958; Nelson and Winter 1982.

2. John Pierce, letter to Charles Smith, April 23, 1983, Stanford University Archives, SC0634. Unless otherwise noted, all letters, memos, reports, and miscellaneous documents cited in this chapter can be found in the Stanford University Archives, SC0634.

3. John Chowning, memo to Ewell Thomas, November 22, 1989.

4. Interview with Moorer. As Moorer later clarifies, the numbers of students were not exact; instead, his point is that many more students were affiliated with com-

puter music than with early music. It also is worth noting that Rice is a talented classical pianist.

5. John Chowning, letter to Laurent Boyle, September 26, 1994.

6. Parrish 2000. Jan Mattox, a CCRMA-affiliated composer, recalled in a 1984 interview that appeared in *Smithsonian Magazine*, "Several of the Grateful Dead have been coming to our concerts for years" (Rich 1984). Mattox herself would collaborate with Grateful Dead vocalist Bob Weir on her composition *Shaman*.

7. Grant application to the National Endowment for the Arts, "Composers Program," November 24, 1979.

8. Ibid.

9. Interview with Kirk.

10. John Chowning, memo to Ewell Thomas, November 22, 1989.

11. John Chowning, memo to Anne Peck, December 4, 1992.

12. Interview with Chowning, May 13, 2008.

13. Blau 1970.

14. Handwritten notes on "CCRMA Funding," January 21, 1987.

15. Following the 1989 Loma Prieta earthquake, the third floor of the Knoll was condemned and it stayed so for sixteen years, until the Knoll was completely renovated in 2005. As a result, CCRMA was housed, in part, in trailers next to the Knoll for the decade of the 1990s. (An adjacent trailer would house Yahoo as that company was just beginning.) The remodeled Knoll, incidentally, leverages architecture to reinforce collaboration: there are few assigned spaces and even fewer offices with doors. Instead, most people simply find an open workspace to do their work. The computers themselves are in a few large clusters, occupying the original ballroom and reception of the grand mansion. The conference rooms and classrooms feature walls that open to enlarge the spaces and to invite people in. Upstairs, there is a foosball table, couches, and a small kitchen—all with sweeping views of the San Francisco Bay. Arrayed throughout the building are musical sculptures, experimental instrument interfaces, various computer peripherals, posters and programs from past concerts, and, on the lowest level, a CCRMA "museum" that houses some of the earliest equipment (including a full array of historic Yamaha keyboards). These features of the space all serve functional roles. The foosball table, couches, and kitchen encourage informal conversations; open walls invite people into meetings and classes; the lack of formal offices and assigned spaces brings together new combinations of people on a continual basis; and the museum and concert posters provide a sense of shared history.

16. John Chowning, letter to Sherrill Milnes, February 4, 1985.

17. John Pierce, letter to William Hewlett, November 5, 1984; John Pierce, letter to David Packard, November 5, 1984.

18. John Pierce, letter to William Hewlett, November 5, 1984.

19. William Hewlett, letter to John Pierce, November 20, 1984. Hewlett's son, Walter, had already visited CCRMA. As Pierce wrote in a response letter to Packard, "[Walter Hewlett] has already been here, and it looks as if he will collaborate in work on a project here that is close to his interests. We heard a good deal about your son [Packard's son, David Woodley] from him." John Pierce, letter to David Packard, December 20, 1984.

20. David Packard, letter to John Pierce, December 13, 1984

21. The visit apparently happened on January 9, 1985, per a handwritten note by John Pierce. Unfortunately, Pierce did not have time to share with them details of CCRMA's financial needs. John Pierce, letter to William Hewlett, January 15, 1985;. John Pierce, letter to David Packard, January 15, 1985.

22. Nancy Bruno, office memo to John Chowning, February 1, 1985.

23. John Gilliland, office memo to Bill Dailey, John Hays, and David Mitchell, December 11, 1985.

24. "The World's Billionaires," *Forbes Magazine*, accessed April 22, 2014, http://www.forbes.com/profile/gordon-getty/.

25. John Gilliland, office memo to Bill Dailey, John Hays, and David Mitchell, December 11, 1985.

26. Ibid.

27. Interview with Chowning, May 13, 2008. John Chowning, letter to Gordon Getty, January 22, 1986.

28. John Chowning, letter to Louise Davies, November 12, 1984.

29. John Chowning, letter to Doreen Townsend, April 12, 1984.

30. Ibid.

31. John Gilliland, memo to Al Cohen and Nancy Bruno, December 13, 1985.

32. Donna Lawrence, memo to the record, August 6, 1986.

33. John Chowning, memo to Carolyn Lougee and Susan Schofield, January 14, 1985.

34. David and Greenstein 1990; Farrell and Saloner 1985; Katz and Shapiro 1985. Much of the literature on standards also addresses the possibility that a standard will be difficult to change, even if a majority of users would benefit from such a change. See David 1985; David and Greenstein 1990.

35. John Chowning, letter to Grant Smith, February 6, 1985; Grant Smith, letter to John Chowning, February 25, 1985.

36. John Chowning, letter to Howard Klein, October 31, 1979.

37. John Pierce, letter to Charles Smith, April 23, 1983.

38. John Chowning, letter to System Development Foundation, November 23, 1981.

39. Interview with Loy.

40. Schedule for SDF Music Group meeting at MIT, November 5–6, 1982.

41. Overview of research topics and groups for SDF meeting, February 4, 1983.

42. MIT Experimental Music Studio, Stanford CCRMA, and UCSD CARL, proposal to conduct research in computer music (preliminary).

43. Rob Poor, memo to Charlie Smith, March 29, 1984. Knuth had presented a proposed computer-generated music notation system at an early CCRMA colloquium.

44. John Chowning, email to Shoichi Suzuki, November 12, 1985.

45. Interview with Chowning, April 18, 2008.

46. Chowning used the book proceeds to purchase a Yamaha grand piano for the CCRMA recording studio.

47. John Chowning, letter to Yasunori Mochida, September 11, 1985.

48. Interview with J. Smith, April 17, 2008.

49. "Some of the History of Hardware at CCRMA," accessed April 22, 2014, https://ccrma.stanford.edu/guides/planetccrma/Some.html.

50. Interview with Moorer.

51. Interview with J. Smith, April 17, 2008.

52. Interview with Jaffe. Jaffe's full name is David Aaron Jaffe and he usually goes by David A. Jaffe to distinguish himself from another David Jaffe active in video games.

53. Interview with J. Smith, April 17, 2008.

54. Interview with Chowning, April 18, 2008.

55. Interview with J. Smith, April 17, 2008.

56. "Some of the History of Hardware at CCRMA."

57. Patte Wood, memo "To all users and formers users of the Foonly and Samson-box at CCRMA," November 15, 1990. The actual event appears to have been delayed until April 3, 1992, according to a later CCRMA report. Igoudin 1996, 16.

58. Patte Wood, memo "To all users and formers users of the Foonly and Samson-box at CCRMA," November 15, 1990. Gareth Loy (2013) provides a detailed overview of the Samson Box.

59. The double compact disk *Intercambio/Exchange* and its accompanying report capture the first three years of the exchange program. Robert Willey, "Report on Residency and Exchange Program in New Music Technology," Center for Research in Computing and the Arts, University of California at San Diego, accessed April 22, 2014, http://willshare.com/willeyrk/creative/recordings/intercambio.html.

60. In fact, CCRMA soon after appointed him as a lecturer and systems administrator, where he remains today. Ironically, López-Lezcano nearly failed to make it to Stanford: he was slated to go to UCSD. When the wife of the participant who was slated to go to Stanford became pregnant and when this participant's replacement expressed a preference to go to UCSD, López-Lezcano took the Stanford spot. Interview with López-Lezcano.

61. Interview with López-Lezcano. The first set of 68040 upgrade boards had been shipped to LIPM, but the truck was robbed between the airport and LIPM. López-Lezcano speculates that the boards ended up in a landfill.

62. Jaffe and Boynton 1989; Smith 1989.

63. Interview with J. Smith, April 17, 2008.

64. Julius Smith to the Music Kit distribution list, August 31, 1992. An email from John Chowning to Steve Jobs that May expresses Chowning's intention to assign graduate students to the MusicKit program. John Chowning, email to Steve Jobs, May 15, 1992.

65. David A. Jaffe to the Music Kit distribution list, October 28, 1992.

66. Interview with McNabb.

67. "Kalvos and Damian" 1997.

68. Pampin 1999.

69. Mike McNabb's website contains a detailed description of the piece, along with some photographs. Michael McNabb, "Musical and Electronic Media Compositions," accessed April 22, 2014, http://www.mcnabb.com/music/.

70. Mike McNabb, memo to John Chowning, Patte Wood, and Gayle Curtis, November 1, 1985.

71. John Chowning, letter to Steve Wozniak and Steve Jobs, May 21, 1984.

72. John Chowning, letter to Joseph Engelberger, January 15, 1985.

73. Joseph Engelberger, letter to John Chowning, February 11, 1985.

74. Ibid.

75. Michael McNabb, "Musical and Electronic Media Compositions."

76. Lokken 1986.

77. Hertelendy 1985.

78. Hertelendy 1986.

79. Grant application to the National Endowment for the Arts, March 14, 1986; Alvin H. Perimutter, Inc., proposal for "Computer Jam," May 21, 1987.

80. The same letter notes, "Bill Cosby's producer is also aware of the program with an interest in possibly having Cosby do the introduction." George Olczak, letter to Stephen Peeps, July 17, 1987.

81. Interview with Schottstaedt.

82. Interview with Cook.

83. John Chowning, memo to the National Endowment for the Arts, August 17, 1989.

84. Perry Cook and Dexter Morrill, Stanford University Invention Disclosure for "An Acoustical Brass MIDI Instrument."

85. Amato 1989.

86. Masaharu Kuwabara, letter to John Chowning, August 5, 1991.

87. Hugh Lusted, letter to Earl Schubert, December 9, 1991.

88. John Chowning, memo to Bob Byer, May 3, 1992. Today, BioControl Systems, the company that Knapp and Lusted started to commercialize their system, counts clients ranging from Johnson & Johnson to Sony to NASA.

89. Park 2009.

90. Manning 2004.

91. Grunwald 1995; Manning 2004.

92. Max Mathews, letter to G. L. Miller, February 29, 1988.

93. Joe Koepnick, letter to Roland Corp. president Ikutapo Kakehashi, April 16, 1990.

94. Max Mathews, memo, "Disposition of Radio Batons Made at CCRMA," March 7, 1991. Mathews continued his work on alternate controllers until his death in 2011, at the age of 84. A 2007 concert, appropriately titled "Influences: A Tribute Concert," celebrated his accomplishments and his numerous contributions to the field

of computer music. Compositions by Jon Appleton, Dexter Morrill, and Chris Chafe used Mathews's Radio Baton.

Chapter 7

1. Harris 1985.

2. Johnstone 1999.

3. Johnson 1982.

4. Of course, observers found fault with other US practices, too. In an influential 1980 article in the *Harvard Business Review*, Robert Hayes and William Abernathy (1980) blamed US underperformance on poor management practices and, specifically, on the ascendance of management by metrics rather than an emphasis on hands-on experience with technologies. A respondent article (Hill, Hitt, and Hoskisson 1988) in the *Academy of Management Executive* charged that diversification strategies and capital market pressures, too, were responsible for the crisis. The larger point, however, is that the 1970s and 1980s marked a period in which the United States worried about growing Japanese success tied to technology development efforts.

5. Hughes 2001.

6. Berman 2012.

7. Jaffe's own description of the work is available on his website, accessed April 22, 2014, http://www.jaffe.com.

8. Interview with Jaffe.

9. Smith 2010.

10. Interview with J. Smith, April 17, 2008.

11. Ibid.

12. Interview with J. Smith, May 13, 2008. Smith may have received reassurance, too, from the fact that Jim Angel, an electrical engineering professor, also served as the Stanford carillonneur for several decades.

13. Jaffe's comments are captured on the Internet Archive: David Jaffe, "Silicon Valley Breakdown," accessed April 22, 2014, http://archive.org/details/G_JAF_DAV_01.

14. Interview with Jaffe.

15. Joe Koepnick, memo to Anna Ranieri, October 24, 1988, Stanford University Archives, SC0634. Unless otherwise noted, all letters, memos, reports, and miscella-

neous documents cited in this chapter can be found in the Stanford University Archives, SC0634.

16. Schrieberg 1988.

17. Interview with Koepnick.

18. Joe Koepnick, letter to Maki Kamiya, August 31, 1988.

19. Kosuke Kamo, letter to Joe Koepnick, November 8, 1988.

20. Subsequent material in this chapter draws heavily on Nelson 2014.

21. Julius Smith, letter to Yohei Nagai, March 9, 1989.

22. Interview with Sandelin.

23. An overview of Smith's development of waveguide and of the initial licensees can be found in Grunwald 1992. The detailed licensing agreement for MediaVision is in the Stanford University archives: "Sondius Technology License Agreement," May 19, 1995. The OTL trademark plan details the strategy and components of the trademark: Office of Technology Licensing, "Technology Trademark Plan," May 13, 1993, Stanford OTL files.

24. The Stanford Office of Technology Licensing Docket for rDNA includes the full list of 464 licensees. These licensees are summarized in Nelson 2009.

25. Grunwald 1992.

26. Niels Reimers, Telex to Maki Kamiya, November 2, 1983.

27. Office of Technology Licensing, "Technology Trademark Plan," May 13, 1993, Stanford OTL files.

28. Interview with J. Smith, May 13, 2008.

29. Another challenge, according to Smith, was that the inventor receives licensing revenue from patents, but not trademark revenue. As Smith remarked, "The inventor pays for it, but doesn't get the benefit." Interview with J. Smith, July 28, 2004.

30. Interview with Watanabe.

31. Interview with J. Smith, May 13, 2008; Minnick 1990.

32. Porcaro et al. 1996.

33. Mary Watanabe, memo to Jim McGraw regarding Docket S97-500, November 1999, Stanford OTL files. Confirmation of the contracts with these developers is provided in: Joe Koepnick, letter to David A. Jaffe, October 7, 1993; Joe Koepnick, letter to Nick Porcaro, October 18, 1993.

34. Joe Koepnick, letter to Pat Scandalis, September 2, 1994.

35. Interview with Scandalis.

36. Robert Byer, letter to John Chowning, May 31, 1991; Patricia Devaney, memo to John Chowning and Julius Smith, June 10, 1992; Patricia Devaney, memo to Julius Smith, April 18, 1994.

37. John Chowning, letter to Robert Byer, April 2, 1991.

38. John Chowning, memo to Robert Byer, May 3, 1992.

39. Gregory (Pat) Scandalis, email message to Mary Watanabe, March 27, 1996, Stanford OTL files.

40. Interview with Schottstaedt.

41. Campbell et al. 2002; Hong and Walsh 2009; Walsh and Hong 2003.

42. Interview with Van Duyne.

43. Perry Cook, email to Julius Smith and Mary Watanabe, December 5, 1995, Stanford OTL files.

44. Cowell 2002.

45. Sondius accounting worksheets for fiscal year 1995–96.

46. Gary Williams, memo to Mary Watanabe, September 13, 1995.

47. Such behind-the-scenes relationships were not uncommon to resolve differences connected with Stanford's OTL. Jon Sandelin, a senior licensing associate, relayed one case in which the Stanford provost and a senior vice president at Motorola—the two were friends—stepped in to resolve an intellectual property disagreement between the two organizations. Interview with Sandelin.

48. Julius Smith, email to Patte Wood, April 5, 1994.

49. "VL1 at a glance," Sonicstate, accessed April 22, 2014, http://www.sonicstate.com/synth/yamaha_vl1/.

50. Ibid. Emphasis in original.

51. Colbeck 1996, 187.

52. Schrieberg 1998.

53. Ibid.

54. The Staccato licensing agreement is attached to Kosuke Kamo's letter to Mary Watanabe, July 9, 1997.

55. Interview with Koepnick.

56. Interview with J. Smith, May 13, 2008.

57. Interview with Scandalis.

58. Cowell 2002.

59. Interview with Scandalis. Recall Yamaha's initial response to the license option, in which they wrote that "FM is capable of producing tones of every tone color while DWT is applicable [only] to a specific tone color or colors." Kosuke Kamo, letter to Joe Koepnick, November 8, 1988.

60. Interview with Watanabe.

61. Interview with J. Smith, July 28, 2004.

62. Ibid.

63. Ibid.

Chapter 8

1. Interview with Schottstaedt.

2. López-Lezcano 2009. It is important to note that other computer music centers, too, contributed much to the free and open sharing of software. CCRMA graduates Dick Moore and Gareth Loy, for example, founded the Computer Audio Research Laboratory (CARL) at UC San Diego in 1980, with the explicit intention of creating and distributing open source software. (This idea, in fact, lured Loy away from Apple to UCSD.) The Carl System was a software package that UCSD distributed on magnetic tape, providing access to the various applications on the UCSD computer. Loy noted that they distributed 300–400 copies to both academia (e.g., MIT and Northwestern, though not Stanford since the Stanford system was not compatible) and industry (e.g., to EMU/Creative, which used it for product development). The package is still available on the Internet. Interview with Loy. See also Alex Di Nunzio, "Carl System," accessed April 22, 2014, http://www.musicainformatica.org/topics/carl-system.php.

3. Edwards et al. 2001.

4. Ibid.

5. Interview with Chowning, May 13, 2008.

6. Interview with Cook.

7. Ibid.

8. López-Lezcano 2009.

9. López-Lezcano 2005, 109.

10. Recall from chapter 6 that López-Lezcano first engaged with CCRMA through an exchange program facilitated by the move to standardized NeXT machines.

11. López-Lezcano 2005. Material in this section also derives from interview with López-Lezcano.

12. López-Lezcano 2009.

13. López-Lezcano 2005; Fernando López-Lezcano to PlanetCCRMA mailing list, January 31, 2004, http://ccrma-mail.stanford.edu/pipermail/planetccrma/2004-January/004141.html.

14. López-Lezcano 2005.

15. López-Lezcano 2009.

16. Interview with López-Lezcano.

17. Nelson 2012; Kline and Rosenberg 1986; Rosenberg 2004.

18. Julius Smith, email to author, February 12, 2014.

19. "The Industrial Affiliates Program," accessed April 22, 2014, https://ccrma.stanford.edu/affiliates/.

20. Ibid.

21. Interview with J. Smith, May 13, 2008.

22. The analysis in Nelson 2012 provides a quantitative sense of these different means of engaging with CCRMA. Far more commercial relationships transpire through employment agreements and open sharing through publications and performances than through patents and licenses. Murray (2004) elaborates on the importance of social capital in commercialization efforts, and Murray and O'Mahony (2007) describe the ways in which openness facilitates follow-on innovation.

23. Cook also serves on Smule's Board of Advisors.

24. Interview with Wang.

25. Ibid.

26. Ibid.

27. Kosman 2010.

28. Interview with Wang.

29. Ibid.

30. Hoge 2011. Notably, Shah and Tripsas (2007) use the phrase "accidental entrepreneur" in their research article on how users "create, evaluate, share and commercialize their ideas."

31. The "Method for Evaluating the Quality of Service of a Digital Network Connection" is US Patent 6,801,939. The "Distributed Acoustic Reverberator for Audio Collaboration" is US Patent 7,522,734.

32. CCRMA professor Jonathan Berger, among others, has also made important contributions to sonification, drawing upon the technique for several of his compositions. Supper (2012) reviews the role of sonfication as a scientific method. Sterne and Akiyama (2012) discuss the connections between sonification and other sonic practices.

33. Eisenberg 2002.

34. LaTempa 2007.

35. Hart 2010.

36. Ibid.

37. John Chowning's program notes for a 12 February 2012 concert at the Eastman Computer Music Center, accessed April 22, 2014, http://ecmc.rochester.edu/ecmc/ecmc.feb15.2011.program.pdf.

38. Interview with Abel.

39. Watson and Keating 1999.

40. A complete project description can be found online, accessed April 22, 2014, http://iconsofsound.stanford.edu.

41. Interview with Abel.

42. Ibid.

43. Ibid.

44. John Chowning, Leland Smith, and Albert Cohen, "The Computer Music Facility: A New Musical Medium," proposal to the National Endowment for the Arts, June 18, 1974, Stanford University Archives, SC0634.

Chapter 9

1. Interview with Chowning, April 18, 2008.

2. See also Owen-Smith and Powell 2001a.

3. See, e.g., Bozeman 2000; Friedman and Silberman 2003; Jensen and Thursby 2001; Kenney and Patton 2011; Owen-Smith and Powell 2001a,b; Siegel, Waldman, and Link 2003.

4. Of course, there are exceptions. See, e.g., Perkmann and Walsh 2007.

5. Chesbrough 2003. See also Chesbrough, Vanhaverbeke, and West 2008; Dahlander and Gann 2010; Jeppesen and Frederiksen 2006; Perkmann and West 2013.

6. Again, there are exceptions. Most notably, Katherine Strandburg (2009) has argued that most university inventors are "user innovators" who invent primarily to serve their own needs. Also, Cyrus Mody (2011) offers a detailed history of the development and commercialization of the scanning tunneling microscope, tying university involvement in its commercialization to a change in academic disciplines that used the tool.

7. See, e.g., Barry and Born 2013; Jacobs and Frickel 2009; Rhoten and Parker 2004. The portion of this literature that emphasizes "applied" work as a focus of interdisciplinary research gets closest to considering these relationships. Nevertheless, there are important differences between applied research on one hand and commercialization and its effects on the other.

8. Padgett and Powell 2012.

9. For a related discussion on transposition, see Powell, Packalen and Whittington 2012.

10. Interview with Kirk.

11. Lehrman 2005a.

12. Interview with Wang.

13. Interview with Kirk.

14. In fact, this point is the unifying theme of science and technology studies. For canonical texts, see Bijker, Hughes, and Pinch 1987; Hughes 1989; Latour and Woolgar 1986.

15. Bechky 2003; Carlile 2002; Star 2010; Star and Griesemer 1989.

16. Bijker 1987; Orlikowski 1992; Pinch and Bijker 1987.

17. In so doing, boundary objects can also give rise to what Cyrus Mody (2011) calls an *instrumental community*—a network of diverse people with a common interest in a particular scientific instrument. Of course, CCRMA differs from Mody's case in that the identity of the "instrument" itself as "scientific" versus "musical" is ambiguous, reflecting the more diverse groups that assemble around it.

18. Star 2010.

19. John Chowning, Leland Smith, and Albert Cohen, "The Computer Music Facility: A New Musical Medium," proposal to the National Endowment for the Arts, June 18, 1974, Stanford University Archives, SC0634.

20. Moore 1979.

21. John Pierce, letter to Wolfgang Kuhn [undated], John Pierce papers, Huntington Library, Box 5, Folder Misc. Correspondence H–Z, 1973–79.

22. See, e.g., Bechky 2003; Carlile 2002; Star and Griesemer 1989.

23. In this way, boundary objects at CCRMA represent what Pinch and Trocco label "liminal entities" that "can pass between different worlds ... can take on different meanings in these worlds and in the process transform these worlds" (Pinch and Trocco 2009, 208).

24. Interview with J. Smith, April 17, 2008.

25. For a discussion of strategic ambiguity, see Gioia, Nag, and Corley 2012. For examples of studies foregrounding closure around interpretive flexibility, see Bijker 1987; Klein and Kleinman 2002; Pinch and Bijker 1987.

26. Mathews joined the CCRMA faculty in 1997 and worked there until his death in 2011. In a 2008 interview that appeared in the *Computer Music Journal* (Park 2009), Mathews shared, "My training is as an engineer, and I consider that I'm not a composer. I'm not a professional performer of any instrument. I do love music. If I've done anything, I am an inventor of new instruments, and almost all the instruments I have invented are computer programs. ... If I am remembered for anything, I would like to be remembered as one of the inventors of new instruments." John Pierce also spent his final days at CCRMA, serving as a visiting professor until his death in 2002.

27. Interview with Chafe.

28. Ibid.

29. Julie Thompson Klein and Richard Parncutt (2010) argue that music may be inherently interdisciplinary since it is vested in creativity, it is widely appreciated beyond the academy, and it is nonverbal and thus amenable to different translations.

30. Brand 1987, 83.

31. For a deep analysis of MIT's engagement with the arts through the Center for Advanced Visual Studies, which predated the Media Lab, see Wisnioski 2013.

32. Interview with Moorer.

33. Ibid.

34. Interview with Grey.

35. Interview with Moorer.

36. Interview with Wang.

References

Agrawal, Ajay, and Rebecca Henderson. 2002. Putting patents in context: Exploring knowledge transfer from MIT. *Management Science* 48 (1): 44–60.

Allen, Thomas. 2007. Architecture and communication among product development engineers. *California Management Review* 49 (2): 23–41.

Amato, Ivan. 1989. Muscle melodies and brain refrains: Turning bioelectric signals into music. *Science News* 135 (April 1): 202–203.

Antonucci, Mike. 2013. Return to Mars. *Stanford Magazine* (May–June).

Ashley, Holt. 1971. New directions for engineering research. *Grindstone* 1 (February 22).

Association of University Technology Managers (AUTM). 2014. *AUTM U.S. Licensing Activity Survey, FY2012*. Deerfield, IL: AUTM.

Audretsch, David, Isabel Grilo, and Roy Thurik. 2007. *Handbook of Research on Entrepreneurship Policy*. Cheltenham: Edward Elgar.

Autio, Erkko, and Tomi Laamanen. 1995. Measurement and evaluation of technology transfer: Review of technology transfer mechanisms and indicators. *International Journal of Technology Management* 10 (7–8): 643–664.

Bailie, J. 1982. Computer music: A trend that's caught fire. *Stanford Daily*, July 20, 7.

Balsiger, Philiip. 2004. Supradisciplinary research practices: History, objectives and rationale. *Futures* 36 (4): 407–421.

Barry, Andrew, and Georgina Born. 2013. *Interdisciplinarity*. London: Routledge.

Becher, Tony, and Paul Trowler. 2001. *Academic Tribes and Territories: Intellectual Enquiry and the Culture of Disciplines*, 2nd ed. Buckingham: Open University Press.

Bechky, Beth. 2003. Object lessons: Workplace artifacts as representations of occupational jurisdiction. *American Journal of Sociology* 109:720–752.

Berman, Elizabeth Popp. 2012. *Creating the Market University: How Academic Science Became an Economic Engine*. Princeton, NJ: Princeton University Press.

Bernstein, David. 2008. *The San Francisco Tape Music Center: 1960s Counterculture and the Avant-Garde*. Berkeley: University of California Press.

Besen, Stanley, and Joseph Farrell. 1994. Choosing how to compete: Strategies and tactics in standardization. *Journal of Economic Perspectives* 8 (2): 117–131.

Bijker, W. E. 1987. The social construction of Bakelite: Toward a theory of invention. In *The Social Construction of Technological Systems: New Directions in the Sociology and History of Technology*, ed. W. Bijker, T. Hughes, and T. Pinch, 159–187. Cambridge, MA: MIT Press.

Bijker, Wiebe, Thomas Hughes, and Trevor Pinch, eds. 1987. *The Social Construction of Technological Systems: New Directions in the Sociology and History of Technology*. Cambridge, MA: MIT Press.

Blank, Steve. 2009. The secret life of Silicon Valley, part 6. http://steveblank.com/2009/04/27/the-secret-history-of-silicon-valley-part-vi-the-secret-life-of-fred-terman-and-stanford.

Blau, Peter. 1970. A formal theory of differentiation in organizations. *American Sociological Review* 35:201–218.

Born, Georgina. 1995. *Rationalizing Culture*. Berkeley, CA: University of California Press.

Bozeman, Barry. 2000. Technology transfer and public policy: A review of research and theory. *Research Policy* 29 (4): 627–655.

Brand, Stewart. 1987. *The Media Lab: Inventing the Future at MIT*. New York: Viking.

Brown, Louis. 1999. *A Radar History of World War II*. Philadelphia, PA: Institute of Physics Publishing.

Buchanan, Bruce. 1983. Introduction to the COMTEX Microfiche edition of memos from the Stanford University Artificial Intelligence Laboratory. *AI Magazine* 4 (4): 37–42.

Burt, Ronald. 1992. *Structural Holes: The Social Structure of Competition*. Cambridge, MA: Harvard University Press.

Campbell, Eric, Brian Clarridge, Manjusha Gokhale, Lauren Birenbaum, Stephen Hilgartner, Neil Holtzman, and David Blumenthal. 2002. Data withholding in academic genetics: Evidence from a national survey. *Journal of the American Medical Association* 287 (4): 473–480.

Carlile, Paul. 2002. A pragmatic view of knowledge and boundaries: Boundary objects in new product development. *Organization Science* 13:442–455.

Chadabe, Joel. 2000. The electronic century, part III: Computers and analog synthesizers. *Electronic Musician* (April 1).

Chesbrough, Henry. 2003. *Open Innovation: The New Imperative for Creating and Profiting from Technology*. Boston: Harvard Business Press.

Chesbrough, Henry, Wim Vanhaverbeke, and Joel West. 2008. *Open Innovation: Researching a New Paradigm*. Oxford: Oxford University Press.

Chowning, John. 1971. The simulation of moving sound sources. *Journal of the Audio Engineering Society* 19 (1): 2–6.

Chowning, John. 1973. The synthesis of complex audio spectra by means of frequency modulation. *Journal of the Audio Engineering Society* 21 (7): 526–534.

Chowning, John. 1993. Computer music: A grand adventure and some thoughts about loudness. In *Proceedings of the 1993 International Computer Music Conference* (Waseda University, Tokyo, Japan), September 10–15, 1993. San Francisco: International Computer Music Association.

Chowning, John, and David Bristow. 1987. *FM Theory and Applications: By Musicians, For Musicians*. Tokto: Yamaha Music Foundation.

Cohen, Wesley, Richard Nelson, and John Walsh. 2002. Links and impacts: The influence of public research on industrial R&D. *Management Science* 48:1–23.

Colbeck, Julian. 1996. *Keyfax: Omnibus Edition*. Emeryville, CA: MixBooks.

Colyvas, Jeannette. 2007. From divergent meanings to common practices: The early institutionalization of technology transfer in the life sciences at Stanford University. *Research Policy* 36 (4): 456–476.

Colyvas, Jeannette, Michael Crow, Annetine Gelijns, Roberto Mazzoleni, Richard R. Nelson, Nathan Rosenberg, and Bhaven N. Sampat. 2002. How do university inventions get into practice? *Management Science* 48 (1): 61–72.

Colyvas, Jeannette, and Walter Powell. 2006. Roads to institutionalization: The remaking of boundaries between public and private science. *Research in Organizational Behavior* 27:305–353.

Cowan, Robin, Paul David, and Dominique Foray. 2000. The explicit economics of knowledge codification and tacitness. *Industrial and Corporate Change* 9 (2): 211–253.

Cowell, Brian. 2002. Interview of Joe Bryan. *SonikMatter*. Accessed January 9, 2007, http://interview.sonikmatter.com/bryan/ (website no longer available).

Dahlander, Linus, and David Gann. 2010. How open is innovation? *Research Policy* 39 (6): 699–709.

Dasgupta, Partha, and Paul David. 1994. Toward a new economics of science. *Research Policy* 23:487–521.

David, Paul. 1985. Clio and the economics of QWERTY. *American Economic Review* 75 (2): 332–337.

David, Paul. 1987. Some new standards for the economics of standardization in the information age. In *Economic Policy and Technological Performance*, ed. P. Dasgupta and P. Stoneman, 206–239. London: Cambridge University Press.

David, Paul, and Shane Greenstein. 1990. The economics of compatibility standards: An introduction to recent research. *Economics of Innovation and New Technology* 1 (1–2): 3–41.

Davis, Margo, and Roxanne Nilan. 1989. *The Stanford Album: A Photographic History, 1885–1945*. Stanford: Stanford University Press.

Dayal, Geeta. 2011. Interview with Max Mathews. *Frieze Magazine*, May 9.

Derrick, Edward, Holly Falk-Krzesinski, and Melanie Roberts, eds. 2011. *Facilitating Interdisciplinary Research and Education: A Practical Guide*. Washington, DC: American Association for the Advancement of Science.

Doornbusch, Paul. 2005. *The Music of CSIRAC: Australia's First Computer Music*. Champaign, IL: Common Ground.

Earnest, Lester. 1973. Final report: The first ten years of artificial intelligence research at Stanford. Stanford Artificial Intelligence Laboratory Memo AIM-228, July.

Edwards, Michael, Johannes Goebel, Margaret Schedel, and John Young. 2001. CCRMA and intellectual property. *Computer Music Journal* 25 (1): 6–7.

Eisenberg, Anne. 2002. What's next; An aria with hiccups: The music of data networks. *New York Times*, December 19.

Elliott, Orrin Leslie. [1937] 1977. *Stanford University: The First Twenty-Five Years*. New York: Arno Press.

Farjoun, Moshe. 2002. The dialectics of institutional development in emerging and turbulent fields: The history of pricing conventions in the on-line database industry. *Academy of Management Journal* 45 (5): 848–874.

Farrell, Joseph, and Garth Saloner. 1985. Standardization, compatibility, and innovation. *Rand Journal of Economics* 16:70–83.

Ferraro, Fabrizio, Dror Etzion, and Joel Gehman. 2014. Tackling grand challenges pragmatically: Robust action revisited. Working paper. IESE Business School.

Ferraro, Fabrizio, and Siobhán O'Mahony. 2012. Managing the boundaries of an "open" project. In *The Emergence of Organizations and Markets*, ed. J. Padgett and W. W. Powell, 545–565. Princeton, NJ: Princeton University Press.

Franke, Nikolaus, and Sonali Shah. 2003. How communities support innovative activities: An exploration of assistance and sharing among end-users. *Research Policy* 32 (1): 157–178.

Friedman, Joseph, and Jonathan Silberman. 2003. University technology transfer: Do incentives, management, and location matter? *Journal of Technology Transfer* 28 (1): 17–30.

Frodeman, Robert, Julie Thompson Klein, and Carl Mitcham, eds. 2010. *The Oxford Handbook of Interdisciplinarity*. Oxford: Oxford University Press.

Gallini, Nancy, and Suzanne Scotchmer. 2002. Intellectual property: What is the best incentive system? In *Innovation Policy and the Economy*, vol. 2, ed. NBER. Cambridge, MA: MIT Press, 51–78.

Garud, Raghu. 1997. On the distinction between know-how, know-why, and know-what. *Advances in Strategic Management* 14:81–101.

Geiger, Roger, and Creso Sá. 2008. *Tapping the Riches of Science: Universities and the Promise of Economic Growth*. Cambridge, MA: Harvard University Press.

George, Gerry. 2005. Learning to be capable: Patenting and licensing at the Wisconsin Alumni Research Foundation 1925–2002. *Industrial and Corporate Change* 14 (1): 119–151.

Gibbons, Michael, Camille Limoges, Helga Nowotny, Simon Schwartzman, Peter Scott, and Martin Trow. 1994. *The New Production of Knowledge: The Dynamics of Science and Research in Contemporary Societies*. London: Sage.

Gillmor, C. Stewart. 2004. *Fred Terman at Stanford: Building a Discipline, a University, and Silicon Valley*. Stanford: Stanford University Press.

Gioia, Dennis, Rajiv Nag, and Kevin Corley. 2012. Visionary ambiguity and strategic change: The virtue of vagueness in launching major organizational change. *Journal of Management Inquiry* 21 (4): 364–375.

Greenberg, Herb. 1996. Media Vision: The saga continues, and employees tell all. *SFGate*, April 16.

Grey, John. 1975. An exploration of musical timbre. Stanford Department of Music, Report No. STAN-M-2 (February).

Grimpe, Cristoph, and Heide Fier. 2010. Informal university technology transfer: A comparison between the United States and Germany. *Journal of Technology Transfer* 35 (6): 637–650.

Grunwald, Eric. 1992. OTL licenses "Waveguide Synthesis" to Sierra, Crystal. *Stanford University Brainstorm* 3(2).

Grunwald, Eric. 1995. "Father of computer music" still conducting himself well. *Stanford Technology Brainstorm* 4(2).

Haken, Lippold, Ed Tellman, and Patrick Wolfe. 1998. An indiscrete music keyboard. *Computer Music Journal* 22(1): 30–48.

Hargadon, Andrew, and Yellowlees Douglas. 2001. When innovations meet institutions: Edison and the design of the electric light. *Administrative Science Quarterly* 46 (3): 476–501.

Harmon, Brian, Alexander Ardishvili, Richard Cardozo, Tait Elder, John Leuthold, John Parshall, Michael Raghian, and Donald Smith. 1997. Mapping the university technology transfer process. *Journal of Business Venturing* 12 (6): 423–434.

Harris, Michael. 1985. Why inventions flee overseas. *San Francisco Chronicle*, April 25, 29, 34.

Hart, Hugh. 2010. Smog musicians turn pollution data into jagged melodies. *Wired*, October. http://www.wired.com/2010/10/smog-music/.

Hayes, Robert, and William Abernathy. Managing our way to economic decline. *Harvard Business Review* 58 (4): 67–77.

Heller, Michael, and Rebecca Eisenberg. 1998. Can patents deter innovation? The anticommons in biomedical research. *Science* 280 (5364): 698–701.

Hertelendy, Paul. 1975. Stanford's musical "marriage." *Oakland Tribune*, January 12, 1975, 20.

Hertelendy, Paul. 1985. Robot ballet bold but unrefined. *San Jose Mercury News*, December 7, 1C (Living).

Hertelendy, Paul. 1986. High-stepping season sends sparks flying with fresh approaches. *San Jose Mercury News*, July 27, 26 (Arts).

Hill, Charles, Michael Hitt, and Robert Hoskisson. 1988. Declining US competitiveness: Reflections on a crisis. *Academy of Management Executive* 2 (1): 51–60.

Hoge, Patrick. 2011. Music apps make prof an "accidental entrepreneur." *San Francisco Business Times*, December 9.

Holm, Petter. 1995. The dynamics of institutionalization: Transformation processes in Norwegian fisheries. *Administrative Science Quarterly* 40 (3): 398–422.

Holmes, Thom. 2008. *Electronic and Experimental Music: Technology, Music, and Culture*, 3rd ed. New York: Routledge.

Hong, Wei, and John Walsh. 2009. For money or glory? Commercialization, competition, and secrecy in the entrepreneurial university. *Sociological Quarterly* 50: 145–171.

Hughes, Sally Smith. 2001. Making dollars out of DNA: The first major patent in biotechnology and the commercialization of molecular biology, 1974–1980. *Isis* 92 (3): 541–575.

Hughes, Thomas. 1989. *American Genesis: A Century of Invention and Technological Enthusiasm*. New York: Penguin.

Hughes, Thomas. 1993. *Networks of Power: Electrification in Western Society, 1880–1930*. Baltimore: Johns Hopkins University Press.

Igoudin, Alex. 1996. CCRMA Report. Report No. Stan-M-98 (August).

Innovation's Golden Goose. 2002. *Economist*, December 12, 3.

Jackson, Myles. 2013. From scientific instruments to musical instruments: The tuning fork, the metronome, and the siren. In *The Oxford Handbook of Sound Studies*, ed. T. Pinch and K. Bijsterveld. Oxford: Oxford University Press.

Jacobs, Jerry. 2014. *In Defense of Disciplines: Interdisciplinarity and Specialization in the Research University*. Chicago: University of Chicago Press.

Jacobs, Jerry, and Scott Frickel. 2009. Interdisciplinarity: A critical assessment. *Annual Review of Sociology* 35:43–65.

Jaffe, David, and Lee Boynton. 1989. An overview of the sound and music kits for the NeXT computer. *Computer Music Journal* 13 (2): 48–55.

Jantsch, Erich. 1947. Inter⊠and transdisciplinary university: A systems approach to education and innovation. *Higher Education Quarterly* 1 (1): 7–37.

Jensen, Richard, and Marie Thursby. 2001. Proofs and prototypes for sale: The licensing of university inventions. *American Economic Review* 91 (1): 240–259.

Jeppesen, Lars, and Lars Frederiksen. 2006. Why do users contribute to firm-hosted user communities? The case of computer-controlled music instruments. *Organization Science* 17 (1): 45–63.

Johnson, Chalmers. 1982. *MITI and the Japanese Miracle: The Growth of Industrial Policy, 1925–1975*. Stanford, CA: Stanford University Press.

Johnstone, Bob. 1994. Wave of the future. *Wired* 2 (3).

Johnstone, Bob. 1999. *We Were Burning: Japanese Entrepreneurs and the Forging of the Electronic Age*. New York: Basic Books.

Jungleib, Stanley. 1987. Stanford's Computer Music Lab. *Keyboard* 13 (December): 58–65.

"Kalvos and Damian." 1997. Interview with Matthew H. Fields (a.k.a. The Doctor), part 1. November 22. http://kalvos.org/fieless2.html.

Katz, Mark. 2004. *Capturing Sound: How Technology Has Changed Music*. Berkeley, CA: University of California Press.

Katz, Michael, and Carl Shapiro. 1985. Network externalities, competition, and compatibility. *American Economic Review* 75 (3): 424–440.

Kenney, Martin, and David Patton. 2009. Reconsidering the Bayh–Dole Act and the current university invention ownership model. *Research Policy* 38 (9): 1407–1422.

Kenney, Martin, and David Patton. 2011. Does inventor ownership encourage university research-derived entrepreneurship? A six-university comparison. *Research Policy* 40 (8): 1100–1112.

Klein, Hans, and Daniel Kleinman. 2002. The social construction of technology: Structural considerations. *Science, Technology, and Human Values* 27 (1): 28–52.

Klett, Joseph. 2014. Sound on sound: Situating interaction in sonic object settings. *Sociological Theory* 32 (2): 147–161.

Klein, Julie Thompson. 1990. *Interdisciplinarity: History, Theory, and Practice*. Detroit, MI: Wayne State University Press.

Klein, Julie Thompson, and Richard Parncutt. 2010. Art and music research. In *The Oxford Handbook of Interdisciplinarity*, ed. R. Frodeman, J. T. Klein, and C. Mitcham, 133–146. Oxford: Oxford University Press.

Kline, Ronald, and Trevor Pinch. 1996. Users as agents of technological change: The social construction of the automobile in the rural United States. *Technology and Culture* 37 (4): 763–795.

Kline, Stephen. 1971. Values, technology, and society included in experimental program. *Campus Report*, May 19.

Kline, Stephen, and Nathan Rosenberg. 1986. An overview of innovation. In *The Positive Sum Strategy*, ed. R. Landau and N. Rosenberg, 275–304. Washington, DC: National Academy Press, Washington, DC.

Kockelmans, Joseph, ed. 2003. *Interdisciplinarity in Higher Education*. University Park, PA: Penn State University Press.

Kosman, Joshua. 2010. Stanford Laptop Orchestra makes music with Macs. *San Francisco Chronicle Datebook*, June 1.

Kristensen, Tore. 2004. The physical context of creativity. *Creativity and Innovation Management* 13 (2): 89–96.

Lakhani, Karim, and Eric von Hippel. 2003. How open source software works: "Free" user-to-user assistance. *Research Policy* 32 (6): 923–943.

LaTempa, Susan. 2007. Music of the (delicious reddish) spheres. *Los Angeles Times*, August 29 (Food).

Latour, Bruno, and Steve Woolgar. 1986. *Laboratory Life: The Construction of Scientific Facts*. Princeton, NJ: Princeton University Press.

Lattuca, Lisa. 2001. *Creating Interdisciplinarity: Interdisciplinary Research and Teaching among College and University Faculty*. Nashville, TN: Vanderbilt University Press.

Lawrence, Roderick, and Carole Després. 2004. Futures of transdisciplinarity. *Futures* 36 (4): 397–405.

Lécuyer, Christophe. 2006. *Making Silicon Valley: Innovation and the Growth of High Tech, 1930–1970*. Cambridge, MA: MIT Press.

Lehrman, Paul. 2005a. A talk with John Chowning, part 1. *Mix Magazine Online*, February 1. http://mixonline.com/mag/audio_talk_john_chowning/.

Lehrman, Paul. 2005b. A talk with John Chowning, part 2. *Mix Magazine Online*, March 1. http://mixonline.com/mag/audio_talk_john_chowning/.

Lenoir, Timothy, Nathan Rosenberg, Henry Rowen, Cristophe Lécuyer, Jeannette Colyvas, and Brent Goldfarb. 2004. *Inventing the Entrepreneurial University: Stanford and the Co-Evolution of Silicon Valley*. Unpublished book manuscript. http://www.info.sophia.ac.jp/amecana/J2/PDF/22-01Inventing_the_Enterpreneurial_University.pdf.

Leslie, Stuart. 1987. Playing the education game to win: The military and interdisciplinary research at Stanford. *Historical Studies in the Physical Sciences* 18:55–88.

Leslie, Stuart. 1993. *The Cold War and American Science: The Military-Industrial-Academic Complex at MIT and Stanford*. New York: Columbia University Press.

Lessig, Lawrence. 1999. The problem with patents. *Industry Standard*, April 23.

Levinthal, Daniel, and James March. 1993. The myopia of learning. *Strategic Management Journal* 14 (S2): 95–112.

Levitt, Barbara, and James March. 1988. Organizational learning. *Annual Review of Sociology* 14 (1): 319–338.

Link, Albert, Don Siegel, and Barry Bozeman. 2007. An empirical analysis of the propensity of academics to engage in informal university technology transfer. *Industrial and Corporate Change* 16 (4): 641–655.

Lockett, Andy, Donald Siegel, Mike Wright, and Michael D. Ensley. 2005. The creation of spin-off firms at public research institutions: Managerial and policy implications. *Research Policy* 34 (7): 981–993.

Lokken, Dean. 1986. Robots get mixed reviews in drama. *Chicago Tribune*, January 16, 8.

López-Lezcano, Fernando. 2005. Surviving on Planet CCRMA, two years later and still alive. In *Proceedings of the 3rd International Linux Audio Conference*, 109–114. Karlsruhe: Zentrum fur Kunst und Medientechnologie.

López-Lezcano, Fernando. 2009. A very brief history of computing at CCRMA. *eContact!* 11 (3).

Lowen, Rebecca. 1997. *Creating the Cold War University: The Transformation of Stanford*. Berkeley, CA: University of California Press.

Loy, D. Gareth. 2013. Life and times of the Samson Box. *Computer Music Journal* 37 (3): 26–48.

Maisel, Ivan. 2011. A place in the sun. *Stanford Magazine*. May/June.

Manning, Peter. 2004. *Electronic and Computer Music*. Oxford: Oxford University Press.

Mansfield, Edwin. 1986. Patents and innovation: An empirical study. *Management Science* 32 (2): 173–181.

March, James. 2010. *The Ambiguities of Experience*. Ithaca, NY: Cornell University Press.

March, James, and Herb Simon. 1958. *Organizations*. New York: Wiley.

Mathews, Max. 1963. The digital computer as a musical instrument. *Science* 142 (3592): 553–557.

Mathews, Max, Joan Miller, F. Richard Moore, John Pierce, and Jean-Claude Risset. 1969. *The Technology of Computer Music*. Cambridge, MA: MIT Press.

McMillen, Keith. 1994. ZIPI: Origins and motivations. *Computer Music Journal* 18 (4): 47–51.

Means, Loren. 2005a. An interview with John Chowning. *YLEM Journal* 25 (6 and 8): 4–8.

Means, Loren. 2005b. An interview with Max Mathews. *YLEM Journal* 25 (6 and 8): 19–23.

Merton, Robert. 1973. *The Sociology of Science: Theoretical and Empirical Investigations*. Chicago: University of Chicago Press.

Meyer, David. 2003. Political opportunity and nested institutions. *Social Movement Studies* 2 (1): 17–35.

Milne, P. W. 1979. Nine months of labour at SAIL. *DCR Newsletter* 148 (August): 10–12.

Minnick, Michael. 1990. A graphical editor for building unit generator patches. In *International Computer Music Conference Proceedings*, 253–255. San Francisco: International Computer Music Association.

Mintz, Daniel. 2007. Toward timbral synthesis: A new method for synthesizing sound based on timbre description schemes. Master of Science thesis, University of California at Santa Barbara.

Mody, Cyrus. 2011. *Instrumental Community: Probe Microscopy and the Path to Nanotechnology*. Cambridge, MA: MIT Press.

Mody, Cyrus. 2012. Conversions: Sound and Sight, Military and Civilian. In *The Oxford Handbook of Sound Studies*, ed. T. Pinch and K. Bijsterveld. Oxford: Oxford University Press.

Mody, Cyrus, and Andrew Nelson. 2013. "A towering virtue of necessity": Interdisciplinarity and the rise of computer music at Vietnam-era Stanford. *Osiris* 28: 254–277.

Moore, F. Richard. 1979. The nature of music research. *Directions: Center for Music Experiment and Related Research* 4 (1).

Morrison, Pamela, John Roberts, and Eric von Hippel. 2000. Determinants of user innovation and innovation sharing in a local market. *Management Science* 46 (12): 1513–1527.

Mowery, David, Richard Nelson, Bhaven Sampat, and Arvids Ziedonis. 2001. The growth of patenting and licensing by US universities: An assessment of the effects of the Bayh–Dole Act of 1980. *Research Policy* 30 (1): 99–119.

Mowery, David, Richard R. Nelson, Bhaven Sampat, and Arvids Ziedonis. 2004. *Ivory Tower and Industrial Innovation: University-Industry Technology Transfer Before and After the Bayh–Dole Act in the United States*. Stanford, CA: Stanford University Press.

Mowery, David, Nathan Rosenberg, Bhaven Sampat, and Arvids Ziedonis. 1999. The effects of the Bayh–Dole Act on US university research and technology transfer. In *Industrializing Knowledge: University-Industry Linkages in Japan and the United States*, ed. L. Branscomb, F. Kodama, and R. Florida. Cambridge, MA: MIT Press.

Mowery, David, and Bhaven Sampat. 2001. Patenting and licensing university inventions: Lessons from the history of the research corporation. *Industrial and Corporate Change* 10:317–355.

Mowery, David, and Bhaven Sampat. 2005. The Bayh–Dole Act of 1980 and university-industry technology transfer: A model for other OECD governments? *Journal of Technology Transfer* 30 (2): 233–245.

Murray, Fiona. 2002. Innovation as co-evolution of scientific and technological networks: Exploring tissue engineering. *Research Policy* 31 (8): 1389–1403.

Murray, Fiona. 2004. The role of academic inventors in entrepreneurial firms: Sharing the laboratory life. *Research Policy* 33 (4): 643–659.

Murray, Fiona, and Siobhán O'Mahony. 2007. Exploring the foundations of cumulative innovation: Implications for organization science. *Organization Science* 18 (6): 1006–1021.

Murray, Fiona, and Scott Stern. 2007. Do formal intellectual property rights hinder the free flow of scientific knowledge? An empirical test of the anti-commons hypothesis. *Journal of Economic Behavior and Organization* 63 (4): 648–687.

Nelson, Andrew. 2005. Cacophony or harmony? Multivocal logics and technology licensing by the Stanford University Department of Music. *Industrial and Corporate Change* 14 (1): 93–118.

Nelson, Andrew. 2009. Measuring knowledge spillovers: What patents, licenses, and publications reveal about innovation diffusion. *Research Policy* 38 (6): 994–1005.

Nelson, Andrew. 2012. Putting university research in context: Assessing alternative measures of production and diffusion at Stanford. *Research Policy* 41 (4): 678–691.

Nelson, Andrew. 2014. From the ivory tower to the startup garage: Organizational context and commercialization processes. *Research Policy* 43 (7): 1144–1156.

Nelson, Richard, and Sidney Winter. 1982. *An Evolutionary Theory of Economic Change*. Cambridge, MA: Belknap Press.

Nordhaus, William. 1969. *Invention, Growth, and Welfare: A Theoretical Treatment of Technological Change*. Cambridge, MA: MIT Press.

Nowotny, Helga, Peter Scott, and Michael Gibbons. 2001. *Re-thinking Science: Knowledge and the Public in an Age of Uncertainty*. Cambridge: Polity Press.

Obstfeld, David. 2005. Social networks, the tertius iungens orientation, and involvement in innovation. *Administrative Science Quarterly* 50 (1): 100–130.

O'Mahony, Siobhán. 2003. Guarding the commons: How community managed software projects protect their work. *Research Policy* 32 (7): 1179–1198.

Oppenheimer, Larry. 1984. CCRMA: Computer music at Stanford. *MIX Magazine* 8 (6): 14, 16, 18, 22, 24–26.

Organization for Economic Cooperation and Development. 1972. *Interdisciplinarity: Problems of Teaching and Research in Universities*. Paris: OECD.

Orlikowski, W. J. 1992. The duality of technology: Rethinking the concept of technology in organizations. *Organization Science* 3 (3): 398–427.

Oudshoorn, Nelly, and Trevor Pinch. 2003. *How Users Matter: The Co-Construction of Users and Technology*. Cambridge, MA: MIT Press.

Owen-Smith, Jason. 2003. From separate systems to a hybrid order: Accumulative advantage across public and private science at research one universities. *Research Policy* 32 (6): 1081–1104.

Owen-Smith, Jason, and Walter W. Powell. 2001a. Careers and contradictions: Faculty responses to the transformation of knowledge and its uses in the life sciences. *Research in the Sociology of Work* 10:109–140.

Owen-Smith, Jason, and Walter W. Powell. 2001b. To patent or not: Faculty decisions and institutional success at technology transfer. *Journal of Technology Transfer* 26 (1–2): 99–114.

Padgett, John, and Christopher Ansell. 1993. Robust action and the rise of the Medici, 1400–1434. *American Journal of Sociology* 98 (6): 1259–1319.

Padgett, John, and Walter W. Powell. 2012. *The Emergence of Organizations and Markets*. Princeton: Princeton University Press.

Pampin, Juan. 1999. ATS: A Lisp environment for spectral modeling. In *Proceedings of the International Computer Music Conference*, Beijing. San Francisco: International Computer Music Association.

Park, Tae Hong. 2009. An interview with Max Mathews. *Computer Music Journal* 33 (3): 9–22.

Parrish, Michael. 2000. Mickey Hart: Musical healing. *Dirty Linen* 86 (Feb./Mar.).

Perkmann, Markus, and Kathryn Walsh. 2007. University–industry relationships and open innovation: Towards a research agenda. *International Journal of Management Reviews* 9 (4): 259–280.

Perkmann, Markus, and Joel West. 2013. Open science and open innovation: Sourcing technology from universities. In *Handbook of University Technology Transfer*, ed. A. Link, D. Siegel, and M. Wright. Chicago: University of Chicago Press.

Pinch, Trevor, and Wiebe Bijker. 1987. The social construction of facts and artifacts: Or how the sociology of science and the sociology of technology might benefit each other. In *The Social Construction of Technological Systems: New Directions in the Sociology and History of Technology*, ed. W. Bijker, T. Hughes, and T. Pinch, 17–50. Cambridge, MA: MIT Press.

Pinch, Trevor, and Karin Bijsterveld. 2003. Should one applaud? Breaches and boundaries in the reception of new technology in music. *Technology and Culture* 44 (3): 536–559.

Pinch, Trevor, and Frank Trocco. 2009. *Analog Days: The Invention and Impact of the Moog Synthesizer*. Cambridge, MA: Harvard University Press.

Plush, Vincent. 1983. Interview with John Chowning. Conducted on May 31, 1983, in Palo Alto. Palo Alto, CA: Yale Oral History Project.

Porcaro, Nick, William Putnam, Pat Scandalis, Tim Stilson, David Jaffe, Julius Smith and Scott Van Duyne. 1996. SynthBuilder and Frankenstein: Tools for the creation of musical physical models. *ICAD meeting* (November).

Powell, Walter W., Kelley Packalen, and Kjersten Whittington. 2012. Organizational and institutional genesis: The emergence of high-tech clusters in the life sciences. In *The Emergence of Organizations and Markets*, ed. J. Padgett and W. Powell. Princeton: Princeton University Press.

Powell, Walter W., Douglas White, Ken Koput, and Jason Owen-Smith. 2005. Network dynamics and field evolution: The growth of interorganizational collaboration in the life sciences. *American Journal of Sociology* 110 (4): 1132–1205.

Press, Eyal, and Jennifer Washburn. 2000. The kept university. *Atlantic Monthly* 285 (3): 39–42, 44–52, 54.

Rebello, Kathy, and Robert D. Hof. 1994. Mirage at Media Vision. *Business Week*, May 22. http://www.businessweek.com/stories/1994-05-22/mirage-at-media-vision.

Reid, Gordon. 2001. Yamaha GS1 and DX1, part 1: The birth, rise, and further rise of FM synthesis (Retro). *Sound on Sound*, August. http://www.soundonsound.com/sos/Aug01/articles/retrofmpt1.asp.

Rhoten, Diana, and Andrew Parker. 2004. Risks and rewards of an interdisciplinary research path. *Science* 306 (5704): 2046.

Rich, Alan. 1984. A composer whose computer music has a magical twist. *Smithsonian Magazine* (December): 97–104.

Risset, Jean-Claude, and Max Mathews. 1969. Analysis of musical-instrument tones. *Physics Today* 22:23.

Roads, Curtis. 1982. Interview with John Chowning. In *Composers and the Computer*, ed. Curtis Roads, 17–25. Los Altos, CA: William Kaufmann, Inc.

Roberts, Tom. 2012. Algorithm my rhythm: John Chowning's "Stria" and the discovery of FM synthesis. January 25. http://herecomesthesounduk.blogspot.com/2012/01/algorithm-my-rhythm-john-chownings.html.

Roose, Kenneth, and Charles Andersen. 1970. *A Rating of Graduate Programs*. Washington, D.C.: American Council on Education.

Rosenberg, Nathan. 2004. *Innovation and Economic Growth*. Paris: OECD.

Rosenberg, Nathan, and Richard Nelson. 1994. American universities and technical advance in industry. *Research Policy* 23:323–348.

Rosenberg, Nathan, and W. Edward Steinmueller. 2013. Engineering knowledge. *Industrial and Corporate Change* 22 (5): 1129–1158.

Ross, Alex. 2007. *The Rest Is Noise: Listening to the Twentieth Century*. New York: Farrar, Straus & Giroux.

Rothaermel, Frank, Shanti Agung, and Lin Jiang. 2007. University entrepreneurship: A taxonomy of the literature. *Industrial and Corporate Change* 16 (4): 691–791.

Rothaermel, Frank, and Marie Thursby. 2005. Incubator firm failure or graduation? The role of university linkages. *Research Policy* 34 (7): 1076–1090.

Rubin, Michael. 2006. *Droidmaker: George Lucas and the Digital Revolution*. Gainesville, FL: Triad Publishing.

Rubin, Nathan. 1994. *John Cage and the Twenty-Six Pianos of Mills College: Forces in American Music from 1940 to 1990, a History*. Moraga, CA: Sarah's Books.

Salter, Liora, and Alison Hearn. 1996. *Outside the Lines: Issues in Interdisciplinary Research*. Montreal: McGill-Queen's University Press.

Sampat, Bhaven, and Richard Nelson. 2002. The emergence and standardization of university technology transfer offices: A case study of institutional change. *Advances in Strategic Management* 19:135–164.

Schrieberg, David. 1998. The matchmakers. *Stanford Today Online*, January–February.

Scott, W. Richard. 2001. *Institutions and Organizations*, 2nd ed. Thousand Oaks: Sage.

Scott, W. Richard. 2003. *Organizations: Rational, Natural, and Open Systems*. Upper Saddle River, NJ: Prentice-Hall.

Seelig, T. L. 2012. *inGenius: A Crash Course on Creativity*. New York: HarperOne.

Serra, Xavier and Patte Wood. 1988. Overview: Center for Computer Research in Music and Acoustics. Stanford Department of Music, Report No. Stan-M-44 (March).

Shah, Sonali, and Mary Tripsas. 2007. The accidental entrepreneur: The emergent and collective process of user entrepreneurship. *Strategic Entrepreneurship Journal* 1 (1–2): 123–140.

Siegel, Donald, David Waldman, and Albert Link. 2003. Assessing the impact of organizational practices on the relative productivity of university technology transfer offices: An exploratory study. *Research Policy* 32 (1): 27–48.

Smith, Julius. 1989. *Unit-Generator Implementation on the NeXT DSP Chip*. Ann Arbor, MI: MPublishing, University of Michigan Library.

Smith, Julius. 2010. *Physical Audio Signal Processing for Virtual Musical Instruments and AudioEffects*.CreateSpace.http://www.dsprelated.com/dspbooks/pasp/Karplus_Strong_Algorithms.html.

Sommer, Julia. 1982. Computer music audiences mushroom. Stanford News Office press release, June 28.

Stanford University. 1993. György Ligeti to be composer-in-residence at Stanford University. January 12 (press release).

Stanford University Department of Music. 1982. Computer music comes of age. *Music at Stanford,* October. Included with the *Stanford Observer,* section 2.

Stanford University Office of Technology Licensing. 1992. *Connections (Annual Report).*

Star, Susan Leigh. 2010. This is not a boundary object: Reflections on the origin of a concept. *Science, Technology, and Human Values* 35 (5): 601–617.

Star, Susan Leigh, and James Griesemer. 1989. Institutional ecology, "translations," and boundary objects: Amateurs and professionals in Berkeley's Museum of Vertebrate Zoology, 1907–39. *Social Studies of Science* 19:387–420.

Stephan, Paula. 2010. The economics of science. In *Handbook of the Economics of Innovation,* ed. B. Hall and N. Rosenberg, 217–274. Amsterdam: North Holland.

Sterne, Jonathan. 2012. *MP3: The Meaning of a Format.* Durham, NC: Duke University Press.

Sterne, Jonathan, and Mitchell Akiyama. 2012. The recording that never wanted to be heard and other stories of sonification. In *The Oxford Handbook of Sound Studies,* ed. T. Pinch and K. Bijsterveld. Oxford: Oxford University Press.

Strandburg, Katherine. 2009. User innovator community norms at the boundary between academic and industrial research. *Fordham Law Review* 77 (5): 2237–2274.

Supper, Alexandra. 2012. The search for the "killer application": Drawing the boundaries around the sonification of scientific data. In *The Oxford Handbook of Sound Studies,* ed. T. Pinch and K. Bijsterveld. Oxford: Oxford University Press.

Suthers, D. D., K. Lund, C. P. Rosé, C. Teplovs, and N. Law. 2013. *Productive Multivocality in the Analysis of Group Interactions.* New York: Springer.

Taylor, Timothy. 2012. The avant-garde in the family room: American advertising and the domestication of electronic music in the 1960s and 1970s. In *The Oxford Handbook of Sound Studies,* ed. T. Pinch and K. Bijsterveld. Oxford: Oxford University Press.

Terman, Frederick. 1947. *Radio Engineering.* New York: McGraw-Hill.

Théberge, Paul. 1997. *Any Sound You Can Imagine.* Middletown, CT: Wesleyan University Press.

Thursby, Jerry, and Marie Thursby. 2004. Are faculty critical? Their role in university-industry licensing. *Contemporary Economic Policy* 22:162–178.

Tircuit, Heuwell. 1975. Something special in a concert hall. *San Francisco Chronicle,* August 9.

Turner, Fred. 2010. *From Counterculture to Cyberculture: Stewart Brand, the Whole Earth Network, and the Rise of Digital Utopianism*. Chicago: University of Chicago Press.

University of California at San Diego. 1969. Department of Music presents Loren Rush in concert. April 17 (press release). http://libraries.ucsd.edu/historyofucsd/newsreleases/1969/19690417b.html.

Vanhemert, Kyle. 2013. Look Inside Apple's Spaceship Headquarters with 24 all-new renderings. *Wired*, November 11. http://www.wired.com/2013/11/a-glimpse-into-apples-crazy-new-spaceship-headquarters/.

von Hippel, Eric. 2005. *Democratizing Innovation*. Cambridge, MA: MIT Press.

Walsh, John, and Wei Hong. 2003. Secrecy is increasing in step with competition. *Nature* 422:801–802.

Watson, Aaron, and David Keating. 1999. Architecture and sound: An acoustic analysis of megalithic monuments in prehistoric Britain. *Antiquity* 73:325–336.

Weingart, Peter, and Nico Stehr. 2000. *Practising Interdisciplinarity*. Toronto: University of Toronto Press.

West, Joel. 2003. How open is open enough? Melding proprietary and open source platform strategies. *Research Policy* 32 (7): 1259–1285.

West, Joel, and Scott Gallagher. 2006. Challenges of open innovation: The paradox of firm investment in open source software. *R&D Management* 36 (3): 319–331.

West, Joel, Ammon Salter, Wim Vanhaverbeke, and Henry Chesbrough. 2014. Open innovation: The next decade. *Research Policy* 43 (5): 805–811.

White, Harrison. 1985. Agency as control. In *Principals and Agents: The Structure of Business*, ed. J. Pratt and R. Zeckhauser, 187–214. Boston: Harvard Business School Press.

White, Harrison. 1992. *Identity and Control*. Princeton, NJ: Princeton University Press.

Wiesendanger, Hans. 2000. *A History of OTL: Overview*. Stanford: Stanford University Press.

Willey, Robert. Report on residency and exchange program in new music technology. Center for Research in Computing and the Arts, University of California at San Diego. Accessed April 22, 2014: http://willshare.com/willeyrk/creative/recordings/intercambio.html.

Wisnioski, Matthew. 2003. Inside "the system": Engineers, scientists, and the boundaries of social protest in the long 1960s. *History and Technology* 19:313–333.

Wisnioski, Matthew. 2012. *Engineers for Change: Competing Visions of Technology in 1960s America*. Cambridge, MA: MIT Press.

Wisnioski, Matthew. 2013. Why MIT institutionalized the avant-garde: Negotiating aesthetic virtue in the postwar defense institute. *Configurations* 21 (1): 85–116.

Wright, Mike, Sue Birley, and Simon Mosey. 2004. Entrepreneurship and university technology transfer. *Journal of Technology Transfer* 29 (3–4): 235–246.

Yesterday's news. 2013. *Harvard Magazine* 115 (2): 51.

Ziegler, Thomas, and Jason Gross. 2005. *Ohm: The Early Gurus of Electronic Music: 1948–1980*. Special edition 3CD + DVD. Ellipsis Arts.

Zierhofer, Wolgang, and Paul Burger. 2007. Disentangling transdisciplinarity: An analysis of knowledge integration in problem-oriented research. *Science Studies* 20 (1): 51–72.

Index

Page numbers followed by an "f" indicate figures.

Inside Technology

edited by Wiebe E. Bijker, W. Bernard Carlson, and Trevor Pinch

Andrew J. Nelson, *The Sound of Innovation: Stanford and the Computer Music Revolution*

Sonja D. Schmid, *Producing Power: The Pre-Chernobyl History of the Soviet Nuclear Industry*

Casey O'Donnell, *Developer's Dilemma: The Secret World of Videogame Creators*

Christina Dunbar-Hester, *Low Power to the People: Pirates, Protest, and Politics in FM Radio Activism*

Eden Medina, Ivan da Costa Marques, and Christina Holmes, editors, *Beyond Imported Magic: Essays on Science, Technology, and Society in Latin America*

Anique Hommels, Jessica Mesman, and Wiebe E. Bijker, editors, *Vulnerability in Technological Cultures: New Directions in Research and Governance*

Amit Prasad, *Imperial Technoscience: Transnational Histories of MRI in the United States, Britain, and India*

Charis Thompson, *Good Science: The Ethical Choreography of Stem Cell Research*

Tarleton Gillespie, Pablo J. Boczkowski, and Kirsten A. Foot, editors, *Media Technologies: Essays on Communication, Materiality, and Society*

Catelijne Coopmans, Janet Vertesi, Michael Lynch, and Steve Woolgar, editors, *Representation in Scientific Practice Revisited*

Rebecca Slayton, *Arguments that Count: Physics, Computing, and Missile Defense, 1949–2012*

Stathis Arapostathis and Graeme Gooday, *Patently Contestable: Electrical Technologies and Inventor Identities on Trial in Britain*

Jens Lachmund, *Greening Berlin: The Co-Production of Science, Politics, and Urban Nature*

Chikako Takeshita, *The Global Biopolitics of the IUD: How Science Constructs Contraceptive Users and Women's Bodies*

Cyrus C. M. Mody, *Instrumental Community: Probe Microscopy and the Path to Nanotechnology*

Morana Alač, *Handling Digital Brains: A Laboratory Study of Multimodal Semiotic Interaction in the Age of Computers*

Gabrielle Hecht, editor, *Entangled Geographies: Empire and Technopolitics in the Global Cold War*

Michael E. Gorman, editor, *Trading Zones and Interactional Expertise: Creating New Kinds of Collaboration*

Matthias Gross, *Ignorance and Surprise: Science, Society, and Ecological Design*

Andrew Feenberg, *Between Reason and Experience: Essays in Technology and Modernity*

Wiebe E. Bijker, Roland Bal, and Ruud Hendricks, *The Paradox of Scientific Authority: The Role of Scientific Advice in Democracies*

Park Doing, *Velvet Revolution at the Synchrotron: Biology, Physics, and Change in Science*

Gabrielle Hecht, *The Radiance of France: Nuclear Power and National Identity after World War II*

Richard Rottenburg, *Far-Fetched Facts: A Parable of Development Aid*

Michel Callon, Pierre Lascoumes, and Yannick Barthe, *Acting in an Uncertain World: An Essay on Technical Democracy*

Ruth Oldenziel and Karin Zachmann, editors, *Cold War Kitchen: Americanization, Technology, and European Users*

Deborah G. Johnson and Jameson W. Wetmore, editors, *Technology and Society: Building Our Sociotechnical Future*

Trevor Pinch and Richard Swedberg, editors, *Living in a Material World: Economic Sociology Meets Science and Technology Studies*

Christopher R. Henke, *Cultivating Science, Harvesting Power: Science and Industrial Agriculture in California*

Helga Nowotny, *Insatiable Curiosity: Innovation in a Fragile Future*

Karin Bijsterveld, *Mechanical Sound: Technology, Culture, and Public Problems of Noise in the Twentieth Century*

Peter D. Norton, *Fighting Traffic: The Dawn of the Motor Age in the American City*

Joshua M. Greenberg, *From Betamax to Blockbuster: Video Stores and the Invention of Movies on Video*

Mikael Hård and Thomas J. Misa, editors, *Urban Machinery: Inside Modern European Cities*

Christine Hine, *Systematics as Cyberscience: Computers, Change, and Continuity in Science*

Wesley Shrum, Joel Genuth, and Ivan Chompalov, *Structures of Scientific Collaboration*

Shobita Parthasarathy, *Building Genetic Medicine: Breast Cancer, Technology, and the Comparative Politics of Health Care*

Kristen Haring, *Ham Radio's Technical Culture*

Atsushi Akera, *Calculating a Natural World: Scientists, Engineers and Computers during the Rise of U.S. Cold War Research*

Donald MacKenzie, *An Engine, Not a Camera: How Financial Models Shape Markets*

Geoffrey C. Bowker, *Memory Practices in the Sciences*

Christophe Lécuyer, *Making Silicon Valley: Innovation and the Growth of High Tech, 1930–1970*

Anique Hommels, *Unbuilding Cities: Obduracy in Urban Sociotechnical Change*

David Kaiser, editor, *Pedagogy and the Practice of Science: Historical and Contemporary Perspectives*

Charis Thompson, *Making Parents: The Ontological Choreography of Reproductive Technology*

Pablo J. Boczkowski, *Digitizing the News: Innovation in Online Newspapers*

Dominique Vinck, editor, *Everyday Engineering: An Ethnography of Design and Innovation*

Nelly Oudshoorn and Trevor Pinch, editors, *How Users Matter: The Co-Construction of Users and Technology*

Peter Keating and Alberto Cambrosio, *Biomedical Platforms: Realigning the Normal and the Pathological in Late-Twentieth-Century Medicine*

Paul Rosen, *Framing Production: Technology, Culture, and Change in the British Bicycle Industry*

Maggie Mort, *Building the Trident Network: A Study of the Enrollment of People, Knowledge, and Machines*

Donald MacKenzie, *Mechanizing Proof: Computing, Risk, and Trust*

Geoffrey C. Bowker and Susan Leigh Star, *Sorting Things Out: Classification and Its Consequences*

Charles Bazerman, *The Languages of Edison's Light*

Janet Abbate, *Inventing the Internet*

Herbert Gottweis, *Governing Molecules: The Discursive Politics of Genetic Engineering in Europe and the United States*

Kathryn Henderson, *On Line and On Paper: Visual Representation, Visual Culture, and Computer Graphics in Design Engineering*

Susanne K. Schmidt and Raymund Werle, *Coordinating Technology: Studies in the International Standardization of Telecommunications*

Marc Berg, *Rationalizing Medical Work: Decision Support Techniques and Medical Practices*

Eda Kranakis, *Constructing a Bridge: An Exploration of Engineering Culture, Design, and Research in Nineteenth-Century France and America*

Paul N. Edwards, *The Closed World: Computers and the Politics of Discourse in Cold War America*

Donald MacKenzie, *Knowing Machines: Essays on Technical Change*

Wiebe E. Bijker, *Of Bicycles, Bakelites, and Bulbs: Toward a Theory of Sociotechnical Change*

Louis L. Bucciarelli, *Designing Engineers*

Geoffrey C. Bowker, *Science on the Run: Information Management and Industrial Geophysics at Schlumberger, 1920–1940*

Wiebe E. Bijker and John Law, editors, *Shaping Technology/Building Society: Studies in Sociotechnical Change*

Stuart Blume, *Insight and Industry: On the Dynamics of Technological Change in Medicine*

Donald MacKenzie, *Inventing Accuracy: A Historical Sociology of Nuclear Missile Guidance*

Pamela E. Mack, *Viewing the Earth: The Social Construction of the Landsat Satellite System*

H. M. Collins, *Artificial Experts: Social Knowledge and Intelligent Machines*

http://mitpress.mit.edu/books/series/inside-technology

Printed in the United States
by Baker & Taylor Publisher Services